Which?
WAY TO
RUN YOUR CAR

Editor: Alisdair Aird

House Editor: Nigel Fox

Design: Turner Wilks Dandridge Ltd

Illustrations: Hayward and Martin Ltd
Kieth Field
A Good Studio

First Edition
© Consumers' Association 1979

ISBN 0 85202 171 2

Printed and bound in Great Britain
by Butler & Tanner Ltd, Frome and London

INTRODUCTION

This book is to help you run a better car for less money. First, it's meant to help you choose the car which will suit you and your pocket best. Then, it'll help you get the best possible value out of it. It's based on the years of testing and experience which have gone into *Motoring Which?*. This means it's not just general advice: instead, it's highly specific – and, when that'll help, it names names.

This introductory section is simply a set of signposts, to help you find your way through the book.

SECTION ONE, Chapter 1, Knowing What You Want, is for working out what you really need from a car. First, it shows you how to make the most of your own experience, so that you can start the hunt for the best car in the right way. Next, it shows you how to work out your own particular demands: after all, you're unique and so are your needs. The trick in getting car choice right is working out what's special about those needs, so that you can look for the car that suits you and not just some Mr Average. That's the next step: using your analysis of what really matters to you, to pinpoint the car that will suit you best. Finally, this chapter tells how to find out the real facts about cars.

Chapter 2, New or Secondhand?, shows how faults grow as cars get older – picking out particular faults, and particular cars. Then it works out the relationship between age and cost: how the cost of owning

a particular car changes as it gets older; and how you can use this to pick a car which – at the right age – will give you the most for your money. It explains how depreciation works – and shows how you can work out exactly what a car will cost you, depending on how long you keep it. It puts inflation and rising car prices into an easy-to-understand perspective, so that you never get taken unpleasantly by surprise. Finally, it picks out the ways you can profit best from how depreciation works – naming cars that hold their value well.

Chapter 3, Your Monthly Outlay, shows how car costs work out in practice, and what controls them.

Chapter 4, Deciding on Details, goes through all the main variations in any particular range of cars. First, how to make the best choice of engine, bearing performance and economy in mind. Then, in turn, automatic gearchange; body variations, including estates, hatchbacks, coupés and so forth; the various degrees of luxury trim you can get; the string of optional extras which manufacturers fit; colour – there are quite a few practical considerations besides what appeals to you; safety belts; and tyres. All through this chapter, cost is counted.

SECTION TWO, Chapter 1, Buying New, starts with choosing a dealer, then goes through the actual paperwork involved – showing possible savings.

Chapter 2, Buying Secondhand, again starts with where to buy: garages, auctions, private buyers, and so forth. It makes sense of the growing business in used-car guarantees. There are tips on picking the best time to buy – how you can make the most of what the big fleet users do, industrial trouble, VAT changes. It shows how to avoid 'new-modelitis' – the troubles which may afflict a newly-introduced car. Then there's the actual choice of your car: how to choose a good one; using professional inspection services; doing your own test-inspection; special trouble-spots to look out for, depending on the age of the car, and the model.

Chapter 3, Money, Money, Money, is all about getting the most car for the least money. It picks out the best value lenders. Shows how to get the highest price for your old car, as well as the lowest for the new one. It suggests how to get someone else to help pay – your firm, even the taxman, perhaps a leasing arrangement. Finally, it looks into hiring.

Chapter 4, New Cars: the First Year, starts with another money-saver – how to cut the cost of hidden extras when you buy. Then it shows how to check for the faults which are most likely on new cars. It guides you through underbody sealing; running in; making the most of the first service; profiting from the end of the guarantee period. It tells what to do if things ever go badly wrong, and you can't get satisfaction.

SECTION THREE, Chapter 1, Cheering Up Your Car, is about the things you can add to make a car better, *after* you've bought it. Again with a clear eye to value for money, it goes in turn through added safety features; anti-theft devices; performance and economy; and comfort and appearance.

Chapter 2, Insurance, shows how to find a good company; when to use brokers; how to pick the best policy; how to make the most of the no-claims discount system; how to make a claim. It explains what will make your premium either low or high.

Chapter 3, Looking After It, is about the routine basics of maintenance.

Chapter 4, Basic Servicing, should save you both trouble and money. First, choosing a reasonable garage, and making sure it does the job properly. Then, a fool's guide to doing it yourself: the tools you'll need; how to learn about it; using tools safely; and how to do three simple, money-saving jobs that anyone can cope with – oil and filter change (including choice of oil), fanbelt changing and adjustment, and touching up paintwork.

Chapter 5, Saving on Petrol, evaluates gadgets which are supposed to cut fuel costs. It considers garage tune-ups – and tells you how to do the job simply yourself, naming the gadgets which will help. It tips you off on economy-driving.

Chapter 6, Repairs, starts with prevention, signs of trouble ahead, and preparing for winter (including battery choice). Then, a useful emergency spares kit; using breakdown services; diagnosing faults; getting garage repairs done; how to save on spares; and how to win any dispute with your garage.

Chapter 7, Going Abroad, is a short guide to cheap ways of getting there, and making things easy.

SECTION FOUR, Chapter 1, Learning to Drive – or Drive Better, starts with the real learner (and some tips to remember); then sets you on the road to advanced driving; and ends with a Highway Code quiz ... you probably won't do well.

Chapter 2, The Police, is another we hope you won't need to have read: your rights, and those of the police; the courts, and your chances of conviction.

So that you can find a particular topic that you need, an Index starts on page 155.

CONTENTS

SECTION ONE

CHOOSING YOUR CAR

Which way to find the car that truly meets your needs – an action plan to find your best buy, new or used

1. KNOWING WHAT YOU WANT

There's a tremendous thrill for some people in choosing a new car; others dread the complexities; others, secretly hankering for the car of their dreams, are sad that they'll have to settle for something much more sensible; still others are frankly bewildered by the conflicting claims of competing adverts – not to mention the jangling technicalities of the glossy brochures. But whatever you feel – maybe you combine a bit of all these attitudes to car-buying – there's no denying that choosing a car is one of the biggest decisions you have to make. If you know exactly what you want, and the price is no problem, you're lucky: you shouldn't be reading this chapter at all, so shoo! Otherwise, let's look for a few short cuts through all those car-choice complexities.

Where to start
The most important thing is to fix on a firm starting-point in your search for the best choice of car. What you want is an exact reference-point, to give you a clear perspective on all the different factors. There are three possibles – each entirely different from the others – and which of them you take as your reference-point depends on your particular circumstances.

Price is the first possibility. Lots of people automatically think of price as the first and most important factor in starting their search for a car – but price can be misleading, for reasons that will become obvious in Chapter

3 which is all about the cost side. There are two – and only two – cases in which price makes the right starting-point. First, many firms and employers pay for an employee's car, setting a clear price range or price ceiling: if you're getting a car on the firm in this way, then it does make sense for you to use the firm's price limits as your starting-point. But think about the next two possibilities, too: one of them added to your price limits should make choice a lot easier.

Price is also the starting-point for people who can lay their hands on a certain fixed amount of money, and no more, and who know that this is going to be the critical factor in getting a car. This may sound obvious, but it's actually quite a bit more devious than it sounds. For instance, if someone already has a car worth, say, £1,000, and if they plan to part-exchange it using the proceeds as a one-third deposit on another car, they might think that £3,000 is their obvious price limit. But what if there's the ideal car for them, in the long run cheaper to own, with a price-tag of £4,000? Most people in that situation would be able to raise the extra money in one of the ways described in Section 2: so, if they'd started out with that £3,000 price limit, they'd have missed their ideal choice – not only better value, not just affordable, but even maybe cheaper to own in the long run. So, to avoid the risk that you might rule out your perfect car, don't set a price limit unless you have to. These are the most likely cases in which a straightforward price limit is sensible:

£ You've got a certain amount of money to spend, you don't want to draw on any savings (see page 70), and you definitely don't want to borrow money – so you've got a price limit equal to the amount of money you're prepared to spend

£ You've got a certain amount of money to spend, you don't want to or can't draw on any savings, and you can't borrow money (are you sure? see page 72) – again, that's your price limit

£ Again, you've got a certain sum of money to spend, you're not going to use savings, but you can get HP – so you reckon your price limit is the amount you can raise including your money as the deposit: WRONG, because if you get HP you could probably use your credit-worthiness to increase your spending power well beyond that limit – for you, it doesn't make sense to stick to a rigid preliminary price limit.

POINT TO REMEMBER

Even if you're one of the relatively few people for whom a price limit makes a sensible starting-point in choosing a car, remember this: price on its own can be a bad guide to the true cost of having a car – see later.

The second possible reference-point for choosing a car is an **overriding need.** If there's one thing which you need from a car – something much more important to you than anything else – then it makes sense to use that as the starting-point in your search for the right car. Let's say for instance that you've got a caravan, quite a big one: any car you choose must be able to tow it. Or you're so tall that you must have a car with an unusually high roof line so that you can easily see ahead without getting a crick in your neck. Or you live on a farm with such a rutted drive that your car needs an eight-inch ground clearance.

Factors crucial enough to take as your point of reference don't have to be practical, of course. You might for example decide right from the start that your car's got to be an open-topped sports car – nothing else would do. Some people insist above all else on buying British (though in these Common Market days a British name might easily cover a 'naturalised' foreigner like the German Ford Granada, the French Talbot Horizon, or a car of Belgian extraction like the Vauxhall Cavalier). Maybe there's even some unusual colour which you feel you've simply got to have.

Whether it's practical or just a personal fad, if there is some point which matters tremendously to you then it's almost certainly worth using as a preliminary sieve: if a car doesn't give you that point, then for you that car's probably not worth considering. Otherwise, if you just try to pretend that your overriding need is simply one bit of a bigger shopping list of factors you want from a car, you might easily end up with some car in which these other factors had ruled your choice – excluding the one thing that really matters to you.

POINT TO REMEMBER

Treating any single point as seriously as this means that it really has got to be important to you: it's no good elevating some passing whim into a binding major requirement.

Your present car – or some other car that you know really well, warts and all – is the last of the three possible reference-points. Probably, this is the starting-point that's best for most people.

If you already know some car very well, and think carefully about its good points and its bad points, you'll be well on the way towards drawing up a specification for your ideal choice.

One *Motoring Which?* survey asked people what factors they thought were important, in choosing a new car. Then, it asked quite separately how satisfied they were about various points to do with their present car. In the second question many points stood out as being extremely unsatisfactory for them – points which they hadn't put on their new car 'shopping list' in the first question. If they stuck to the 'shopping list' in choosing another car, they could easily find it just as unsatisfactory as the old one.

What this means for you is clear. If you think hard about your own present car – or, if you don't have one, maybe someone's that you know quite well – you can probably point your finger at some things which you find particularly good about it, and other things which have been a bother. Good or bad, the factors concerned are a good short-cut signpost to what you should look out for most carefully in your next car.

So, to recap, these are your possible starting-points in thinking about your best choice of car (and you could combine all three):

● if your firm's paying for your car
● if you've a set sum of money to spend, and can't or won't borrow
– use your price limit as the start of a short list

● if you've got some difficult-to-suit personal characteristic, making special demands on a car
● if your personal circumstances set some particular requirement for a car
● if you've set your heart on some special type of car (and you're sure you won't change your mind)
– use that as a compulsory pass-fail factor, before you consider any car further

● if you've already got a car, or
● if you know some other car well enough to judge
– use your judgement of its good and bad points as the key to what matters most to you in a car.

Of these three possible starting-points, the third is likely to be much the most help to most people. It's also the one needing most effort from you. It's no good just thinking of a few points straight off the top of your head. You've got to be a bit systematic about it – see below.

What you want from a car
As well as fixing on some firm starting-point in your quest for the best choice of car, you need a pretty exact idea of what you really want from a car before you can choose wisely. The questionnaire which follows is designed to kill two birds with one stone. You'll see as you go through it that it's meant to throw up two separate things: first, any key factors so important that they should dominate your car choice right from the beginning; second, the general order of importance to you of various car characteristics, so that you know roughly how much weight to give to a car's various qualities when it comes to the detail of choosing between one short-listed car and another.

The questionnaire isn't meant for you to fill in – though of course there's nothing to stop you doing that if you'd like. But you should at least follow the reasoning through, so that you can see how to apply the principle – an analysis of your particular car requirements, reached through a hard think about your attitude to your present car.

QUESTIONNAIRE: HOW YOUR CAR RATES YOU

If your car — or another car you know well enough to rate, if you don't actually own one yourself — strikes you as being either particularly good or particularly bad for any of the following points, note those points: they're things that matter to you. If you want to be heroically energetic, you could even try scoring each point, with marks out of ten, say, where high marks mean that some point is either specially good or specially bad, and low marks that that point doesn't really strike you either way. But you'll probably find that it's enough of a guide — and quite enough work — just to pick out the points where your present car rates a credit or a black mark.

If your present car doesn't give you a rosy glow of pride when you think of some particular point, and it doesn't make you hot under the collar or burst into tears either, then that point probably isn't important enough to you for it to weigh heavily in your choice of a new car. That's overstating it, of course: but you should know, as you go through each point, whether — in the light of your present car's behaviour — that point matters to you or not.

POINT TO REMEMBER   For points where you're reasonably satisfied with things as they are, think how much less satisfied you'd be with another car **just slightly less good for that thing or how much difference even a small improvement would make. If it would make a lot of difference to you, that point counts as one for you to watch in car choice.**

And it's true that there *might* be something about your car which really does make you feel quite swollen with pride — something which you'd miss enormously in another car, some point where you'd want to be sure that any replacement car did at least as well. There might also be something that infuriates you about your car, some point where it lets you down badly: here you'd want any future car to be radically better. Any of these points, good or bad, are the most important of all in showing your needs — so long as they are truly characteristics of your car, rather than mechanical faults which could be put right. Because you feel so strongly about them, these are the points which you should think of as key factors to start you off in your choice of a future car. Note them separately as binding requirements, things you should check that any car has before you consider it as a possible.

So, here goes with the questionnaire:

Starts easily, and runs smoothly,
— even when it's very cold?
— even when it's damp?

Powerful enough,
— to cruise fast enough for you on motorways?
— to overtake other traffic when you want?
— to pull away all right on steep hills?

— for any towing needed?

Flexible enough for smooth driving without too much gearchanging,
— on the open road?
— in crowded town traffic?

Handling trustworthy,
— on wet roads?
— on bumpy roads?
— in nasty winds?
— with a full load?

Manœuvrability and size ok,
— for parking in town?
— for narrow gaps?
— for your garage?

Brakes trustworthy,
— on wet roads?
— at high speeds?
— for sudden emergency stops?
— to hold you on the handbrake, on hills?

This part has all been about how the car behaves on the road (usually discussed in the 'In action' section of *Motoring Which?* car test reports). If your present car conjures up strong feelings, either good or bad, about many of these points, then you probably set more store than most people by performance, and should concentrate more than them on that side of things when you're choosing a new car.

continued over

Controls convenient,
- steering wheel placed right, light and easy to turn, not too much twirling?
- gearlever placed right, light and quick to use?
- handbrake placed well, light to pull on?
- pedals placed well, no awkward angles, smooth and light to press?
- other controls easy to identify, reach and use?

Instruments convenient,
- easy to read by day?
- easy to read by night?
- tell you all you want to know?

View out good,
- clear view ahead?
- ditto, when it's raining?
- headlights good enough?
- mirrors ok?
- no bodywork blindspots?
- easy to see while you're parking?
- demisting works well?

These points, dealing with actually driving the car (usually discussed in the 'At the wheel' section of *Motoring Which?* tests), should show up how much you're sensitive to ergonomic factors — that's to say, factors directly influencing how easily you can drive the car.

Getting in and out easy,
- in the front?
- in the back?
- unlocking, locking up?

Seats comfortable,
- for driving?
- for people in the front?
- and in the back?
- even on long runs?
- plenty of room for all the passengers you carry?
- seat covering satisfactory?

Ride smooth enough,
- on bumpy roads?
- in slow town traffic?
- going round corners and fast bends?

Quiet enough,
- in town traffic?
- at speed?
- no irritating rattles or whines or whirs?

Pleasant 'climate' in the car,
- heater warm enough?
- not too stuffy, front or back?
- enough fresh air?
- cool enough in hot weather?

Those are the main comfort points.

Enough luggage room,
- in the boot (or back)?
- easy to load?
- space enough inside for odds and ends?
- easy to keep valuables out of sight?

Servicing convenient,
- easy to book in when you want?
- servicing intervals not too frequent?
- costs reasonable?
- simple checks like oil level ok?
- easy to work on yourself, if you do that?
- bigger jobs cheap enough?
- spares cheap enough, easily available?

Reliability satisfactory,
- no niggling repetitive faults?
- not off the road for big repairs too much?
- bodywork stands up to your treatment ok?

Economical,
- petrol mpg good enough?
- easy to get the right grade of petrol?
- tyres last well?
- insurance reasonable?

This last group of points starts with factors to do with the way you use the car, just like the earlier groups. But then it goes on to questions like servicing and reliability, which really boil down to cost — though it's important to think too of the waste-of-time angle. For instance, frequent servicing intervals might mean that servicing costs more; but they also mean that you lose the use of your car more often, which would obviously upset you most if you needed it every day. Again, all these points generally follow on from each other in *Motoring Which?* test reports, coming towards the end of a report.

POINT TO REMEMBER This questionnaire covers only things you can judge for yourself in your present car. There are other points vital to car choice where experience with your present car is no help — like safety and depreciation.

How you use your car

Careful analysis of how you use your car gives you an extra line on choosing well. To take an obvious example, if you know that you use much of your boot space just for a once-a-year trip to the seaside, you might consider a car with a much smaller boot which you could supplement with a roof-rack for that one annual jaunt.

So think about the various different types of trip you make in your car. For each, think about the length of the trip, how often you make it, and what special demands it puts on the car. 'Special demands' includes passengers, especially if there's some problem like an elderly relation who finds it difficult to get in and out; it also includes luggage. What about the less obvious things? Dogs with dirty feet, muddy tools, hard-cornered metal boxes, maybe a bicycle you'd like to fit in, golf clubs, a bulky camera you'd like to keep handy but protected, smelly stuff... Or unusual journeys you might need the car for: particularly bumpy tracks, such frequent trips abroad that you'd like a specially easy way of switching your headlamp dipped beam to the opposite side of the road, hot-weather trips abroad where a dark-coloured car would be like an oven?

If you don't have a car of your own, thinking about the present pattern of your journeys can give you only the roughest idea of how you might use a car. There will of course be the trips that you now make using public transport, or another car, maybe even bicycle. But that won't be all. Going on other people's experience, there are some predictions you can make about a whole set of new journeys that having a car would prompt – trips over and above those you make now.

The two main categories are a great many local trips of the sort that you might make on foot now, and some longer ones. Mostly, these trips are all likely to be to do with leisure activities, rather than work, though you'll almost certainly find that you go farther afield than before for your shopping. If you follow the general pattern, you'll find that with a car you make two or three times as many trips, for fun or for shopping, as people without cars. Judging by government surveys, the car will become the crucial factor in something like 15% of your leisure time. You'll spend far more of your time getting out and about – on average, something like four times as much as people without cars. You'll be able

to visit far more places like sports grounds, cinemas, parks, friends and relations – people with cars go on roughly twice as many trips beyond easy walking distance as people without, and again are about twice as likely to get involved in some sort of outdoor or sporting activity. You'll find yourself going to places you'd have never thought of going to by public transport: probably over twice as many jaunts to the countryside on summer weekends, for instance. In particular, there are lots of beauty spots and remote areas, very poorly served by public transport, where virtually all the visitors come by car. Having a car might well change the way you holiday, too: most car-owners use it for their main holiday – indeed, given the same general circumstances, some people you'd otherwise expect to go away for a full holiday actually don't, just making lots of car excursions instead.

Bearing all that in mind, and the extra travel which getting a car will prompt, you'll probably find that you use your car for about three-quarters of your total travel, excluding very short local walks.

Where you live has a bearing on how much you're likely to use your car, too. Allowing for regional variations in the proportion of people with cars, the National Travel Survey shows that individual car-owners account for a higher proportion of the journeys people make in the North of England, and to a less extent in the North-West, Yorkshire and Humberside, and Scotland, than they do elsewhere.

How odd are you?
Yet another way of laying the foundations for your choice of car, maybe particularly useful if you haven't had one before, is to take a careful look at yourself and think how average you are. One of the most important things in choosing a car is to make sure that it 'fits' you. Just as you wouldn't dream of getting a pair of shoes that were too tight or too loose, you shouldn't get an ill-fitting car. For comfort, especially on long runs, and for perfect control over the car, you have to find the controls spaced right for your hands and feet, you have to be able to see out easily, and the shape of the seat has to conform well to your own shape.

If you're a Mr Average, you shouldn't have much of a problem. Manufacturers design their cars for the average-shaped driver. Also, accepting that people vary quite a lot around this average, they allow for variations, for example by having adjustable seats and steering wheel positions. Even so, the variation between the biggest and smallest drivers, between the fattest and thinnest, is too great for a really good compromise – one that would suit everyone perfectly. For example, Scots are often several inches shorter on average than people in the South-East – that's to say, than the mass of the population for whom cars are most likely to be designed. And cars have primarily been designed for men, not women: on average, women both are shorter than men and tend to have shorter arms and legs even than men of the same overall height.

Then the British Mr Average isn't always the same as his counterparts Monsieur Moyen, Señor Tipico or Daihyooteki Na-san. The difference can work in your favour if you're not the standard shape and size: if you're unusually small by British standards, for instance, you might be bang on the Japanese average; if you think the pedals in British cars are set so long away that you'd need stilts to get at them when the steering wheel's set right for you then you sound the Italian shape – a long arm-stretch without spider-long legs.

Start your short list
So there you are: you've worked out any key factors that you reckon are vital before you'd even consider a car, and you've got quite a list of points affecting your choice, worked out from your analysis of how you get on with your present car, any special jobs the car's going to have to do for you, any special characteristics of your own, and so forth. You're *nearly* ready to start choosing. But wait a moment: have you considered doing without a car altogether? Or making do with one much cheaper than you'd need to meet all your needs,

POINTS TO REMEMBER

Any imminent changes in your circumstances? Moving to the country? Having a baby? Anything else that might change what you need from a car?

and hiring a different one for special jobs? (More about that later.)

Finding the car which meets your needs

To make your best choice of car, you have to solve an equation. One side of the equation is your set of needs, what you want from the car. The other side, the solution, is what the chosen car offers – characteristics which are the exact mirror image of your needs.

Some people like to go about this very systematically. They translate their needs into a list of features, maybe in order of importance to them, perhaps even giving each feature a rating – 10 for crucial, say, and 1 just for something that would be quite nice to have. Then they go through the various possibilities, checking off which features each car has against their shopping list.

This approach is quite fun. But it's got enormous snags. The obvious one is that there are so many cars to choose from that working through the possibles might take you so long that they'd all be on the scrap heap by the time you'd finished – even if you weren't

yourself. It's worth going into the less obvious snags in some detail – not to persuade you that this approach isn't worth while (you probably already don't think much of it), but because understanding these snags will help you avoid two common pitfalls in choosing a car.

The first pitfall: kidding yourself. The trouble with points 'scoring systems' is that they're either so simple that they give the wrong score, or they're so complicated that only a computer could make head or tail of them. In practice, if you tot up points for the various factors you want from a car, you run the grave risk that a whole lot of unimportant details (each getting a plus point) could outweigh something really vital to your choice. Using this approach makes it far too easy to kid yourself about whether a car's really going to meet your needs.

Instead, it's best to see your needs almost as a set of increasingly finer-meshed sieves. The first, coarse, sieve is made up from your overriding needs: when you come to compare cars, you simply sieve out the ones that fail to meet these. Next, there's probably a group of factors that matter quite a lot to you, without being vital – again, chuck out cars that don't get through this second sieve. And so on, down through less and less important stuff. The number of cars to choose from is so great that you should be able to eliminate pretty drastically at each stage. But if you do find that the baby's gone out with the bath water, and that nothing's left after one sieve, you can always go back a stage and fiddle with the sieve's mesh slightly to make sure it still leaves you some choice.

The second pitfall: specificationitis. When you translate your needs into the features you'll look for in your next car, you're in danger of catching one of the most dangerous automotive diseases – specificationitis. You'll come out in a rash of bhps, flying wedges, and transverse FWDs, have a grave attack of trailing arms and maybe a touch of the MacPherson struts, and you might even develop recirculating balls.

When car makers, and technical car magazines, describe cars, often they talk about theoretical details of their design rather than the practical facts of its behaviour. The information may be absolutely raw; or it may be seductively quasi-practical (though in fact little more help than the raw information). Take performance as an example. Raw information that you might be given as a substitute for facts about performance include the car's engine capacity, whether or not it's got electronic ignition, what make and type of carburettor is used, the number of cylinders in the engine, even their exact diameter and the length of the piston stroke – maybe a whole lot of stuff about where the camshaft is, how it's driven, how many bearings the crankshaft has.

It's very important for the manufacturer, when he's designing the car, to get his decisions about all these factors right – after all, the original design of the engine does control its performance. But once the car is off the drawing-board and on to the road, design details like these become virtually irrelevant. For example, even if you're enough of an engineer to know that the first and second orders of moment of an in-line six-cylinder engine are in balance, whether or not the engine will actually pull more smoothly than a V-six or a four-cylinder depends on the way all the other aspects of the design build up together into the engine's overall performance. It's best to treat raw specification data of this type merely as mumbo-jumbo.

Quasi-practical specification details at first sight look much more helpful. In our performance example, they might include the engine's maximum power output, its maximum torque (a measure of the turning force in its output shaft), and – a bit closer to practicality – the car's top speed and the time it takes to accelerate from a standstill to either a particular speed (like 60 mph) or a set distance (like quarter of a mile).

Again, though, even these details can give only the grossest impression of the probable behaviour of the car. Take as an example two cars tested together by *Motoring Which?*, the Honda Accord and the Volkswagen Golf 1600. The Accord's engine is 7% more powerful than the VW's: does that mean it performs better on the road? The VW's top speed was some 5% higher than the Honda's: so is *it* quicker? In fact,

careful track tests showed that the two cars were very closely matched for acceleration and overtaking, and driving experience over ten thousand miles of testing confirmed that in practice it wouldn't be worth trying to choose between them. So, in the case, whether you'd taken the power output measurement or taken the top speed, you'd have been misled into a false idea of how the two cars compared in real-life performance.

So don't use performance specification data as more than a very general guide – a 140-bhp car will be quicker than a 50-bhp car of the same size, and the acceleration and overtaking performance you get from a 110-mph car will be better than from a 70-mph one. But if performance does matter much to you, then you'll be interested in much closer comparisons than that. And when you compare a 100-mph car with a 90-mph one, you could well find that the 90-mph car accelerates more quickly.

The same goes for descriptions of a car's suspension system, or its steering – they won't tell how the car actually behaves on the road.

If **space for luggage** matters to you, then you might pay some attention to cubic capacity figures given by manufacturers. But don't assume that this is actually the measure of how much luggage you could fit in yourself. Different manufacturers use different measuring methods – some even quoting a 'fluid' cubic capacity, that is the total you could squeeze in if the shape of the boot didn't matter. But some use a set of cases of varying shapes and sizes, so that their boot-capacity figures are much closer to what you might find yourself. (This second system is closer to what *Motoring Which?* uses in its tests.)

Manufacturers who do seem to quote a fairly conservative figure for boot space include Alfa Romeo, Honda, Lada, Opel, Saab, Toyota and Vauxhall. To put figures quoted by different makers on very roughly the same footing, getting at least a rough comparison

POINT TO REMEMBER

What really matters, choosing a car, is how it behaves in practice – not what the specification says.

between figures given by different makers, you could reckon that the comparable space in a Talbot, Datsun or Volkswagen might be around two-thirds of what they quote; in a British Leyland, Citroën, Fiat or Ford about three-quarters – slightly less than this in a Volvo, slightly more in a Peugeot; in a Renault you might reckon on allowing some 90% of the space they quote. But this is only a rough rule of thumb.

If you're really interested in carrying capacity, you might be thinking of an estate car or a hatchback (a car with a back loading door), with the possibility of folding the back seat to add extra space. It's difficult to compare their carrying capacity, using any one single figure – best to use a full set of dimensions such as those shown in *Motoring Which?*. If you're just thinking of carrying suitcases and the like, remember that you wouldn't want to heap them up above seat level – they could shoot forwards when you brake. For this, bear in mind that makers' capacity figures generally assume that you *will* fill up the whole of the space: to get a rough idea of how an estate's luggage capacity might compare with a saloon, divide the maker's estate figure by half to allow for this.

Figures quoted by car manufacturers for **fuel consumption** have to be the result of government-approved tests. One simulates town driving – to represent accelerating, slowing, changing gear, stopping, and idling. Another is based on driving at a steady 56 mph; the third, on driving at a steady 75 mph.

None of these figures on their own gives an accurate guide to fuel consumption. *Motoring Which?* computer analysis shows that most people in practice get an mpg somewhere between the town driving figure and the 56-mph figure. But an 'economy-engined' car, for example, might come out relatively well in the official tests – and do much worse in real life, because in practice drivers work the relatively underpowered engine much harder than in a more powerful version.

So it's best to reply on mpg tests over several thousand miles of normal driving (such as those in *Motoring Which?*). But failing that you can get a rough idea of typical mpg, by doing one or two sums developed by the *Motoring Which?* computer:

First sum:

1. subtract the urban-driving figure from the 56-mph figure

2. multiply that result by 0.38

3. add the urban-driving figure to this second result, to get predicted average mpg.

Second sum (using all three test figures):

$$\frac{\text{urban mpg} + \text{mpg at 56 mph}}{2} - \frac{\text{mpg at 75 mph}}{10} - 1$$

Dealers may have copies of the full list of official mpg figures. Otherwise, you can get it from Dept of Energy (Car Fuel List), PO Box 702, London SW20 8SZ.

Motoring Which? found 21 mpg in real life, with the automatic

Petrol tank range is always a convenience factor: the number of gallons the tank can hold, multiplied by its mpg. Now, with the growing frequency of petrol shortages, tank range has growing importance. Try for 300 miles or more.

Hard facts: how to find them out

Accepting specifications as, at best, only a very partial guide to a car's behaviour, how can you find out which car will fit your needs best?

Not surprisingly, we think *Motoring Which?* is much the best source of comparative information about cars. The test reports are backed by analysis of the experience of some 20,000 or more readers each year. They come out quarterly on a subscription basis and cover all popular cars. Old issues can be a help, too – when considering used cars.

Two gaps in *Motoring Which?* test coverage are very newly-introduced cars (the full battery of tests take several months to finish, and even a 'rush job' on some outstanding newcomer takes two or three months at least to get into print) and more unusual or expensive cars. For tests on these you can use the bookstall magazines.

Motor and *Autocar*, weeklies very similar to one another, have been the obvious car-test rivals for many years. Both have gone quite some way towards emulating the rather scientific *Which?* approach to testing. This makes their test results more factual and comparative – easier to use as directly factual evidence than, say, the much more personal 'reviews' of the newspaper motoring writers. Like other motoring magazines, they borrow pre-launch cars from the manufacturers so that they can publish reports on new cars at the time they are first announced, and they both test a good number of expensive or exotic cars as well as popular ones. But you might well want to read their reports on popular cars in addition to *Motoring Which?* reports on them, just to get a broader picture.

What Car? tabulates specification details for all new cars and many used ones (up to five years old). It also tests groups of comparable cars, and includes 'market reviews' – outlines of the choice available if you've some

particular type of car in mind. *Car*, too, has group tests, often quite outspoken: like *Motor Sport* (which also has tests), it tends to concentrate on points to interest really keen drivers more than on day-to-day practical details.

American magazines like *Road & Track* and *Car and Driver* do have quite hard-hitting reports on European cars – but often the versions sold in the US are quite different from those sold here. If you read French, *Autojournal* stands out for its frank no-punches-pulled practical approach – though French cars always seem to do best in its comparative group tests!

The guide to used-car prices which dealers use is *Glass's Guide*: it aims to reflect the prices actually paid for used cars, at various ages and in various states of repair. But only dealers are allowed to subscribe to it – indeed, they use it to set their own prices for used cars. You probably won't be able to borrow a copy from a friendly garage-owner: substitutes you can buy yourself are *Motorists Guide to new and used car prices* and *Parker's New, Used and Trade Car Price Guide*; *What Car?* also has prices. *Motoring Which?* analysis has shown that *Motorists Guide* tends to be best of these on prices.

Using the evidence

Whatever source of facts you use, the approach is the same: you start with your collection of needs (converted into the features you'll be looking for in your next car), checking the facts about cars against your essential needs and preferences. There's the long way round – painstakingly checking off all the possibles against your requirements; and there are various short cuts – arbitrarily cutting down the original list of possibles in one way or another, which of course means that you might rule out your perfect choice simply by leaving it off the list, but at least means that you'll be dealing with a manageable problem, rather than a full-time job for the next year!

The most workable short-cut starting-point is a test report of a group of comparable cars, of the type you're most interested in, or including a particular car that you've always thought of as a possible for you. A typical *Motoring Which?* report, for instance, would include two or three closely comparable cars, and in conclusion may well bring into the comparison maybe ten other possibilities. So, starting with that report, on a type of car in which you were interested, you'd have your attention directed also to cars which you might not have thought of as in the running.

The annual *Motoring Which?* Car Buying Guide, in the October issue, covers about 9 out of 10 of all new cars sold. With your shopping list of needs, you can work through each of the 50 or 60 main models to see which comes up to your requirements best. Or – a short cut within a short cut – use the Guide's value for money summary section as a pointer to just a small number of cars that stand out as worth special consideration.

There are other approaches you might consider. Sometimes, advertisements set out to persuade you that one particular car is a better buy than five or six others. If any of those cars are ones you've thought of as possibles, it would be worth your looking into the others – factually of course, rather than in the terms of the advertisement! Another thing to try is to say to any of your friends that 'know about cars' that you're thinking of getting a new car, and tell them the most important things on your list of needs. Different people are practically bound to suggest different possibilities. Don't let yourself be persuaded by any of your knowledgeable friends into choosing their own favourite: but do make a list of all the possibles they suggest, then work through the list, with your needs in mind, using one of the factual sources of evidence about how cars behave in practice. Yet another approach is to spend a few days looking carefully at other people's cars – not just people you know, but cars you just happen to see in the street. Any that look to you as if they might be the sort of thing you're looking for, make a note of the maker and model name – then check the facts on the cars you've been ogling, in the same way as was outlined above. One special advantage of that approach is that

POINT TO REMEMBER
Your best buy may be a car you hadn't even considered – so spread the net wide.

you'll add into your list not just current cars, but some older ones too.

Test drives

It's a mistake for you to hope for too much from test-driving a new car. The things which you notice in just an hour or less with a car may be quite different from the things which will strike you about it when you're actually living with it. Indeed, almost any new car – especially with the salesman sitting beside you – can seem like perfection itself on first acquaintance, especially as your standard of reference, what you're actually judging it against, is probably your old car which you've decided to get rid of.

Even so, with a cool approach to the test drive you can make it quite useful.

The obvious first step is to go back to your original list of needs, and the features which those needs told you you wanted in your new car. Are any of them things which a test drive, or even a careful look at the car in the showroom, can tell you more about than any other source of information?

A short test drive can't let you make fine comparative judgements about handling, power and so forth, if those things really matter to you. At best, it should show up any gross failings – see that it's not jerky, driving at varying speeds under 30 mph in top gear; see that it doesn't twitch horribly, if you put the brakes on gently while you're going round a bend; see that it can manœuvre and park in small spaces, if that's something you need.

Check all the controls to make sure you can reach them easily and work them conveniently. Again, this won't warn you of a clutch pedal that becomes tiringly heavy in long traffic jams, or some confusingly-placed switch that you keep getting wrong on rainy nights. But it could spot anything really bad, like a steering wheel that needs an all-in wrestler for parking, a gearlever you can't reach, pedals so high off the floor that you can't work them while you're resting your heel on the floor, or a handbrake which snugly keeps the car parked on a hill – so long as it's a gorilla driving.

23

You can check visibility quite well: check ahead, that the roof line wouldn't cut off your view up a hill ahead say, that you can actually see over the steering wheel, that if it was raining the windscreen wiper pattern wouldn't leave a thick blindspot at the edge. Then see how well you can judge the back corners, for reversing; and see that there isn't a blindspot there, which could hide a cyclist say when you were waiting to come out of a side road.

Comfort again is something that you can't judge on a short run – certainly not good points, though anything grotesquely uncomfortable or inconvenient might show up. But you should see how easy it is to get in and out. If you have a regular passenger who tends to find this difficult, they'd be well worth bringing along. And you can check the luggage arrangements, bearing

POINT TO REMEMBER
A short test drive can give a very misleading impression of a car's long-term suitability.

specially in mind any odd luggage needs you have.

Don't pay attention to any good points the salesman brandishes at you unless they happen to be things which you've already worked out that you want. They're bound to be attractive – he wouldn't be mentioning them otherwise – but from your point of view the charm is superficial ... they don't matter to you.

A profitable variation on the test-run theme is to hire a car of the type you want for a couple of days. Then, you can really put it through its paces. Try it in all the circumstances where you know that your particular requirements set an important test. Go on the routes you'd be going on normally, and keep driving for a long time – a car's faults don't really start showing until you're getting a bit tired yourself.

If you do plan to do this, it could be worth trying to find a garage which is a dealer for the car you want *and* which hires cars itself. You might well be able to arrange that if you did buy the car you'd be able to have the whole of your hiring charge knocked off the bill.

2. NEW OR SECONDHAND?

Most people who buy new cars do so not because they've worked out that it's actually better for them than buying a used car, but simply because to them that's what car-buying means. Similarly, most people who buy used have assumed from the start that they're in the used-car market, and that's that.

If you really are determined to start from those assumptions, taking for granted your own position as either a new-car buyer or a used-car buyer, then that's fine. People might have very strong, even if irrational, reasons for wanting to buy new – that unmistakable smell that survives for a few weeks, that smart new registration letter, the feeling that it's really and truly yours because it's never been anyone else's.

But you can make the decision between buying new and buying used on rational grounds, instead.

Reliability is one factor to consider. People expect new cars to be more reliable than older ones, and know they can rely on a guarantee usually for a year if they can't actually rely on the car itself.

In fact, new cars are by no means fault-free. In all its years of testing, *Motoring Which?* has never found a single car delivered new without any faults. Moreover, even after those first faults are sorted out, things start going wrong with most cars almost immediately.

From the point of view of sheer inconvenience – having to put your car in for repairs when you'd rather be able to use it – new cars don't score at all over cars which are a year or two old. Most people get faults fixed when they have their car serviced. For the first few years of its life, the average car spends four days or so each year off the road, for this.

However, a lot of the faults that hit young cars are less serious than the things that happen to them as they get older. The chart shows how the number of parts needing replacement or overhaul each year increases as the car gets older:

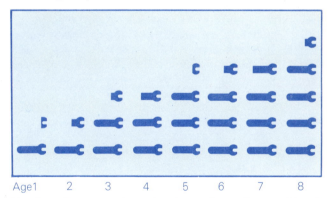

Number of spanners in each column shows the number of major repairs likely each year: e.g. 4 in 7th year.

There's an increase, too, in the total number of faults including little niggling things that can wait a while to get fixed – but again the car even when it's new starts with some of these smaller faults.

Perhaps the most important index of how inconvenient a fault is, is whether that fault makes the

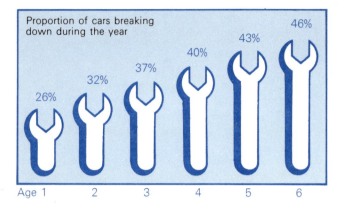

Proportion of cars breaking down during the year

26% — Age 1
32% — 2
37% — 3
40% — 4
43% — 5
46% — 6

car break down. On that index, new cars don't have much of a margin over ones a year or so older, as the chart above shows. However, they are quite a lot less likely to break down than cars four or five years old.

Garage bills relate to how expensive a car was when it was new – rather than to its secondhand value. Obviously, if you have the same amount of money to spend buying a secondhand car as buying a new car, the secondhand one when it was new would have been a more expensive car than the new car which today carries the same price tag. In other words, if you pick up an old Jaguar for the same price as a new Mini, you've got to remember that your servicing and repairs will come at Jaguar prices, not Mini ones.

Taking account of this factor, as well as the increased risk of faults in older cars and the protection against repair costs which you get with a new car's guarantee, you should reckon that garage bills for say a two-year-old car might cost you nearly three times as much as for a new car with the same price-tag – at least in the first year. Garage bills for a four-year-old car might cost you over four times as much. (See the graph on page 29 later on in this section – it shows how much you might expect to have to spend on garage bills during

(See the graph on page 29 later on in this section

POINT TO REMEMBER – THE GUARANTEE

In the first year of a car's life, it cuts garage bills to about 60% of what they would have been if you'd had to pay for all the faults yourself.

the year, as a proportion of what you'd pay to buy a car of a particular age.)

This really brings us to the crucial point in the new-versus-used comparison – how total costs of owning new and used cars compare.

New versus used – value for money
There are two ways of comparing the value you get for your money, buying new or used. The first compares the cost of owning an identical car – new in one case, used in the other (and of course thinking about used cars of varying ages). The second compares what you can get, new or used, assuming you're going to spend a set amount of money buying and running the car. So, in the first case the car is fixed – what you're interested in is how much the age of the car affects your owner-ship costs. In the second case it's these costs that are fixed – you're interested in the variations in what that money buys, instead.

CASE ONE: How age affects costs
The cost of owning a car includes some things that usu-ally aren't affected by which car it is: particularly, road tax and parking or garaging costs. In comparing the cost of different cars you can forget about these. The costs that do matter to any comparison can be split into two different sorts of thing.

First, there are 'standing costs': costs which you have to meet regardless of how much or how little you use the car. These include depreciation (discussed much more fully in its own special section, opposite), pur-chasing costs and insurance. Then there are 'running costs' which depend on how much you use the car – the more you use it, the higher the costs. These include petrol and oil, servicing and repairs.

If you are thinking simply about one particular car – and how its costs vary at different times of its life – the amount you'll be using it doesn't affect the issue too critically. And some costs, like insurance, are going to be pretty much the same for any one car however old it is (though the premium should be slightly lower for an older car). So the costs to consider really boil down to:

- depreciation
- purchasing cost
- repairs and servicing.

DEPRECIATION

Because depreciation is the biggest factor in car costs, it's worth understanding how it works.

Depreciation is the amount of value a car loses, as it gets older. In the old days, it was relatively simple to weigh this up. If a car cost £3,000 at the start of a year, when you bought it, and at the end of that year you could sell it for £2,000, then it would have depreciated by £1,000, or 33%. Inflation's changed all that. Now, secondhand car prices are yanked up by the inflation of new car prices. If during the year the price of the £3,000 car is inflated by 15%, to £3,450, this price-rise reverberates through the secondhand market, too. You find at the end of the year that you can get maybe £2,300 for your car. So on paper it looks as if your depreciation has been only £700 – 23% instead of 33%. Jolly good, you think. The snag is that when you then come to buy another car, you find that as car prices have risen by 15% your £2,300 can buy only what £2,000 would have bought at the start of the year.

So, in real-life values rather than merely in paper money, you're right back to the beginning. Effectively, that 23% depreciation coupled with the 15% inflation is just the same as the 33% depreciation that you'd have had without the inflation. Remember, depreciation doesn't cost you anything until you sell. But as soon as you do sell, what you need to know about isn't some arbitrary number of pound notes, it's what your car is worth in terms of what you can buy.

So in this book we've used real-life figures for depreciation – that's to say, figures that do reflect the true value of your car when the time comes to sell. This means that future changes in the rate of inflation shouldn't affect the figures much. Although any major change would make nonsense of predictions based merely on the number of pounds a car will fetch when it's sold, it won't alter the underlying value of what you're selling or buying.

Strictly speaking, 'depreciation' is the fall in the value you get from the car, as wear and tear, obsolescence and its declining ability to meet your needs take their toll. In practice, 'depreciation' is usually taken to be the money difference between what you pay for the car and what you eventually get when you sell it, divided by the number of years you keep it for.

As the depreciation box on the left shows, however, high present-day rates of inflation mean that you can no longer simply think in terms of the falling number of pounds your car will cost to buy with each passing year. If you did reckon just on that, you'd get a nasty and perhaps almost insurmountable shock when you found eventually that replacing your car cost far more than its face-value depreciation. So any practical calculation throughout this book includes the eventual cost of replacement.

Although different cars certainly vary in how well they keep their value, there is a general pattern which many cars fit quite well. It's quite simple: you can assume that the moment you drive the car away from the showroom, it'll *instantly* lose about one-sixth of its value if it's new, about one-tenth if it's used; and that each year that you keep it will cut its value by another one-sixth or more (depending on how well you look after it).

The chart below, based on analysis of the depreciation behaviour of over 200 different models, shows how

Chart 1   RESALE VALUE

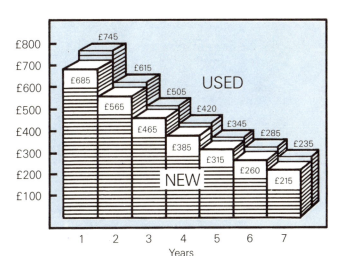

this works in practice. It shows the resale value you might expect, for each £1,000 spent now on either a new or a used car.

Remember, this isn't simply the falling number of £s which the car will fetch. Instead, it takes into account the car's value in terms of what you might be able to buy for the money it brings when you sell. This gives a truer and simpler picture of depreciation, as it won't be upset by any changes in the rate of inflation from year to year – which can make a nonsense of the 'falling number of ££s' method of describing depreciation (see page 27).

Purchasing cost depends a lot on how you actually pay for the car. If you pay for it outright, with your own money, you lose the value of what you might otherwise have used that money for. For instance, if you'd had the money in a building society, you'll lose the interest you'd have got. If you'd have spent the money on something other than a car, which held its value better than a car, then that's what you lose: say for example you'd have spent it instead on buying a more expensive house, your loss should be measured instead in terms of the rise in value of houses over the period that you keep the car for.

If instead you borrow the money or at least part of the money, then your buying cost is simply the cost of borrowing the money. As the later section on paying for cars shows, this cost will vary depending on who lends you the money. Generally, the cost would be more if you borrowed than if you used your own money.

In these examples, we've taken 8% a year as the cost of using your own money (and assumed that even if you borrow you'll pay a deposit of one-third the price yourself, borrowing only two-thirds). For borrowing, we've given a choice between 16% (a bank loan) and 26% (HP). Just a passing word of warning: this is the right way to compare money costs when you're simply thinking about the true costs of owning different cars. But of course, as the later section on actually paying for the car shows, when you're working out how much you can afford you're interested in a different figure – the level

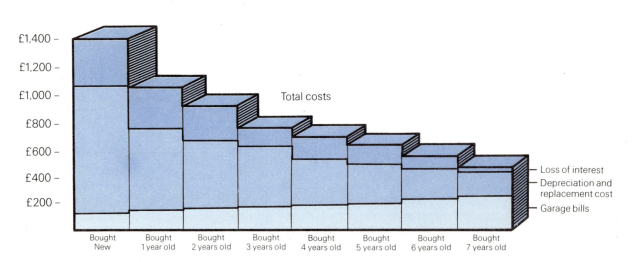

Chart 2   ANNUAL COSTS OF OWNING A TYPICAL CAR

Total costs

Loss of interest
Depreciation and replacement cost
Garage bills

£1,400							
£1,200							
£1,000							
£800							
£600							
£400							
£200							

Bought New — Bought 1 year old — Bought 2 years old — Bought 3 years old — Bought 4 years old — Bought 5 years old — Bought 6 years old — Bought 7 years old

of your monthly outgoings. If you borrow money, your monthly outgoings include both interest and capital repayments. But here we can forget about that, and concentrate just on the interest.

The third and final part of this cost comparison between new and used is the increasing cost of repair and servicing, as the car gets older. In practice, people's actual garage bills tend to flatten out with older cars. This partly reflects the generally poorer state of repair that people with much older cars put up with, partly the fact that people tend to cover lower annual mileages as their car gets older. So for these examples we've assumed that repair costs continue to increase with age – that's to say, that if something went wrong you'd be just as likely to fix it with an old car as with a new one.

The effect of all these components – depreciation, buying costs and repairs – on the choice between buying a particular car new and buying it used is shown in the charts (pages 27 to 29). Chart 2 shows how the different costs contribute. It sets out how buying costs, depreciation and garage bills compare, for someone buying a £4,300 car – using their own money to pay for it, and keeping it for two years before selling. The costs are for a car worth £4,300 *new*.

You can see from this that the way the car's age brings down its price – and therefore the cost of depreciation and the loss of interest – is much more important than the way that increasing age pushes up garage bills. So, the older the car is, the cheaper it is to own. Moreover, the difference is by far the greatest between a new car and one just one year old: the one-year-old car costs only three-quarters as much as the new car to own (before paying for petrol, etc). To make as big a saving as this over a three-year-old car, you'd have to buy one about twice as old.

POINT TO REMEMBER

The cheaper buying costs of older cars almost invariably outweigh their higher repair bills.

Of course, not everyone's interested in that £4,300 car – and not everyone's able to find all the money

Chart 3   COST OF OWNING A CAR PER YEAR, PER £1000 OF ITS NEW LIST PRICE NOW

	if bought	new	1 yr old	2 yr old	3 yr old	4 yr old	5 yr old	6 yr old	7 yr old
using all your own money	kept for 1 year	£520	£370	£320	£270	£250	£220	£210	£190
	kept for two years	£410	£310	£270	£230	£210	£190	£170	£160
	kept for 3 years	£370	£280	£250	£220	£190	£170	£160	£150
	kept for 4 years	£340	£270	£230	£200	£180	£160	£150	—
	kept for 5 years	£320	£250	£220	£200	£180	£160	—	—
with 12% loan	kept for 1 year	£560	£390	£340	£290	£270	£230	£220	£200
	kept for 2 years	£440	£340	£290	£250	£230	£200	£180	£170
	kept for 3 years	£400	£310	£270	£230	£210	£190	£170	£150
	kept for 4 years	£370	£290	£250	£220	£200	£180	£160	—
	kept for 5 years	£350	£280	£240	£210	£190	£160	—	—
with 26% loan	kept for 1 year	£680	£480	£410	£350	£320	£280	£250	£230
	kept for 2 years	£560	£430	£360	£310	£280	£240	£220	£200
	kept for 3 years	£520	£400	£340	£290	£260	£230	£210	£190
	kept for 4 years	£490	£380	£330	£280	£250	£220	£200	—
	kept for 5 years	£470	£370	£320	£270	£240	£210	—	—

themselves, to buy. So Chart 3 gives the information simply as total ownership cost: breaking it down into the three component parts of the cost would have made it far too complex to read.

In Chart 3, the first section shows costs for people putting up all the money themselves; the second, for people borrowing most of it cheaply (a bank loan); the third, for people borrowing more expensively (on HP). Each section shows how the length of time you keep the car affects costs. So that you can use the information for any car you're thinking of buying, it's given in annual cost per £1,000 of a car's current list price when new. This means that if you're thinking of a £6,000 car, you can multiply the figures in the chart by 6 – and so on. There's one small proviso. Although garage bills are higher for expensive cars than for cheap ones, they don't keep absolutely in line with price. In the chart you can allow for this, by knocking about £10 off the cost-per-£1,000 shown if you're thinking of an expensive car (but adding £10 for a really cheap one).

Chart 3 underlines the two main lessons: the older you buy, the less it costs; and the vital cost difference is between new and used – because of the much bigger price drop in the car's first year than at any later time in its life. But the chart adds some extra points.

Most important, the longer you keep the car, the cheaper that makes it. For example, if you keep a car for five years instead of just one year before changing it, it'll cut the expense of owning it by between a quarter and one-third. This is entirely because of the way that depreciation becomes less serious the longer you keep the car. Although the actual rate of depreciation stays much the same in percentage terms, because the value of the car is less the depreciation slice of that value has to get smaller, too. While garage bills do get worse as the car gets older, this isn't enough to balance the less costly depreciation of the older car, except towards the very end of its life. Which does raise a point that it's important to make:

POINT TO REMEMBER
The longer you keep the car, the more you'll save.

With older cars, there is an increasing risk of catastrophic mechanical trouble – or, more likely, of desperate rust. So there is a risk that in the later years you might have not a car but a heap of scrap – with no chance whatsoever of scraping through its MoT Test unless you spent absurd amounts of money on repair. The figures in the charts are based on the assumption that you keep the car in good condition, and that real disasters are unlikely. Nevertheless, unless you're one of those people who can spot warnings of mechanical trouble very far in advance – or unless you've always been able to make cars struggle on valiantly, long after the point when they should have gone to the wreckers – you should probably play safe, by not planning on keeping a car very long after its sixth year, say.

CASE TWO: How age affects what you can buy
The components of this comparison are the same as the last: depreciation, purchasing cost and repairs. But the answer is different – what you can buy, rather than how much you have to pay for it.

This time, assume you've got a fixed budget, and you're comparing what you might get if you bought new with what you might get if you bought used. Chart 4 shows the comparison. The figures in it represent 'new list price' values, so that for each £1,000-worth of a new car that you might buy you can see how much used car you might buy instead. For example, say you had £4,000 to spend, or rather to be strictly accurate that your budget for buying costs, depreciation and garage bills would allow you to buy a £4,000 new car. If you multiply any of the figures in the chart by four, you would see how expensive a used car of that age you could get instead – the 'expensiveness' of the used car is measured in terms of the current list price of a new car of that model. So, for example, instead of your £4,000 new car, you could buy a four-year-old specimen of a car whose current price is £1,950 × 4, that is £7,800.

This time, the way you pay for the car makes no difference to the results – assuming of course that you would be using the same payment method, whichever age of car you bought. The length of time you keep the car does make a slight difference – if you're going to keep the car for a long time, you can't get quite such an 'expensive' used car for the same outlay – but the difference is too small to tabulate separately. Knocking £100 off the values quoted above would be about right.

You can see that there isn't very much difference between one year and the next – about 10%. That's actually well within the range of cost differences that would probably get swallowed up anyway in other aspects of your choice. That's to say, you shouldn't buy a car one year older just for the saving involved. The time to do it would be when you were right at the limit of your budgeting, and reckoned that this was the only way you could possibly afford a particular car that you'd set your heart on.

On the other hand, you might at least think about buying a *much* older car. If you get it four or five years old, instead of new, you can afford twice as expensive a car as you'd otherwise be able to buy. That takes you

Chart 4   USED CAR VALUES

1 year old		£1,325
2 years old		£1,525
3 years old		£1,675
4 years old		£1,950
5 years old		£2,200
6 years old		£2,375
7 years old		£2,600

into a quite different price range – worth exploring, before you make your mind up.

How cars vary in keeping their value
Now that the car market is so international, and no longer dominated by our home producers, depreciation rates are affected by economic trends in the country in which a car was made, which may be quite different from economic trends here. If a country's economy is more vigorous than ours, and if as a result its currency tends to hold its value better than ours, then even if its cars' prices stay the same when they're sold in that country's home market, they tend to rise in terms of our currency – which of course is what we have to use to pay for them, if they're exported here.

So, if you buy a foreign car (or even a British one, come to that), to some extent you're speculating in the currency of its country of origin. If that currency tends to strengthen while you've got the car, when you come to sell it you'll find that it has tended to depreciate less than if that currency has weakened. But don't set too much store by this point. First, as their depreciation performance is helped by the fact that the price of those cars, new, has risen faster than average, you wouldn't be able to cash in on this advantage unless – when replacement time came – you bought instead a car from a weak-currency country like Italy. Second, and more important, the effect that new prices have on second-hand prices matters much less than how much people want a particular make of used car. The car's general reputation, and its relative reliability, contributes much more to its secondhand value.

So how can you choose a car which is going to hold its value relatively well? The simplest way is to use the predictions in *Motoring Which?* test reports. These have proved a good guide to how depreciation costs work out in practice. There are also some general rules which help.

Unless they're very uncommon, cars which have particularly long waiting lists for delivery new tend to hold their value very well indeed in their first year or two. Indeed, if there's a delivery delay of some six months or more, 'slightly used' cars may actually be higher-priced than the same cars brand new, because they're a way of avoiding the long waiting list for new ones. But beware – if the waiting list is long simply because that particular car is a very recent introduction, depreciation in the longer run may turn out to be actually greater than average: this happened with the Jaguar XJ, for example. Cars where the rule works best are ones which have been in production for quite some time, but where demand still outstrips supply far enough to make for a long queue waiting for delivery – eg, Mercedes. If the reason for the queue is simply chronic industrial trouble at the factory (which seems far more common with British cars than with foreign ones), the rule holds good only in the short term – for as long as the delivery hold-up takes to clear.

Another important rule is that if the car maker does a radical face-lift of some car, or replaces it with a new version or new model entirely, then the old model usually takes quite a sharp dip in its secondhand value. Even worse is the effect on resale values if the car maker simply stops making that model altogether – then, it depreciates about one-third as fast again as it would have done otherwise. The rule affects you in practice in several different ways.

If for example you've already got a car which you'll be selling in the next year or two, you want to avoid being overtaken by some radical change in production which would cut your car's value sharply. If it's been in production without major changes for five years or so, a change might well be imminent – ask knowledgeable friends if there's anything in the wind. If your car's still fairly young, getting rid of it before the change rather than after it could save you £100 or so.

Or maybe you're thinking of some used car which got a face-lift affecting cars of about the age you're thinking of buying. Depending on how radical the changes were, the price difference could be from about £80 to about £200. But that's a once-for-all difference; the depreciation rate tends to stay much the same, otherwise. So if the changes in themselves don't matter a great deal to you, you'd probably be marginally better off getting the slightly older car, just before the face-lift.

POINT TO REMEMBER
Cars no longer made lose their value faster.

It's worth noting that in general estate cars depreciate at much the same rate as their saloon car versions – if anything, they tend to hold their value very slightly better. Similarly, an automatic gearchange version of a car normally loses value at much the same rate as the manual version. And sports cars or sporting coupés tend to depreciate no more quickly than saloons. But extras don't usually add to a car's value – so if they're things you've paid for, rather than simply inherited from a previous owner, don't expect to get your money back on them when you sell.

Different versions of the same car also tend to depreciate at much the same rate as one another. An exception to this is if some version is really quite out of the run of its 'cousins' – diesel-engined versions tend to lose much more of their value in their first year, for example, though after this they depreciate at the 'normal' rate. If a car's got the general reputation of being good value as a utility family saloon, then the ordinary middle-of-the-road versions may tend to hold their value better than ones less in demand, at the high-priced top of the range which run to particularly luxurious trimmings or unusually powerful engines. Conversely, when a car has a basically sporty or exclusive image, the versions which mirror this image best tend to hold their value best.

Over the years, the 'champions' for holding their value relatively well have tended to be cars with the best reputations for reliability. This is specially important with older cars. First of all, people buying used cars obviously don't want them to fall to bits. Secondly, the dealers who take them in part-exchange and then sell them have to allow for their expenses in making the cars more or less ship-shape. It's because of this that the dealer's mark-up, which is usually around 10% or even less on a newish car, rises to 20% or more on older cars. Of course, it's not just reliability on its own that matters here, but the overall cost of repairs – which involves spares prices too (see later). As these tend to be greater for foreign cars – and as spares costs are particularly important for older cars – foreign cars in general tend to lose their value rather more quickly than British cars in general. Again, there are exceptions.

Some Japanese cars with a growing reputation for reliability tend to depreciate at much the same rate as British cars now. German cars also tend to hold their value here as well as British ones – with Mercedes-Benz depreciating less quickly than most. Among British cars themselves, British Leyland cars have tended to lose value a little more quickly than other big manufacturers': in particular, Jaguars (and the equivalent Daimlers) have recently tended to lose value very quickly, though Rovers have held their value well. Lotus, too, have lost value faster than most cars. Best of all – with very long waiting lists – have been Morgan, and Bentley and Rolls-Royce.

Wait for that new model?
A question more for new-car buyers than used-car buyers is whether it's worth waiting for some updated version of a car, or an entirely new replacement model.

If the changes are small ones, they won't usually make the car much better, though they're likely to bump up its price by a few per cent. That can be a particularly good moment to buy the original version. Manufacturers – to make sure their dealers can get rid of these old-model cars and stock up with the new ones – sometimes give them a 'run-out' special discount on the old version. Even if they don't, dealers tend to cut the prices of the old version themselves, to get rid of old stock quickly. On a typical car, this could save you about £200. Although, when you come to sell, you won't get such a good price as if you'd bought the latest version, you're certainly unlikely to lose as much as you'd gained originally.

If the changes are big ones, or if it's an entirely new model, you can't always rely on all the changes being changes for the better. The history of automotive progress is littered with perverse backward steps. A simple, straighforward dashboard may suddenly be cluttered up with so many unnecessary instruments that the switches you need to get at have to be stuffed away out of reach. Stylists – or smooth aerodynamics – may decree that this year ungainly windscreen wipers are out, hiding them in a little recess at the bottom of the screen – where snow and ice lock them in a winter's grave just when they're most needed. A car with perfectly comfortable if unglamorous seats has to be given much grander-looking ones – which don't turn out nearly so comfortable in the long run. A car with an ordinary but quite adequate four-speed gearbox is suddenly given an irksomely recalcitrant five-speed one instead. The latest body shape has elegantly sloping sides – much more squash for the people inside, and much more difficult to judge when parking. Indeed, as cars have become more and more refined, it's become more and more difficult for their makers to give them the periodic changes which the marketing men demand, without these changes turning out to be at least partly changes for the worse.

Another reason for waiting might be that genuinely new models, with different mechanical and body parts, can be a problem in their first year or two. First, the longer a car stays in production the more time the maker has to put right recurrent faults and weaknesses. Secondly, when things do go wrong on a newly-introduced car you're likely to have much more difficulty getting them fixed. This is because it's often difficult to get spare parts for new cars: until the factory has experience of what things need replacement most commonly, it can't plan an effective spares programme. Even after the factory's got this under way, it'll take time before spares stocks for this new car are nearly as substantial as for some older car which has been around for years – and which therefore greatly outnumbers the new one.

3. YOUR MONTHLY OUTLAY

Buying a car, you can split your costs into three groups. The first two are things which you actually pay for – you can tell how much you're spending, as you spend it. But with the third group, the costs are hidden: just as real, but you can't tell how much they are so easily.

The first group is *standing costs*. However you're paying for the car itself, and whichever car you buy, one part of the standing costs is fixed: Road Fund tax. The next part is insurance – this of course does vary from car to car, and from driver to driver (see section 3). More tricky is the third and final part of this group of costs – because not everyone has to pay it. It's the monthly payment on a loan or HP agreement: obviously if you've used your own money entirely to pay for the car outright, you don't have to pay this. But if you are buying on a loan or HP, this monthly payment will be your biggest single regular outlay.

The second group is *running costs*: things which depend on how much you drive. Again, they're costs which you actually pay out, week by week or month by month. The main elements in this group, starting with the most expensive, are petrol costs, general garage servicing and repair bills, and tyre replacement costs.

Finally, there's the insidious group of *hidden costs*. Again, these depend on how you're buying the car. For someone using their own money to buy the car outright, they fall into two parts. First, there's the cost of using that money – the loss of interest it might have earned if it had been left in a building society, for example.

Second, there's the cost of depreciation – the loss of the car's value which takes place all the time but only hits you when you sell or exchange it.

If you borrow money to buy the car, though, the pattern of these hidden costs is different. No doubt you'll put down a deposit on the car – say, one-third of its price. That first outlay costs you money – by way of loss of interest which it might otherwise have earned – in the same way as the outright buyer's outlay has cost him money.

Then there are your monthly payments to consider. Although they're a direct cost which you can see and easily account for, they've also got a hidden-cost element. They could have been going into a regular monthly savings scheme, and earning you interest just like your original deposit. For a strict comparison with the outright buyer, you should take account of this element too. Finally, there's the question of depreciation. If you and the outright buyer have both bought the same car, in the long run the depreciation cost will obviously be the same for both of you. But it affects you rather differently from the way it affects him. He's got his own money tied up in the car, so his monthly buying cost is the hidden cost of loss of interest on his money. When he sells the car, depreciation suddenly hits him as the extra cost of the loss of value of that money. But you, buying on HP, have been paying money each month to the finance company until the loan's paid off. When you've paid off the loan, any money you get from the sale of the car which exceeds the original deposit is a (small) gain, to offset against the (large) cost of all those monthly payments. So instead of a hidden monthly cost, you've got a hidden monthly clawback here: a small eventual gain to set against your large and direct monthly outlay on the loan payments.

Here's how the monthly costs, direct and hidden, might compare for two people both buying the same car new: say it cost £4,300, and is sold after two years, doing 10,000 miles each year. To replace it then, they'd have to find £1,870 (its effective loss in value).

First, the outright buyer:

Monthly standing costs

insurance	£16	
tax	£4	**Total: £20**

Monthly running costs

petrol	£38	
garage bills	£10	
tyres	£ 4	**Total: £52**

Monthly hidden costs

loss of interest	£29	
depreciation	£78	**Total: £107**
		Grand total: £179

Next, someone putting down a $\frac{1}{3}$ deposit, and buying on HP:

Monthly standing costs

insurance	£16	
tax	£4	
HP monthly payment	£151	**Total: £171**

Monthly running costs

petrol	£38	
garage bills	£10	
tyres	£ 4	**Total: £52**

Monthly hidden costs

loss of interest on deposit	£10

loss of interest on monthly payments	£12	
clawback *gain* from eventual sale	(£41)	
		Total (gain): (£19)
		Grand total: £204

From this you can see that the outright buyer has a monthly outlay of about £72 — money he'll be well aware of spending. But he's got a much bigger parcel of hidden costs — about £107 a month that he won't realise he's spent till he comes to sell or exchange the car.

By contrast, the HP buyer can actually see himself spending much more: over £220 a month. But this is offset to the tune of nearly £20 a month by the hidden gain from what he'll eventually get back when he sells the car.

We've already shown (pages 26 to 31) how the overall cost of the car is affected by how long you keep it, how you pay for it, how old it is and so forth. But here, it's worth considering how the monthly outlay might be affected in different ways by either your own circumstances or other aspects of your buying choice.

First, let's take the things that may depend on your own circumstances.

What if you drive a lot less, or a lot more, than average? That'll affect petrol bills, and to some extent garage and tyre bills. Roughly, each 2,000 miles' difference in your annual mileage might affect petrol bills by £7 or £8 a month, garage bills by £1 or so. There'd have to be a big difference to affect tyre costs — it would have to be enough either to save you a tyre-change altogether, or to make you have to pay for an extra set. That's to say, if you drove only a very little you could probably assume that you wouldn't have any tyre costs at all — you'd save the whole £4 a month, because you'd never have needed replacements by the time you sold. Or if you drove nearer 20,000 miles a year tyre replacement costs might work out double — £8 a month.

So driving less — say, 6,000 miles a year instead of 10,000 — might save you perhaps £15 to £20 a month.

This 40% cut in your annual mileage would be equivalent to about 10% of your total costs saved. Say instead you drove 20,000 miles a year – a 100% increase. This might cost you some £40 extra a month – a bit over 20% of your total motoring costs.

Moral: differences in driving habits have to be really dramatic to affect motoring costs much, at least if you've bought a new car. If you buy a used car and keep it much longer, changes in your running costs would have rather more impact on your total costs. Even then, a 40% change in how much you drove would probably change your total costs by less than 20%.

Where you live, and your driving experience, will make a difference to your insurance costs (see section 3). The figure we've suggested would be typical for someone with two or three years' no-claims discount (explained in Insurance), living outside London in a country town. If you lived in the remote country side, you'd save a few pounds a month: if you lived in central London you'd pay a few pounds more. If you had an extremely good record, you'd again pay a few pounds a month less; a bad one and you'd pay maybe much more. Taking all these factors into account, you might pay around £25 to £30 a month in inner London, without any no-claims discount. You might get away with under £10 a month, living miles from anywhere with a 60% no-claims discount. (And that might also cut your garage bills very slightly, because of lower labour charges.)

So, overall, being a relatively poor insurance risk could add some 5 to 10% to your total motoring costs. Being a particularly good risk could save you up to maybe 5%.

POINT TO REMEMBER

In the long run driving carefully may be an easier way of saving money than driving less.

Next, what about the sort of car you buy? We'll describe in the next chapter how the amount of petrol it uses could make a lot of difference to your costs – *if* it's really thirsty. And page 29 shows how the age of car you get, and how long you keep it, affect the issue.

If you get a car which insurance companies rate as a bad risk, your costs could shoot up. Typically, you might pay an extra £20 a month. If you weren't a fairly good risk yourself to start with, the extra cost might be over £40 a month. And even a driver with an excellent record would have to reckon on his car choice costing him an extra £10 a month or so. So choosing a very high-powered car, or one likely to have very high accident repair costs, could add between 5% and over 20% to your total motoring costs. Moral: check carefully on the insurance consequences before you splash out on your dream car.

As explained on page 31, depreciation varies from car to car. Getting a car with relatively low depreciation (however long you keep it, and however old it is when you buy) can be a big saving: say, £15 a month at best – or nearly 10% of your total motoring costs. Conversely, getting a car that loses its value quickly could (for the same buying price to start with) add a bit over £20 a month to your hidden costs. That's over 10% extra, on your total motoring bill. Moral: taking the trouble to learn how depreciation works, and checking on the *Motoring Which?* prediction before you buy, can pay really big dividends.

POINT TO REMEMBER

For your most economical buy, concentrate most on differences in depreciation. Differences in insurance rating – not nearly so important for most people – can matter rather more than differences in repair costs.

4. DECIDING ON DETAILS

The specification of most cars is so elastic and full of variations and 'versions' that you've got quite a lot of deciding to do, even after you've chosen a particular model.

Choosing an engine

Engines are the first variable. Popular saloons may have four or five different engines to choose from. In general, the bigger and more expensive the engine, the faster the car – and the more petrol it uses. But there are exceptions. In some cars, bigger-engined versions may actually give better fuel economy. And in others, the bigger-engined versions may not be best for fast driving.

With petrol costs so high, you may particularly want to go for the most economical engine. It's getting more common for manufacturers to offer a special 'economy' engine. Don't buy it simply on its name, though. See how the tested petrol consumption compares with the regular engine version. The chart converts mpg into monthly petrol costs.

It's based on someone driving 10,000 miles a year

MONTHLY PETROL COSTS

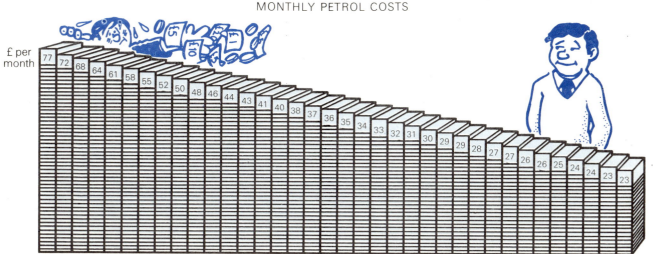

£ per month

77 72 68 64 61 58 55 52 50 48 46 44 43 41 40 38 37 36 35 34 33 32 31 30 29 29 28 27 27 26 26 25 24 24 23 23

15 16 17 18 19 20 21 22 23 24 25 26 27 28 29 30 31 32 33 34 35 36 37 38 39 40 41 42 43 44 45 46 47 48 49 50 mpg

– slightly more than the national average of around 9,000 miles a year, but slightly less than for people with new cars (who do tend to use them rather more than people with older ones). Incidentally, over the years there's been an underlying trend for car owners to drive more, but this is masked from year to year by changes in the price of petrol. When petrol prices go up faster than other prices, as they did in 1974 and again in 1979, people tend to drive a bit less than they'd have otherwise done. But they catch up quickly again when petrol prices rise less quickly than other motoring costs, as they did between 1969 and 1972 and then again between 1975 and the Iranian oil crisis.

Anyway, the chart shows how monthly petrol bills depend on mpg. It's based on petrol costing nearly £1.40 a gallon.

As you can see from the chart, differences of two or three mpg make a lot of difference to monthly petrol costs at the thirsty end of the range. It's here that an economy engine, cutting petrol consumption and improving mpg in cars round the 15 to 20 mpg range, could save you at least £10 a month. Unfortunately, that's not where you find economy engines. They're popular instead for mass-market saloons which even in their normal versions don't use a very great deal of petrol.

POINT TO REMEMBER

Small mpg differences make a big difference to the cost of running a 'thirsty' car – but not much difference with cars that do say 30 mpg.

For example, even government mpg figures (which may be kind to 'economy' engines) suggest a saving of only £1 or so a month for many economy versions. Surveys of *Motoring Which?* readers' mpg confirm that any difference is usually very slight. Sometimes, the 'economy' version even averages slightly *worse* mpg – presumably because with the less powerful engine people keep their foot harder down on the accelerator.

So the savings to be gained from opting for the smallest 'economy' engine are generally small, though

– as with the Renault 5GTL – there are occasional specific exceptions. So always work out what the fuel consumption figures would mean before you choose the small-engined 'economy' version of the car you want.

At the other end of the scale, the most powerful versions of a particular car may be surprisingly economical – if you drive them in just the same way as you'd have driven a less powerful version of that car. This is because things which the maker does to squeeze more power out of an engine tend to make it more efficient. Two carburettors instead of one, redesign of the cylinder head to make the fuel ignite better, a modified exhaust system to suck the burnt exhaust gases out more quickly, even fuel injection instead of carburettors – all these, used primarily to improve performance, have turned out to improve petrol economy too in some cars.

What about **diesel** engines? It's true that these use less fuel than equivalent petrol engines. You can already get one, as an option, on a number of popular cars, and as manufacturers are investing a lot in the further development of diesels for ordinary cars it's likely that many more will come on sale.

Older diesel engines had the drawback of being relatively underpowered – taking nearly twice as long as their petrol-engined versions to accelerate from a standstill to 60 mph, for example. They've had a characteristic noise, too – the clatter of a London taxi, though usually less marked – which, although not necessarily noisy in absolute terms, has tended to draw attention in a way that the noise from a petrol engine doesn't do. In the latest diesel engines lack of power is much less noticeable. Though the quality of the noise they make is different from petrol engines, that's really more a curiosity than a true drawback. So the issue does now boil down to economy.

Diesels, on average costing some 12% more than their basic petrol-engined versions, and even more in small cars, have tended to take a bigger drop in value in their first year, though in the longer run depreciation rates tend to even out. Because of the first-year drop and the higher initial price, it wouldn't make much sense buying a diesel unless you planned to keep it for some time – to let cheaper running costs catch up with more expensive initial price.

Diesel fuel has recently tended to cost *more* than petrol, so that the greater economy of a diesel engine has been partly offset. Again, to buy a diesel version you'd probably need to take the long-term view – that in the interests of national fuel economy diesel should in future cost no more than petrol.

So how might things work out in practice, for some-one keeping a diesel for five years?

Here's one example, taking a typical car costing some £4,300 and assuming that the diesel-engine option is an extra 12%, then over the five years depreciates at the same rate as the basic petrol-engined version. So there's an extra £516 to find to start with, with the pros-pect of getting back £155 of that (or the equivalent in tomorrow's inflated currency) in five years' time. We'll assume too that the petrol-engined version has a pretty typical fuel consumption – averaging 30 mpg. Let's say that the diesel uses a fraction over three-quarters the amount of fuel which the petrol engine does – again, fairly typical. For our example of someone driving 10,000 miles a year and with fuel costing the same, diesel or petrol, this could save around £115 in the first year. It's wise to assume that in future fuel prices are likely to rise a bit faster than prices in general – perhaps by 3% a year extra – so by the fifth year that £115 will have become £130 or more.

Often, the diesel-engined version of a car has a lower insurance rating, and typically this could save another £25 a year or so.

This is what the sums look like:

Initial investment:	£516
Return on investment:	
1st year	£140
2nd year	£143
3rd year	£147
4th year	£151
5th year	£154 + £155 (extra value recovered when car sold)

In this example, the investment's quite a good one. Paying extra for the diesel earns the equivalent of 18% or 19% a year 'interest' on the extra layout – earned through lower fuel and insurance costs. So it would be worth it, using your own money or a bank loan – but not quite, using HP. But note – if you *can't* get that insurance saving, you'd lose.

So, for an average driver, buying a diesel can now be quite a good investment. It's much better, though, for someone driving say 20,000 miles a year. That would double the value of the improved fuel economy, and, over the five-year period of the above example, produce an annual rate of return equivalent to 42%. That's to say, at the end of the period it would leave the driver so much better off than if he'd had the petrol version that it would be as if he'd had the money (the extra cost of the diesel) invested in something paying him 42% a year – far more than enough to pay for his costs in borrowing the money even on HP.

This high-mileage driver would also find the diesel worth while even if it cost much more to start with – say, an extra 20% on the price of the car – and lost its value more quickly than a petrol-engined car.

POINT TO REMEMBER

With increasing fuel costs, diesel engines are now becoming good value – particularly for people who drive more than average.

So diesel-engined versions are certainly becoming an economic proposition for people who drive a great deal more than average.

The choice of gearchange

Something with a bearing on fuel economy, but more important to think about in its own right, is the gear-change. A few small cars, but many medium to large ones, give you the option of either a manual gearchange or an automatic. As a rule, it's the manual gearchange which comes as standard, and you have to pay extra for automatic – usually around 10% of the car's list price, though a lot less with the small Volvo. Some expensive cars come with an automatic gearbox as stan-dard equipment, and occasionally – as with some Mercedes-Benz models – may not even give you the option of choosing manual instead. With other expensive cars there's no price difference between manual and automatic versions.

So, unless it's an expensive car, you can reckon on automatic versions having ownership costs about 10% higher than normal (incidentally, they depreciate at much the same rate as manual versions, as a rule). Running costs are higher, too. This is because the mechanism of the automatic gearbox absorbs more of the engine's power than an ordinary gearbox would do. The government petrol consumption tests don't give a true picture here. The test designed to simulate city driving lays down which gear the car should be in for each section – as automatics change gear themselves, their results from this test compare better with manual cars than they would in real life. But it is unlikely that the extra consumption would be as much as 10% even with a very small-engined car where proportionately more of the engine's power would be soaked up by the automatic.

Generally, people who've got used to driving an automatic wouldn't go back to changing gear manually. There's no doubt that a good automatic gearchange makes driving easier. First, though, there are one or two small drawbacks or rather potential faults, which can be entirely prevented by good maintenance. If the car's engine is wrongly adjusted for idling and very low-speed running, the car may tend to creep forward slightly instead of standing still – in stationary traffic – unless you keep the brakes on. What can be a true snag for poorly maintained cars with automatic transmissions can be the fact that if you can't get the engine started you can't push-start it, or use a tow to get it started: this could seriously mess up the works.

Offsetting this, from the faults point of view, is the way that an automatic gearbox, because it changes gear itself, doesn't have a clutch to be harmed by hamfisted drivers changing manual gears badly. In general automatics don't generate their own faults any more than manual ones – so, taking into account their immunity against mistreament by the driver, they've got quite a good comparative reliability record, though when

things do go wrong they can go badly wrong with the risk of your needing a complete replacement.

Most automatic gearboxes do literally change gear. You 'kick down' to a low gear when you accelerate sharply, or when you push down harder on the accelerator to get the car up a hill for instance. As you take your foot off the accelerator, to cruise more steadily or slow down, they change up. (The Variomatic system developed by the Dutch firm DAF, and used on some Volvos after Volvo took over DAF, is entirely different. In this, a system of belts and pulleys allows continuous adjustment between engine speed and road speed – instead of the adjustment in three or four fixed steps that you get with a conventional gearbox, manual or automatic. In practice, *Motoring Which?* has found this system tends to give a longer lag between the speed you're at and the speed you want than the best conventional automatics, though it's proved reliable apart from routine drive belt replacement.)

On small or medium-sized cars an automatic with four gear speeds can be better than one with three. And many drivers find it helps to be able to 'override' the automatic, for example keeping in a low gear to go down hill or to be ready to overtake. The best override system lets you select each gear individually – just like a manual gearchange but without the clutch. The usual alternative is being able to choose between three driving ranges: one fully automatic, for normal driving; one stopping the car going into top gear; and one keeping it in the lowest gears. A snag with this is that on very slippery surfaces – say, snow or ice – you can't prevent the car selecting first gear so that your wheels spin.

If you do choose an automatic gearbox, you may have to get a slightly more powerful engine version than you'd have done otherwise. This would counterbalance any slight loss in power through the automatic gears.

An option on some rather larger cars, about 4% extra, is **power-assisted steering.** But usually, it's either fitted or not fitted to the particular model you want, and that's that. It uses a small dose of engine power to lighten the effort you need when you turn the steering wheel. And usually you don't have to twirl the steering wheel so much. But the turning circle may be different, too. In general, cars that do offer this option tend to have rather heavy steering on the basic version – so it's probably worth having if you do a lot of town driving, or manœuvring in tight places.

An increasingly common option is light alloy **wheels.** These generally add 5 or 6% to the price of the car, though the extra cost can be less as a proportion of the price of some expensive cars. The advantages that make these essential on racing cars – improved performance at the extreme limit of the car's behaviour – aren't likely to be noticeable in ordinary driving. So you should probably treat this option not so much as something affecting the car's behaviour as instead something influencing its appearance: and only you can make your mind up about that.

Which body?
Many cars give you a choice of body styles. The most common variant is the *estate car*, almost van-shaped with a door or doors for loading at the back; otherwise just the same as the saloon version except that the back seat can be folded flat to take big loads. Although *hatchbacks* are often entirely separate models, they are sometimes sold as versions of saloon cars. They're shaped much more like ordinary saloons than estate cars. The back window lifts up as a tailgate, exposing the boot either under a parcel shelf or simply open, behind the back seat. Again, the back seat can usually be folded flat, for extra load-carrying (obviously much less use for big loads if it can't). Several saloons also have *coupé* versions: usually a bit sportier-looking with the roof line sweeping straight down towards the back rather than a separate boot, and usually much less room in the back. Just one or two cars now have *convertible* versions: with a folding roof.

For sheer luggage-carrying capacity, hatchbacks

Various body types: note particularly the generally rather bigger loading door in an estate, compared with a hatch back

don't have much to recommend them. As they don't have a boot built on separately, their luggage space behind the back seat is really limited by the overall size of the car's passenger compartment. In smaller hatchbacks this tends to mean that (when the back seat is in use) there's actually less luggage space than there would have been in an equivalent saloon car plus boot. In larger hatchbacks the scale of the car allows more space to be devoted to luggage without unbalancing the overall design of the car, so they tend to be able to take as much luggage as an equivalent saloon – but not usually any more.

Although in both the luggage space is enormously increased when you fold down the back seat, for carrying a lot of luggage this advantage over conventional saloons is more a matter of tidiness than of real capacity. And some hatchbacks are anyway designed for sleekness rather than load-carrying – the tailgate just happens to fit in with the sloping back. After all, if you're only using the front of the car for passengers you can put luggage on the back seat, and on the floor there, as well as in the boot of an ordinary saloon: this gives you about as much overall space as you'd have had in the hatchback with its back sat folded down. The real load-carrying advantage of hatchbacks is the advantage of being able to carry big things which simply wouldn't fit in an ordinary car – large objects which need the back loading hatch, or the back seat folded down too, for you to be able to get them in. This is really the advantage of estate cars, too, although some also have more luggage space than their saloon versions even with the back seat in use. But some have less.

POINT TO REMEMBER

Don't take it on trust that a hatchback can carry a lot of luggage – or that estates can, when they're carrying passengers too.

Before you get either a hatchback or an estate, think carefully about the sort of big things which you'd be using them for. If it would be boxes, chests of drawers, that sort of thing, then that's fine: just what they're best

at. But odder shapes – long and thin like planks of wood or stepladders, maybe just odd like bicycles – might do as well or even better in the boot of a conventional car. Remember, you can leave the boot-lid open in an ordinary saloon; you can't do this in an estate or hatchback without the serious risk of drawing in poisonous engine fumes. Also, if some of your loads are going to be smelly, it's worth remembering that putting them in a boot would partly isolate you from the smell, whereas having them in an estate or hatchback with you wouldn't.

Estates and hatchbacks have three further drawbacks. The first is general with estates, quite common with hatchbacks: their back windows tend to get very dirty. A few have a special washer and wiper at the back because of this, sometimes as an extra for about 2% of the cost of the car. The second is that if you've got small children, any safety restraints you fit for them may cause problems when you fold the back seat down. And the strap mountings tend to get in the way of the luggage. The third depends on the make: there can be a higher risk of noise, particularly rather booming bodywork and road noise.

If you decide you do want the ability of an estate or a hatchback to handle big objects, here are some further points to consider before you choose between them. First, cost: hatchbacks tend to cost very little more than their saloon versions, estates to cost about 10% extra, though often more. Second, convenience: a divided back seat, letting you fold down just one half, can be a help. Remember that a carpeted load area may look nice, but won't be practical for messy loads. A low loading height, and luggage doors swinging well clear – often best with estates – are specially worth looking out for. Third, thief-tempting: some hatchbacks shut luggage away from sight under a shelf behind the back seat; in others, and in conventional estate cars, it's exposed to passers-by. Finally, sheer size. Generally, estates have more upright back doors which give more space for big squarish things than the sloping-shaped hatchbacks. Generally, the bigger the car the greater the width and height of the loading area – but differences here are far smaller than in the length of the loading area. You should probably reckon on about four feet for a hatchback – more in a big one, slightly less in a small one. Estate cars, depending on size, range from around 5½ feet to nearer 7 feet.

Coupés have to have a strong appeal to you to be worth while. They generally have less room than their saloon equivalent, but cost about 15 to 20% more. Convertibles might have even more appeal to you, but unfortunately you probably won't be able to get one as very few makers produce convertible versions. If you can find one, it may not cost you that much extra: one costs 6% more than its ordinary version – but sadly that 6% works out to be about £3,000, as it's a Rolls-Royce (and even then there's been a waiting list of several years for it!).

You can get fresh air instead from a **sliding roof.** When these are fitted as an option by the manufacturer, they cost about 4 or 5% extra – and when you come to sell the car you'll probably find that the sunroof doesn't add to its secondhand value, though it may make it easier to sell to a private buyer. You can usually have sunroofs fitted separately to cars which don't offer

them as a factory option. See page 84 for exactly when to have this and other extras fitted – either before or after you've taken delivery of the car.

Most popular cars come in various different levels of **luxuriousness.** The basic version is sometimes sold only to firms running a fleet of cars for their staff. It could well have plastic or vinyl seat-covering material which tends to feel unpleasantly hot and sticky in hot weather, and fixed seat backs which you can't adjust to the most comfortable position. It may also have rubber floor mats rather than carpets, and just one sun visor (for the driver). Safety belts are likely to be of the fixed type, rather than the inertia-reel type which let you lean forward without unbuckling, and which don't need setting to the individual size of each passenger.

The next version up might have quite a bit extra in terms of practical comfort: things like carpets, cloth-covered seats, adjusters to set the backrest at the best angle, passenger sun visor, maybe an electric screen-wash, a heated back window and inertia-reel safety belts, perhaps reversing lights, hazard warning lights,

better tyres, even a radio. More elevated versions of luxury go rather beyond the practical sphere, into things like extra chrome outside, black vinyl roofs, tinted window glass, wood veneer dashboards, electrically-operated windows. On practical grounds, it's probably best to go one up from the very basic, which is really a bit spartan in practice, and to judge the more elaborate refinements in terms of your own personal taste.

It's often quite hard working out exactly which version is which. Ford have a perfectly straightforward naming system: the basic version is simply the basic version, the next up is distinguished by the letter L, and the next by GL; they may have an S or Sport version, more sporty; and the top of each model range is usually called Ghia. But with others the L or De Luxe version is often actually the most basic. In general, 'Super' is better than 'De Luxe', and 'Special' is better than 'Super' – but the most reliable guide is simply the price list. Price steps are commonly around 10% – the first step up costing about 10% more than the very basic, and so on up. Price differences can be counted as straightforward differences in ownership costs, as the different versions of the same model all tend to depreciate at much the same rate.

Once you've chosen your basic body style and the level of luxury trim you want, you can often in a popular saloon or estate choose between either just two doors or four doors. The price difference is close to 4% extra for four doors (again, depreciation is much the same for both versions). Because getting in and out of the back seats is much more awkward in a two-door version, it isn't worth economising on getting one unless your backseat passengers are likely to be both rare and agile.

There are some other options for you to decide on – generally a lot less common than those already mentioned, and likely to 'disappear' in terms of what you'll get for the car when you sell it. That's to say, the car's resale value won't take account of them, so that you should consider their cost a one-off expenditure by you, none of which you'll get back.

Tinted glass is about 3% of the car's price, if available, proportionately less on very expensive cars. There's a practical disadvantage. At night it's particularly important that nothing should dim your view out – which even very slight tinting will do. So if bright sunlight bothers you it would be better, in practical terms, to use sunglasses – and of course that would be very much cheaper. Tinted glass should help to keep the inside of the car a bit cooler in hot weather, though, and if (perhaps because you'll be in a hot country) you've decided that's a critical requirement for you then maybe that's an advantage that would be worth having. But normally you should go for tinted glass only if you think it looks nice.

You might find **electric window winders** fun, and sometimes a marginal convenience. You've usually got to remember to shut them before you switch off the ignition. Again, worth the 5% or so that they add to the car's cost only on non-practical grounds of personal appeal.

A high-penetration-resistance **laminated windscreen,** at up to 2% of the car's price, is a good safety buy. In an accident you're less likely to get cut by this than by normal safety glass. Additionally, it won't shatter if a flying pebble or chunk of road-grit hits it.

Centre door locking – the driver has one control to lock or unlock all the doors – adds 1% or so to the the price, if it's an option (it hardly ever is). You're perfectly capable of living without it, though people who have lived with it tend to find it a boon (particularly if the system also locks the boot and/or tailgate – not all do).

Air conditioning is nice, but as it adds around 10 to 15% to the car's price it's hardly a practical proposition – except if you'll be going to a really hot country where you might count it almost an essential.

You may be given an option on **upholstery:** usually cloth at around 2% extra, occasionally leather at nearly 10% extra. Ventilated leather is superbly comfortable but at that sort of price must be a 'money's-no-object' sort of choice.

Metallic or **special paint** finishes add about 1% to the car's cost – quite a bit more with some foreign makes. Deciding about this is obviously a matter of

ANNUAL COST OF VARIOUS NEW-CAR OPTIONS

	bought with own money		bought on HP	
	kept for 2 yrs	kept for 5 yrs	kept for 2 yrs	kept for 5 yrs
Things which add to the secondhand value:				
estate version	£130	£95	£160	£110
hatchback version	£65	£45	£80	£55
coupe version	£220	£160	£270	£190
slightly luxurious trim	£130	£95	£160	£110
more luxurious	£270	£200	£330	£230
very smart indeed	£420	£310	£520	£360
automatic gearbox	£130	£95	£160	£110
Things which you shouldn't count on getting your money back on, so:				
centre door-locking	£35	£20	£35	£20
HPR windscreen	£60	£30	£65	£35
cloth seats	£70	£35	£75	£40
servo disc brakes	£70	£35	£75	£40
tinted glass	£100	£55	£110	£60
power steering	£140	£70	£150	£80
sunroof	£150	£80	£170	£90
electric window winders	£170	£90	£190	£95
leather seats	£310	£160	£330	£180
air conditioning*	£410	£220	£450	£230

The air-conditioning cost estimates may well be on the pessimistic side – but better safe than sorry.

taste, but a practical point to consider is that future patching up – after a minor accident, say – is likely to be more difficult and expensive than with normal paint finishes. These finishes may involve two separate coats, one for the colour and one for the metallic lustre. It can be virtually impossible to 'touch in' small scratches without leaving some detectable evidence.

Cars have to have an outside mirror on the driver's

POINT TO REMEMBER

Many optional extras, expensive to have on a car you'll be selling after a year or two, work out much better value if you'll be keeping it for a long time.

side. They may offer a matching one on the passenger's side. Or – usually rather expensive – the driver's mirror may be remotely adjustable.

This brings us to the end of the various options – and to the general question of which colour to choose. Before going into that, it's worth summarising the 'ownership costs' of various options. The chart above shows how much each option might add to the annual cost of owning a typical new car – first, assuming you're buying it with all your own money, second, that it's on HP.

As you can see from the chart, the second type of option – which costs you money, but doesn't add significantly to the secondhand value of your car – can work out surprisingly expensive, compared to the first type of option. If you're going to get rid of the car after a couple of years, having electric window winders for it could end up costing you almost as much as (say) having the estate version or having an automatic gearbox. However, if you plan to keep the car for a long time the difference between these two types of optional extra does fade away a bit.

So, back to **colour.** Apart from the metallic paint point mentioned earlier, there are some practical points to bear in mind.

Resale value isn't directly affected by colour. Indirectly, it can however be affected in two ways. First, if you choose a very unusual colour indeed you may find private buyers hesitant about it. Although you should be able to get the same price as for a more conventional colour, it may take you longer – you may find it harder work finding a buyer, because you've got to find someone who at best shares your enthusiasm for that colour, or who at least isn't horrified by it.

Secondly, it's important that when the car's sold its paintwork should look smart – bodywork condition's by far the most important factor in determining how the price you get will compare with the average for that particular model. It's now very rare to find one particular colour within a manufacturer's range deteriorating more than others with time (years ago there used to be problems with some reds, for example). However, some shades can prove more difficult to match perfectly, if they're being touched up after minor damage, or even if a new body panel has to be fitted.

You can see this effect for yourself if you look very carefully at parked cars, two or three years old. It's a fair bet that most of them will have had some minor grazes at least. If the weather's good and the light's bright (so that the cars are clean and their colours show up strongly) you may be surprised at how patchy their bodywork looks. In particular, the human eye is very much better at detecting very small differences in shades of green than in any other colour. So, in a green car, the slightest deviation from the car's basic colour shows up particularly strongly. Clear yellows may show

colour mismatches, too (though a lot less), perhaps because yellow is close to green in the spectrum. If you're interested in looking for yourself, the most susceptible points seem to be doors, and the junction between different panels, such as wings and the rest of the body (bonnet or boot-lid, say, or on some cars the chrome strip which serves as a margin between the lower side part of the wing and its top part). It's most often here that you can see a slight difference in shade or texture between one part of the bodywork and the rest.

Red, black and brown seem virtually immune to this potential problem.

Oddly enough, there's a safety factor in colour choice. In twilight and poor light black cars and dull or muddy colours are much less easy to see than others, and in mist or rain grey or white cars can become a bit indistinct, too. It has been shown that this can be a hazard in some circumstances (though a relatively very small one compared say to mistakes that a driver might make in the way he or she drives). So, from this point of view, bright colours are best. Although of course all colours get equally dirty, some *look* more dirty than others. White – as you'd expect, being so light – shows up dirt and blemishes plainly. Much less predictably, so does black. This is because black, to look bright and clean, depends solely on the reflections of lights and other colours from its surface. Dust stops these reflections, making it look dowdy and dim.

There's a special point to bear in mind, choosing a colour, if you'll be spending time in countries with hot bright sunlight. Light colours, and in particular white, bounce the sun's heat back away from the car more effectively, keeping it cooler inside than dark colours would.

You may have no choice of colour inside, once you've chosen a body colour. So bear this in mind, if your car's going to have to put up with muddy feet or grubby children.

Finally, before you plump for some particular combination of exterior paintwork and interior trim, check carefully that a car with this specification is already in the pipeline, on its way to the dealer of your choice. If it isn't, your order would have to be fed into the programming of the factory's assembly lines, which of course would put you right at the back of any queue there might be.

Two essential 'extras'

When the car's delivered to you, it obviously has to have all its tyres. Also, by law, it has to have front-seat safety belts. So, with both these, you've got to exercise any choice you have before you take delivery of the car.

Don't assume that the tyres which normally come with the car will necessarily be the best ones for it. To keep the car's selling price down, the maker may have chosen tyres which are cheap to buy in the first place but work out expensive in the longer run because they wear out relatively quickly. Luckily, this is becoming much less common nowadays.

Road test reports on the car by say *Motoring Which?* would warn against tyres that came with it but weren't really a good choice for it. For example, Russian-made tyres that came with a Lada tested in 1977 gave the car worse handling than British ones, and wore out nearly

three times as fast. One general rule (which applied in the Lada case and crops up quite commonly among cheaper cars) is that 'cross-ply' tyres are poorer value than 'radial-ply' ones: they may not hold the road so well, and they don't last nearly so long. The difference is caused primarily by a special belt of very strong fabric – often reinforced with steel threads – between the tread of the tyre and the inner flexible rubber-and-fabric casing of the tyre. This belt round the tyre's circumference helps to hold the tread firmly against the road. This helps when cornering: when a car's front wheels are turned for a corner, their angle is greater than the angle of the corner itself. This extra angle (called the 'slip angle') is what leads to skids on slippery roads on the one hand, and to friction and scuffing – and therefore wear – on the other. The extra bracing of radial-ply tyres lets the tyres' tread follow the actual line of the car more exactly, so that much of the 'slip angle' is in fact soaked up by the tyres' casing, which can flex more than in a cross-ply tyre. A tell-tale of this extra flexibility, incidentally, is the rather squishy bulgy look that the sidewalls of many radial-ply tyres

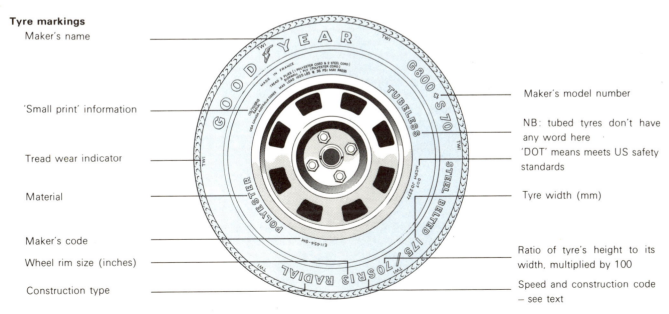

Tyre markings

Maker's name

'Small print' information

Tread wear indicator

Material

Maker's code

Wheel rim size (inches)

Construction type

Maker's model number

NB: tubed tyres don't have any word here

'DOT' means meets US safety standards

Tyre width (mm)

Ratio of tyre's height to its width, multiplied by 100

Speed and construction code – see text

have, compared with cross-plies.

So, by and large, the tyres to have are radial-plies. And for safety's sake don't mix types of tyre: it's anyway illegal to have different types on the same axle, or cross-plies on the back wheels if you've got radials on the front. Also, don't mix the two different types of radial – steel-belted and fabric-belted.

Some people like tubeless tyres. They have a slight advantage with some sorts of puncture. Because the inside of the tyre is coated with a layer of very flexible rubber, the air under pressure in the tyre can force this into a small puncture, perhaps sealing it temporarily and at least tending to let the air seep out more slowly than it would have done in an ordinary tyre. However, on a 'belts and braces' principle, fast drivers – putting extra punishment on their tyres – sometimes prefer to have inner tubes as well. And inner tubes are absolutely essential if you have tubeless tyres fitted to a car with spoked wire wheels.

An expensive option is the safety tyre such as the Denovo made by Dunlop. This is available only for some cars. These tyres come fixed to special wheels. If

CAR TYRE CONSTRUCTION

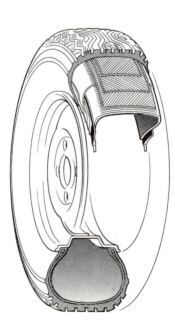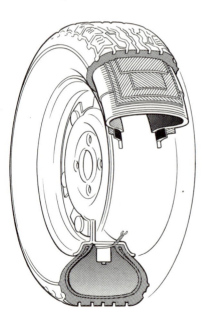

The cross-ply tyre (left) has now been largely superseded by the radial-ply (centre): stiff belts of reinforcing cord increase grip and cut wear. The expensive run-flat tyre (right) is fixed to a special wheel with containers (bottom) to inject a special fluid which keeps the tyre drivable even after a burst.

a tyre is punctured it stays in place on the wheel, instantly refreshed (rather after the style of Heineken beer advertisements) by a special fluid pumped into the tyre from the wheel. *Motoring Which?* tests have shown that these really work, preventing catastrophe if a tyre bursts, and letting you go on driving much as if nothing had happened after a puncture or even a burst. But they cost much more than ordinary tyes.

Whatever tyres you choose, make sure that they're the right rating for your car. In particular, it's important to tell the person you're buying from what speed-rating you want. Tyres are graded for the maximum speed of the car they'll be fitted to. Under the Type Approval Scheme for new cars tyres have to carry a code letter showing this rating.

The code letters now go as follows:

L	up to 75 mph	R	up to 105 mph
M	up to 80 mph	S	up to 111 mph
N	up to 86 mph	T	up to 118 mph
P	up to 93 mph	U	up to 124 mph
Q	up to 99 mph	H	up to 130 mph.

If the tyre's a cross-ply, the speed-code letter will be on its own between the size markings – 175 L 13, say. But radials have an extra R, for radial: 175 SR 13, say.

If you do have non-standard tyres fitted, don't let the garage make out that you'll have to pay for the whole of their cost – that is, not subtracting the cost of the tyres which would have been original equipment instead. It could be a fight, but he should eventually be persuaded when he realises that that's the only way you're going to buy the car.

The law requiring that all new cars should come fitted with safety belts has changed the old situation – where, if you wanted them, it was usually up to you to choose the make of safety belt that you wanted. Now, they're often built into the car in a way that leaves you no choice, at least for the front seats.

The most important point about safety belts – now that the safety angle itself is decently covered by a good compulsory standard – is that they should be comfortable and convenient to use. If they aren't, you or your passengers may be much more tempted not to use them; even if you do, it's obviously a bind if they are inconvenient.

This gives inertia-reel safety belts a commanding advantage over ordinary fixed-type ones. The inertia reel is a mechanism which automatically pulls the belt reasonably tight around you – and pulls it away neatly when you're not using it. Wearing it, you can move about quite freely in your seat – if you lean right forward, for example, the belt unreels to let you, reeling up tight again when you lean back. But in a crash the belt locks, holding you as firmly as the fixed type. By contrast, you have to fiddle with adjustment buckles to get the ordinary fixed type fitting you securely; you have to undo it, then do it up again, if you want to move much more than a squirm in your seat; and if you don't take the trouble to hook it away neatly it tends to get tangled and scrumpled down by the seat when you're not using it.

POINT TO REMEMBER

Inertia-reel safety belts are a good buy.

SECTION TWO

BUYING YOUR CAR

Which way to make the most of your money – or
someone else's – buying and selling on the best
terms, and packing in the best extras

1. BUYING NEW

Over the last decade there's been a trend away from the old pattern of car dealerships – where one garage was often agent for several different makes – to a system where each dealer usually represents only one manufacturer: he's that manufacturer's 'appointed' or 'franchised' dealer. Theoretically, this is useful to buyers. First, specialisation in one manufacturer's cars should make a dealer more expert at least in those cars. Secondly, manufacturers may make arrangements under which a dealer who wants to order, say, four of the most popular model in the range which is selling like hot cakes, has also to order one or two other models which aren't in such demand. Because that dealer doesn't want to have these less popular cars lying in his stocks for long, he may offer specially attractive terms on them to buyers.

If the dealer stocks only one make, he's not likely to give you impartial advice about the comparative advantages and disadvantages of some car you're interested in. If you want to look over several different makes, perhaps test-driving them, you'll probably have to go to several different dealers now – and that could be jolly awkward if you don't live in or near a big town.

So how can you make the most of the present system?

First, if you have a long-standing and happy relationship with a particular garage, there's nothing to stop you at least trying to buy your new car from them, whether or not they are an appointed dealer for the make you want. It's so difficult to find an entirely reliable garage that, once you've got one, it's certainly worth trying to keep it. But if they're *not* a dealer for the make you want, you lose a lot of flexibility. If there's a waiting list for your car, you'll certainly be at the bottom. And – unless the dealer's every bit as keen to keep you as a customer as you are to keep him as your garage – you won't be able to get the price cut. This is because the price which he has to pay the distributor is higher than the price which appointed dealers for that make have to pay.

Moreover, there's a slight difficulty with any guarantee repairs which you might need. Car guarantees say that major repairs have to be done by appointed agents – ie, not your friendly garage. As the rate which manufacturers pay dealers for guarantee repairs is rather lower than the rate which dealers would normally charge ordinary customers, dealers aren't keen on doing these repairs on cars which they haven't sold themselves. But don't be too put off by this: about one in four people actually do have work done under guarantee by garages that they haven't bought the car from, and don't in practice have too much trouble over this.

You might think it more important that garages which don't have a franchise for the make you want almost certainly won't have had their mechanics trained in work on cars of that make; they probably won't keep spares of that make, or have any special servicing tools needed for it; and they may never have had a single car of the model you want in their workshops before. Again, don't let this be an out-and-out disqualifier. In the past, tests by *Motoring Which?* in which cars were taken to different garages for servicing didn't find that appointed dealers were notably better than garages without a franchise for the car concerned. But – as one of the chief points in choosing a garage is to make sure that you are going to get good servicing – don't just trust to luck over this. Your only sound reason for buying from an unfranchised dealer would be if you were sure that his servicing standards were exceptionally high – and that the dealer had absolutely no reservations about working on the car you wanted to buy.

So that you can have some idea of the dealer's scope for giving you special terms, you ought to remember that usually the total amount he has to play with is up to about £140 for each £1,000 of the car's total price including taxes. But, within that margin, he has to allow some £50 or more per £1,000 for his direct costs related to that car – preparing it for sale, guarantee work, first free service.

He shouldn't have to allow much for his financial costs in 'stocking' the car. He may well have specially attractive loan arrangements, and gains a bit from the way VAT works – he doesn't have to pay in VAT until on average two or three months after he's received it from customers.

So, all told, you can reckon that, for each £1,000 of the full quoted price of your car including taxes, the dealer has rather less than £100 'profit' out of which to meet his overheads, pay his sales staff – and earn a true profit for himself. Remember that figure: we'll come back to it in a minute, as it's the basis of how you'll bargain with the dealer over the actual price you're going to pay.

First, though, there are some more points to consider before you decide on a garage.

A big dealer may well have a wider range of demonstrator models for you to try than a smaller one. That's hardly a deciding factor, though: all you need to do is make sure that you've tried the car you want – and there's no reason why you should have to buy the car from the garage where you try it!

More usefully, some dealers keep a wider range of spares in stock than others. This could easily save you

delays later – and money (because when a garage has to send someone out to pick up a crucial spare, they may charge you for that person's time). It's therefore well worth asking particularly about this before you decide on a dealer. Some manufacturers label some of their dealers specifically as 'parts distributors', and these are supposed to keep a particularly full range of spares.

Simply being big gives dealers some other advantages. It should mean that they can bank on a more or less regular flow of sales. If their predictions prove to have been too optimistic, and they're left with unsold cars on their hands for a bit longer than anticipated, they'll be able to absorb the financial shock of that in their general turnover much more easily than a small dealer. So, while a small dealer might wait for firm orders from customers before ordering from the maker, big dealers will usually have ordered many cars – often in a good range of colours – before getting orders. This means that they can often deliver what you want quite quickly, even when there's a waiting list. Conversely, you may stand more chance of getting *exactly* the car you want, having to order from a small dealer.

Again, the big firm can much more easily afford expensive pieces of servicing equipment – rolling roads which let the car 'run' in the workshop and should help diagnose faults quickly, the latest electronic tuning equipment, and so forth. Although none of these is a substitute for the really good mechanic, they're all things which help that good mechanic do his work well.

Against that, it must be said that *Motoring Which?* tests have never confirmed in practice that big garages are better at servicing cars than little garages. And, purely for buying a car, the small garage might have one advantage. In a big garage, the person who actually sells you the car will almost always be employed as a salesman, and will get commission on the firm's profit from that sale. When it comes to bargaining with you over the price, the salesman is concerned purely with the sale – and naturally doesn't want to whittle down the margin out of which his commission is paid, and which determines the actual rate he gets. By contrast, you might deal with a director or even owner in a really small garage – concerned about the full business of his firm. His longer-term view might prompt him to be more generous with you over price, if he thinks it'll make you more of a loyal customer for the future.

So most of the factors to consider before you decide on a garage boil down to common sense. If you've dealt before with some garage that you trust – especially over servicing – stick to that garage, and try to get your new car from them. This would almost certainly be worth while, even if they're not dealers for the make you want. After all, you can always try a demonstration model of that car at a different garage first. But do make sure that your garage is confident about servicing – including the guarantee period. If you don't already have some favourite trusted garage, then you should shop around. See what terms you can get, how long you'd have to wait for delivery, and whether the car you'd then get would be exactly what you wanted in terms of colour and equipment. Be politely impressed if the garage can point to banks of sophisticated servicing equipment – but give much more weight to whether or not it keeps a good stock of spares.

Finally, remember that you'll want servicing attention to be as convenient as possible. This means that it's a mistake to buy your car from some garage at the opposite end of the county, unless it offers you a price you can't refuse and you can make sure in advance that you'd be able to get servicing locally even under guarantee. It also means that you won't want to have to wait for days or even weeks to get something put right: ask the servicing receptionist (not the salesman) how far ahead you'd have to book for a routine service, and what arrangements the garage has for dealing promptly with sudden major faults. Although a long waiting list for servicing may mean that garage has a very good reputation with its customers, unless you're an unusually well-organised sort of person you'd probably find it far too much of a drag to cope with in practice.

Ordering your car

When you've finally decided what you want – and agreed the lowest possible price, remembering the dealer's margin of nearly 10% – you sign a contract with him. The contract's actually called the Order Form. It lays down the specification of the car you've agreed to buy, the price you've agreed to pay, and the date when it should be delivered.

The small print on the back of the form may set out various conditions. The law, under the Supply of Goods (Implied Terms) Act, protects you with the valuable general provision that nothing you sign can take away from you legal rights which would otherwise have been yours, when you buy anything new. So you don't really have to read any of this small print carefully. But you should be aware of common conditions which would probably be upheld by any court of law, if it ever came to a dispute between you and the garage. For example:

● If the car doesn't come by the promised date, you won't be able to make any claim for damages against the dealer

● If the car's price goes up between now and when it's delivered, you usually either have to pay up or cancel

● When the car is ready, you have to take it: if you don't, you lose your deposit, and the garage would have a case against you if it then took a long time to sell the car and the delay cost it more than your deposit.

● If you're putting in an old car in part exchange, it's got to be in as good condition as when it was originally seen by the garage, or you'd have to pay for the cost of bringing it up to that condition. Also, the garage may reserve the right to cut the part-exchange allowance to take account of your car's greater age, if delivery of the new car is delayed. If there is a clause saying that the part-exchange value will be reduced in this way, it's much better to have the agreement saying 'by an agreed amount' than by a fixed percentage – the stated percentage tends to be much greater than the actual drop in value of your old car.

If there is a greater delivery delay than you were promised, it's worth getting the garage to find out why. It may be because of some minor thing you've ordered which you're not actually desperately keen to have – you might be able to get the car right away without that extra thing.

There's one circumstance in which it can pay you a lot to ask for a delivery delay, yourself. A car registered at the start of the new year will be worth much more – maybe hundreds of pounds – than one registered at the end of the old year. So January 1982 would be much better than December 1981. The registration letter changes at the beginning of August. The new letter is also worth rather more, when you sell.

In general, it pays a bit to have the car registered early in a month. The car's road fund licence runs from the first day of the month in which you've registered the car. So if you get only one day in the car's first month of being taxed, you lose nearly a whole month's tax – nearly £5.

Getting the car registered and insured

Before you can drive your car away, it's got to be registered, taxed and insured.

The dealer will arrange registration automatically. Usually, he'll have been allocated a batch of registration numbers – what goes on the number plates – and simply takes one off the top of the list for your car. If you want a slightly distinctive number, it costs you nothing to ask him what choice of numbers he's got – there might be one on his list with special appeal for you.

If you want some particular number, the dealer may ask the registration authority if they can make that available for you. If it's a high number there shouldn't be too much difficulty, but a low number would mean that you'd have to wait until a new letter had started, so that the numbering could go back to 1. Obviously, the wait would be much longer in a small town than a big city – each local authority has its own registration letters (the *last* two letters of the three-letter prefix, incidentally).

You can also – if you're prepared to pay extra for the privilege – have the number that's on your old car

transferred to the new one. This is called the 'cherished number' scheme; you've got to have had the old car for at least six months before you can do it. That's one of the ways that those really distinctive numbers like HYM1E and RAB81T turn up, even on much newer cars than their registration letters would suggest – someone's bought an older car with the special number, paying up to £1,000 more than the car's worth for its number, and had it transferred to a new car.

A much less expensive way of getting a really special number is to work one out for yourself, one that works with next year's letter say, then try and buy a car with that registration letter from a dealer in the area covered by that letter (so, for instance, you'd have to go to N Ireland to get MIA10W; or what about BED50X for a real dream-car, or SEB81X for the car with dandruff?). AA and RAC handbooks list all the different registration letters, for each area.

The trouble with any special-number plan that involves the registration authority is that at any given moment the authority's working rules may simply rule out your plan – so before you set your heart on immortalising your initials or your wit on a car's licence plates, check with the Department of the Environment's vehicle licensing centre, DVLC, Swansea SA99 1AR, that your plan is currently acceptable.

The next step is insurance: you need a current certificate of insurance before you can have the car taxed. If you've already got another car, this step's easy. Your insurance certificate (not the big policy document, but the small sheet of paper which you're sent each year when you renew your policy) nowadays may say simply that you're insured to drive any car belonging to you, without specifying the individual car. So, for the purpose of getting the car taxed, you can use that existing certificate. Of course, if you don't have a car yet you'll have to get insurance for the new one (see Insurance) – and until you've got that you won't be able to get the car taxed, so theoretically won't be able to drive it. If you're not insured already the dealer that you're buying the new car from may issue you with a temporary 'cover note' which you can use to get the car taxed even before you've arranged a full insurance policy for it (but of course it's important to try and get the full policy effective from the moment you drive the new car from the garage).

Even if you are insured, you should tell your insurers about the new car right away. A letter simply saying 'Today I bought a new Ford Granada GL estate car, with a 2792 cc engine, costing £8,872', and quoting the number and renewal date of your policy, is fine. Your policy may keep your old car covered at the same time, if you're trying to sell it privately.

If you use your car in connection with your work – but it's still your responsibility to buy it – you should give them the same information. The firm's insurance policy may cover you while you're using the car on their business, so they need the same information as your own insurers. Usually in a small or medium firm the personnel office or accounts office deal with this: in a big firm you may have to ask in the personnel office to find out just who is responsible. Again, it's best to set the information out in a letter.

Finally, there's tax. As you have to have a current vehicle excise licence disc on the car before you can drive it – and as this can take a week or longer to arrange – it's best to make advance plans. Simplest of all is to make sure that the dealer will fix this, along with the car's registration: he'll need your insurance certificate for this, as it's needed with the form of application.

Incidentally, if you put a little note saying 'tax in post' in the place for the tax disc at the top of the car's screen, you're theoretically breaking the law driving it – unless you are simply driving it direct to the licensing office.

2. BUYING SECONDHAND

Buying secondhand, your choice is even wider – and therefore more difficult – than buying new. This is because you can choose not only among all the cars in production today, but also among cars no longer in production.

A lot of what's been said already, about buying and choosing new cars, applies if you're buying used, too. In particular, you need to think about how the 'extras' information, on pages 37 to 46, affects you.

Where the new-car owner stands to lose, by buying extras which don't add significantly to the car's resale value, you stand to gain. The car which a loving owner has converted into an air-conditioned paradise full of every conceivable luxury could come to you for much the same price as the same car without all those extras. But of course, you can't just order an extra that you want – you'd have to search, to find a car with it.

If you've followed the advice on choosing in earlier chapters, you'll have found that the basic process is much the same as for a person choosing a new car. The crucial difference (as with extras) is that often the new-car buyer's loss is your gain. For example, because there's a huge chunk of depreciation in the car's first year, followed by a much slower rate, that's a particularly good time for you to buy – when the car's almost new. Again, a car that depreciates at a faster rate than average might be a particularly attractive buy secondhand – because after a few years with so much of the car's initial value gone anyway the actual money difference between a high rate of depreciation and a low

one becomes less severe. (But why has that car depreciated so quickly? Perhaps repairs are horrendously expensive; perhaps its bodywork is notoriously bad; perhaps it's just an altogether dreadful car!)

But anyway, those are just reminders: by now, following the earlier suggestions, you should have at least a shortlist of potential buys. So now your four vital decisions are:

- where to buy
- when to buy
- which individual car to buy
- how to pay.

Where to buy secondhand

Buying from a *garage* has some advantages. In particular, you have some legal protection against the garage which you wouldn't have against a private seller, and will probably get some sort of guarantee.

Under the old Sale of Goods Act and the much more recent Supply of Goods (Implied Terms) Act, the car sold by a garage must be of 'merchantable quality' and fit for its purpose. This could be a help if the car turned out to be an immediate disaster – you'd have a claim if some very expensive major fault cropped up almost at once, unless it was something you were warned about when you bought, or might reasonably have been expected to find signs of then. Much more important in practice is that the car's got to be just what the garage claimed for it. If for example you say that it's important that the car should be able to tow a particular caravan, and the garage man says that's no problem, then the car's got to live up to that. If it doesn't – if it can't cope properly with the caravan – then you can return the car and get your money back. If the garage man says that the car's just had a new exhaust system it would be reasonable for you to expect at least a year's life from that – so if the exhaust went within the year you could claim for the costs of repair. Obviously, you'd need evidence – preferably written, at the very least a witness.

Unless the garage makes clear to you that the car isn't roadworthy and needs repair before you could drive it, then the dealer is legally responsible for making sure that the car can meet the Motor Vehicles (Construction and Use) Regulations. Although the roadworthiness requirements of these regulations are not exactly the same as the requirements of the MoT Test, any car meeting the regulations should be able to get through the Test – so if you get the car tested immediately and it fails you'd have a strong case for having the garage put the fault right free. You can have any three-year-old or older car officially tested regardless of whether it's got an up-to-date Test Certificate or not.

Long hassles over your legal rights aren't in practice nearly so useful as a friendly and co-operative garage honouring a guarantee. The guarantee may be sponsored by a car manufacturer (covering other makes as well as the manufacturer's own). But even then, there's nothing fixed and final about the terms of the guarantee. In practice, individual dealers can offer you much better terms than the minimum set out in the basic guarantee – and this should be an important part of your negotiations with any dealer. For example, many guarantees cover only the cost of spare parts: it's essential that you should get labour costs included too (they are usually). If the guarantee is limited to only three months, try for something longer. An alternative is the sliding scale guarantee, which covers a full year but not always on generous terms: for two-thirds of the year the garage's contribution could be only 15p in the £. On the whole, the thing to shoot for is probably at least six months, with full payment for both parts and labour.

For choosing a garage, the advice on page 54 holds – in fact, servicing ability is probably even more important with used cars. The car manufacturers' quality used-car schemes can be a buying pointer: dealers within these schemes generally have to check cars carefully before letting them be covered (otherwise the schemes would lose money on an over-high proportion of expensive repairs), so that their used cars – the ones they've kept to sell themselves, instead of getting rid of to scruffier dealers – should tend to be relatively good. But of course, the same general principle applies to any garage giving a good guarantee on a used car – he won't, unless he thinks the car is relatively sound. And that could mean that the price he asks is high.

Another possible quality pointer is whether or not the garage sells many *new* cars. If it's primarily a new-car garage, it could worry about scruffy secondhand cars scaring off its most valuable new-car customers. So again, it might quickly get rid of shoddy part-exchanged cars to other dealers, keeping only the smarter ones that fitted in well with its general new-car image.

A much riskier trade source of used cars is the car auction. Their prices tend to be much lower than garages' – indeed, lower than what garages themselves are usually prepared to pay for a car. On the other hand, you've got far less chance of checking out the condition of the car than in a garage, and virtually no come-back if it turns out to be a wreck. What rights you have don't go beyond the auction's Conditions of Sale. This might give you the right to return the car and get your money back if you discover some major fault within *one* hour, or if you find that the car's age is different from what you were told, within a fortnight. But even given general conditions like that, many cars are sold 'as seen' or 'as seen without warranty' or 'with all faults as found': if the car's sold as seen or as found, you don't have any grounds for claiming, however much you find wrong, and however quickly you find it.

You'll have no chance to carry out any of the road-test or engine-test checks suggested later for used cars, on page 65 – but you can at least look over the cars in a pound, before they're sold. As each car in turn is driven into the 'ring' for bidding on it, you can get a rough idea of any mechanical disasters by watching carefully while it's started up and driven off (beware of clouds of smoke, lots of rattles, squeaks and jerks). There may be a clue to the car's condition in the auctioneer's spiel, too; and in the attitude of the dealers – it's a bad sign if their bidding isn't brisk. (Most of the people at car auctions are dealers, incidentally.)

If you do decide to risk an auction – because you're confident that you could cope with any hidden mechanical problems – go to one or two first as rehearsals. The selling's very brisk, and until you got the hang of it you could easily be flapped into a mistake. But for most people – who wouldn't have the mechanical know-how to sort out and even spot in advance a really bad buy – car auctions aren't worth the risk. Even though that's where you'd pay the lowest prices of all, that's no use if the car itself turns out to be a catastrophe.

Buying privately is a bit less of a gamble, because the owner will probably give you far more chance to check the car over, and usually take you for a drive in it. Moreover, you can get an expert to check the car, just as you can buying from a garage (see below, page 61). But again, you don't have any general legal rights against a private seller. If he says something specific about the car which turns out to be untrue, you could claim against him in the County Court (see *How to sue in the County Court*, published by Consumers' Association). But of course you'd have to prove it – if he was planning to cheat you he'd hardly give you his fraudulent claim in writing. In general a private sale tends to be cheaper than a garage sale, though not nearly so cheap as an auction.

Finding private sellers is a matter of looking at advertisements. Local newspapers are a good source, including dailies and evenings. Rather more expensive cars have been advertised in the *Observer* and *Sunday Times*, and in the *Guardian*, *Times* and *Telegraph*. Except for the *Telegraph* which concentrates on Wednesdays, adverts tend to crop up most towards the end of the week. There are now several magazines devoted to car sales adverts, including *Car Advertiser*, *Motoring*

Exchange & Mart, and in the London area *Automart*. Motoring magazines with a useful number of ads include *Autocar*, *Motor* and (particularly for older or sports cars) *Motor Sport*. All these include garages with cars to sell, as well as private owners. If you really want to buy from a private owner, check by telephone before you go round to follow up the advertisement: dealers sometimes imply that they're just private sellers, using individual small private-sounding ads for each car, instead of a display ad for all of them together. Even after that check, you may be taken in. Some dealers work on a very small scale from their own homes – buying from auctions say, then reselling quickly without putting faults right. So check the car's registration document, which tells you the date of the last change of keeper.

A newer means of finding a seller is the telephone or postal car-exchange bureau. With these, the idea is that you say what you want – either over the telephone, or filling in a form – giving a price range and any factors that matter to you (colour maybe, or a particular set of extras). Your wants are then checked against the details of cars whose sellers have paid to have them put on the bureau's register: if the details match, buyer and seller are put together. These bureaux advertise in the same papers as sellers themselves: so you might try one if you can't find what you want through the paper itself.

Vaguely similar is the car swop shop – a shop window full of car ads, rather like an estate agent's.

When to buy
Secondhand prices in general tend to be controlled by new-car prices. Events affecting the new-car market affect secondhand prices too. Inflation, for example, tends to push secondhand prices up in two ways. First, the mere fact that the new version of a particular car has had its price increased tends to pull up the prices of used versions of that car, in sympathy – this direct relationship between new and used prices is a dominant factor in controlling how the price of used cars behaves. But there's an additional indirect effect, too. The main body of the secondhand market is built round a firm skeleton of a few very widely selling popular cars.

These market leaders, such as the Ford Cortina, are bought new in large numbers by firms who run fleets of cars, for their employees or perhaps for hire. Their secondhand price levels tend to influence secondhand price levels generally. So the way that fleet users are currently buying and selling these few market leaders tends to affect secondhand prices quite generally. When inflation is sharp, as for example it was in the mid-70s, fleet users who would normally replace their cars after two years, say, may put off buying replacements for an extra year. This cuts down the supply of secondhand cars and therefore tends to push up the price of those that are available to an even higher level than it would have reached anyway. By contrast, when inflation eases a bit, and the firms which run fleets can raise money more readily, they'll return to their normal buying programme – releasing a sudden surge of secondhand cars on to the market, which of course pushes prices down (or at least stops them rising as quickly as they'd have otherwise done). This happened in 1978, for example. And of course, although they may not work it out so carefully, private owners tend to behave in the same sort of way.

Another comparable influence on secondhand prices is exerted by industrial trouble. Anything that cuts the supply of new cars obviously prevents people disposing of used cars, in part-exchange. This tends to hold the price of the used car concerned to a higher level than usual – and if the car is one of the market leaders, this effect tends to ripple through used-car prices in general. This happened for example in 1979, when a rash of industrial problems including a serious strike at Fords kept secondhand prices well above their normal levels.

What lessons can you draw from this, as a buyer? If you can allow yourself several months' leeway in deciding exactly when to buy, you'd be wise to keep your eye on car industry news. Long-running strikes, or anything else causing production shortages, mean the likelihood of higher-than-normal used-car prices. But announcements of record numbers of recent sales, new, should mean relatively low used prices. You may even be able to anticipate events to some extent. Of course, car makers will generally charge what they feel people are prepared to pay, but a round of big pay increases in the car industry, or a sharp rise in the cost of raw materials, may over the next few months turn into higher car prices. That makes it sensible to buy soon – doubly so, because fleet users anticipating higher prices may rush to replace cars a bit early, so pushing more used cars on to the market than usual. One thing which shouldn't affect car prices much, though, is any marked change in the cost of borrowing money. A sharply rising bank rate, it's true, makes it more difficult for new-car buyers to raise money and therefore means fewer cars on the market. But the high cost of borrowing will make it difficult for used-car buyers, too, so a shortage of buyers for used cars compensating for the shortage of cars themselves should stabilise their prices.

There are some general cyclic factors in used-car prices, too. Used-car sales tend to be briskest in spring and early summer – that keeps prices up. Late autumn and early winter tends by contrast to be a rather lean time for car dealers, so they may hold prices down then in an effort to encourage buyers. In particular, if there's been brisk buying of new cars in the late summer and early autumn, by people cashing in on the new registration letter – this is again something you can check by keeping your eye on the monthly figures for new-car sales, maybe published in the papers – there'll be a bigger stock than usual of used cars in the autumn. So November, say, after that supply surge and at the beginning of the dealers' hard winter, can be a specially good time to buy used.

Often the Budget has a strong influence on car sales – it may alter the compulsory minimum amount of deposits, for example, or the amount of car tax or VAT. Here, it's not just what actually happens that affects your chances of getting a bargain, but what people think is going to happen. Unless the general direction of the Budget is quite clear in advance, there's quite a tendency for people to buy new or used before the Budget – to avoid what they suspect may be bad news. Well, that's a gamble of course – one that you might be tempted to try yourself. But like all gambles you're probably more likely to lose than to win. Luckily, with car buying you may have a chance to put your money on instead *after* the horse has passed the winning post. If there's been heavy new-car buying because people have expected car tax and VAT to go up, and it doesn't, there could be a temporary glut of used cars on the market just *after* the Budget — something for you to cash in on. If you're finding the money to buy with yourself (or borrowing an outright sum — say from a bank), you can time your buying in other ways, too. Say the Budget increases the minimum deposit for HP on cars: because about one-third of used-car buyers use HP, this would have an immediately depressing effect on the used-car market — but this, the time when a lot of buyers would find things more difficult, would be just the time for you to buy.

What time in the life of a particular model to buy depends on how much you want to pay — and on for example the risk of 'new-modelitis', the rash of faults that may have troubled the early months of a car's production run (see page 33).

Which individual car to buy
Once you've chosen your model, and decided on any special extras you need, colours and so forth, you have the problem which you don't have with new cars — of choosing an individual sample. Mainly, this boils down to reliability — sound bodywork, sound mechanical condition.

Don't set store only by the age of the car, the number of owners it's had, or even the mileage it's clocked up. Age is of course the main factor in setting the car's price, so by and large — as far as age on its own is concerned — you more or less get what you pay for. There's certainly nothing magic about a car having had just one owner. Fleet cars and hire cars, for example, used by a great variety of people who most likely won't have cherished them much, tend to be registered in the name of one private individual. On the other hand, three or four successive private owners might each have taken a great deal of care of the car — just as much as if it had one single owner all its life. It's now illegal for sellers to set the mileage recorder to a false reading. But

even if an unscrupulous seller hasn't broken the law, the reading can be misleading in any event. For a start, the reading may simply have been wound back to zero — not illegal, but obviously no help whatsoever in gauging how far the car really has travelled. Any reading there is, though it may not have been wilfully falsified, may simply be inaccurate. Either the speedometer or mileage recorder may have gone wrong and needed replacement (with one set at zero) sometime. Or, in a very hard-used car, it may have gone right round through 99,999 miles and back to zero to start again. And the number of miles which a car's done can be a very poor guide to its state of health. Ten miles of bumping along a farm track, for example, could be much more damaging than a thousand miles of motorway. A car parked on a salty seaside promenade for most of its life is likely to rust away much more quickly than one driven continuously, inland. A car given a careful weekly outing by One Fastidious Owner, and therefore never getting its engine really hot, could be pumping round all sorts of nasty substances in the engine oil, that would have been quickly and harmlessly boiled off by the hard-driving team of commercial travellers.

POINT TO REMEMBER
The condition of the car is much more important than its age, mileage, number of owners etc.

You can pay for an inspection by an expert. Both AA and RAC arrange this for their members, though you may have to wait a week or two for an appointment. Commercial firms such as Automobile Consultants (head office 3 High St, Banstead, Surrey SM7 2NA) and Vehicle Surveys (local offices in phone book) may be able to get it done in a day or two. *Motoring Which?* has tested the quality of these services, and found them useful for people with little mechanical knowledge. Although they're unlikely to spot every single fault and risk of trouble, they do spot a lot and could therefore save you the risk of big losses. Also, as the reports are generally made against a background of experience of other samples of the same model, they can give you some idea of whether the car concerned is a better or a worse example than average. And they can warn you of the cost of particular repairs that are looming. Against all this, you'll be lucky to get a report for much under £20.

So, even if you do plan on getting an expert's report, you'll no doubt want to check over your prospective buy yourself first, to make sure that it looks at least worth spending up to £20 on for a report. And obviously, if you're going to rely solely on your own judgement it's essential that you should nose over the car very thoroughly indeed.

First, go armed with what you need: paper and pencil, a screwdriver, cleaning rags, something you can wear to grovel under the car, a powerful torch for shady bits, perhaps a magnet – and a friend. Go on a dry, bright day. (Also, take a cassette if you expect the car to have a cassette recorder fitted.)

Bodywork checks come first. Sadly, you can't really treat rust as a pass/fail test – even relatively new cars are almost bound to show some rust, on a close inspection. But rust is an expensive enemy, so at least make sure it hasn't got a severe hold anywhere, and that it's no worse than average for that model at that age. Look most closely at bodywork seams, at door, bonnet and boot edges, and at the bodywork behind the wheels. Even a small pimple or blister in the paint can be a sign of a big patch of rust ravenously munching through from underneath. Open the doors, bonnet and boot to check the inside edges, and the inner sills. Then wriggle underneath with your torch and screwdriver to check the car's vulnerable underbelly. (*Don't* rely on a jack to hold up the car: people have been crushed to death by jacks collapsing.) The most dangerous places for rust here are any parts of the body which have been strengthened into girder-like box sections (rust here would weaken the car's structure); the mounting points for the car's suspension and engine; and the brake lines. If you find a patch you're suspicious about, poke at it with the screwdriver to make sure it's entirely firm: although there's nothing much wrong with a sprinkling of surface corrosion, you've got to make sure it hasn't

taken enough of a hold to be weakening. A growing potential trouble-spot is underbody sealing: a slightly loose or cracked flap of sealing compound close to the metal body, like some monstrous tarry scab, actually provides the perfect microclimate for a rust-nursery.

A final but essential rust-check is to see that the jack can actually lift the car without the bodywork giving way.

The next thing to look out for is some sign of major bodywork repairs. These are bad news, because they may have been an attempt to deal with a bad case of rust (and the rust will soon be back, you can be sure of that); if not, they'll have been to make good accident damage, which means that there's a risk of subtler difficult-to-spot damage still uncorrected. The most obvious tell-tale signs of poor workmanship: patches of paint spray over brightwork or rubber sealing strips or even window glass. Or you may notice a very slight colour contrast between one body panel and another, or perhaps a slightly different level of glossiness. Sometimes you can see a tidemark of new paint contrasting with the old, just inside a door, bonnet or boot.

Even more worrying is a botched bodywork job: this is where your magnet comes in. Filler, a paste which sets firm when it dries and can then be painted over, is sometimes used to cover dents and slashes in the bodywork, and even to fill in gaps where the metal has been entirely eaten away by rust. If there's a good polish on the car, you'll be able to spot botched-in repairs, by wriggles and distortions in the reflections along the bodywork. Otherwise, bend close to the surface yourself and squint along it, looking out for any odd bulges or hollows. Run your fingers along vulnerable points and places where you might have expected rust: filler doesn't feel quite so cold to the touch as metal. If you do find anything really suspect, try your magnet: it won't be attracted by a big patch of filler.

Incidentally, when you do run your fingers along the bodywork, see how much comes off on you, and sniff. A cheap trick which has been used by some dealers to make a shoddy car look bright and new is to spray its bodywork with paraffin and water – nice and shiny for a couple of days, but that's all.

POINTS TO CHECK ON BODYWORK
Cars needing special check are picked out by name

Rust: check
- seams
- door, bonnet and boot edges (open and shut)
- behind wheels
- paintwork and brightwork generally
- underbody generally
- faulty underbody sealing
- box sections
- suspension and engine mounts
- brake lines
- jacking points

FRONT WINGS
Cortina
Vauxhaull VX (*older*)
Simca 1100
Alfasud
Fiat 127 (*older*)
Fiat 128
Lancia Beta
Datsun Bluebird (*older*)
Datsun Sunny

FLOORS
Mini (*older*)
Austin 1100/1300
Escort
Renault 4
Renault 6 (*older*)
Renault 16

BACK WINGS
Rover 2000
Imp
Citroën Ami
Dyane
2CV (*older*)
Simca 1100
Renault 5 (*older*)
Fiat 127 (*older*)

BOX SECTIONS
Citroen GS (*older*)
Renault 16 (*older*)

SUSPENSION
Escort

JACKING POINTS
Princess (*older*)
Renault 6 (*older*)

DOORS
MGB
Cortina
Granada (*older*)
Renault 16 (*older*)
Alfasud
Fiat 131
Lancia Beta (*older*)

DOOR SILLS
Maxi (*older*)
Mini
Marina
Cortina
Renault 16 (*older*)
Alfasud
Fiat 127
Lancia Beta (*older*)

Body damage: check
- paint spray on sealing strips, glass, brightwork
- new paint tidemarks inside doors, bonnet, boot
- colour or gloss contrast between body panels
- body filler used (the squint-and-magnet tests)
- paraffin-and-water fake polish

Other body checks:
- doors, windows, bonnet, boot open and shut well
- ditto sunroof (check for water stains)
- dry under carpets and boot coverings
- seat padding, covers, trim and carpets, pedal covers
- seat adjustment
- safety belts
- radio/cassette

63

If the car stands up to your rust standards, and hasn't obviously been through major bodywork surgery, you should check some finer bodywork points. Do doors and windows, and bonnet and boot, open and close smoothly, and fit snugly? Is the car completely dry inside, even under the boot coverings and carpets? If there's a sunroof, check how well it fits, opens and shuts particularly carefully, looking out for the smallest signs of water-leak stains round it.

Have the seats still got plenty of padding? (The driver's seat should still look and feel as plump and firm as the passenger's.) Do the seats move in their runners, and if necessary tip up, smoothly? Is the roof lining in good condition (it's a most awkward thing to replace)? Do the safety belts do up, adjust and undo properly? Are they free from dangerous fraying: check contact points such as belt guides, sliding buckles, the mountings. Are seat covers, pedal pads, carpets and other bits of trim satisfactory? Does the radio work – and, if applicable, does it play your cassette decently?

Unless you've a wide choice of other samples of that model, individual bodywork flaws other than rust or major repairs shouldn't put you off buying – they're all things you can put right yourself, usually for a few pounds. But ill-fitting doors etc can cost a lot more: if you want that particular car, see if the garage will have them put right without charging.

Mechanical checks come next. The chart opposite shows the main checks (the following paragraphs describe them in detail). The figures at the bottom of the opposite page show how likely faults are, in each main component. Based on numbers of *Which?* readers reporting faults in their cars over a full year, they indicate how age affects the issue, and which areas deserve the most thorough check. Individual models of cars which are named opposite are ones where faults in that component have been found more likely than in other popular used cars. But less common cars which have not been listed don't necessarily have a clean bill of health, as we don't have enough evidence on them.

Electrical faults are the most common. Switch every-thing on in turn, remembering the brake lights, the horn and the heater fan. (Remember that some things may not work until the engine's on.) When you start the engine, listen for an over-loud noise from the starter, or any odd clunk or whine from it when the engine starts firing itself. Check that there's a *very* slight but noticeable increase in the brightness of lights and in the noise of the heater fan when you increase the engine speed just a little above idling: if there's a very marked change, it probably means the battery's a bit flat (a battery could cost you well over £20); if there's no change, the generator may be faulty (a reconditioned exchange could cost £35, a brand-new replacement about £75, for a typical family car – with fitting labour charges on top). Check under the bonnet that the battery isn't damaged or covered with white corrosion, and that its terminals and mountings are clean and firm. Check that wiring hasn't frayed on anything; check too that drive belts are good and strong.

Exhaust systems tend to last for two years or so, then rust through. So in your gropings under the car, checks on this are important. The silencers are weak points: so are any seams and joints. Poke there with your screwdriver. With the engine running, listen under the car for any suggestion of louder-than-usual noise. Any exhaust smoke leaking out under the car is the worst sign of all. On the other hand you may be lucky and have a car which has recently had its exhaust replaced: it'll still look relatively clean, and if you tap the silencers sharply with the screwdriver they'll give a good clear metallic ring, instead of the rather soggy muffled sound of silencers with tired inside baffles and wodges of rust. A new exhaust system for a typical family car might cost around £40, though often a lot more, particularly if it's foreign. But you can get them fitted free of labour charges at some garages specialising in replacement exhaust systems.

Fuel and ignition faults are quite common, but not easy to spot. If the starter motor churns away briskly (showing that the battery isn't flat), but can't get the engine started easily, don't let the salesman convince

MECHANICAL CHECKS TO MAKE

Cars needing special check are picked out by name

Electrical
- all switches, lights etc working
- battery condition
- wiring condition
- drive belt condition
- start up:
    - ?starting problems
    - ?generator charging well

Marina, Princess: Citroen GS: Capri: Jaguar XJ: Lancia Beta: Triumph TR

Exhaust
- inspection underneath
- noise

Alpine, Honda Civic, Princess: Renault 16 (expensive) Lancia Beta (very expensive)

Fuel and ignition
- starting difficulty, cold or hot
- smooth idling, gentle tick-over

- no exhaust smoke
- optional spark plug check for the enthusiast

Alpine, Imp, Citroen GS (Esp. ignition), Simca 1000 (ditto), Triumph Dolomite, Vauxhall Viva and VX

Cooling system
- worn or leaking hoses
- leaking radiator

Allegro, Marina, Imp, Avenger, Granada, Vauxhall Viva and VX

Transmission
- clutch, gearbox, back axle oil leaks
- underneath, play in prop shaft flexible joint
- clutch starting-in-top-gear test
- underneath, check drive shaft gaiters on

front-wheel-drive cars
Allegro, Marina, Maxi, Princess, Austin 1800/2000 Imp, Triumph 2000/2500

Steering and suspension
- steering wheel free play
- wear in linkage (esp steering joint gaiters)
- shock absorber bounce test
- front wheel bearing jack-up test
- tyres:
    - ?uneven wear
    - ?tread depth
    - ?bulges, scuffs, splits
    - ?radial ply
    - ?tyre types not mixed

Allegro, Marina, Princess, Austin 1800/2000, Avenger, Triumph Dolomite, Toledo and 2000/2500

Brakes
- handbrake action
- footbrake pedal behaviour
- brake fluid level
- brake pipes union with master cylinder
- underneath, brake hose condition

Fiat 127 and 128, Lancia Beta, Peugeot 504

Engine
- oil leaks
- dipstick, tell-tale signs
- oil pressure, just after starting and when warm
- start up:
    - ?rattle from engine
    - ?oil or air bubbles in radiator
    - ?smoke or fumes from oil filler cap
- blue engine smoke

Imp, Avenger, Hunter, Capris and Cortinas since about 1973, Vauxhall Viva and VX

Risk of faults

	1yr old	2yr old	3yr old	4yr old	5yr old	6yr old	7yr old	8yr old
Number of electrical faults per car	.70	.89	1.03	1.14	1.24	1.32	1.40	1.47
% cars with exhaust faults	6	35	58	61	62	62	62	62
% cars with fuel and ignition faults	26	32	36	38	41	43	45	47
% cars with cooling system faults	13	21	28	34	40	45	50	55
% cars with transmission faults	16	21	25	29	33	36	40	43
% cars with steering and suspension faults	11	16	21	25	29	33	36	39
% cars with brake faults	9	15	19	23	26	30	33	36
% cars with engine faults	9	12	15	17	18	20	21	23

you that it's your fault and 'just takes getting used to' – poor starting is one of the commonest signs of trouble. Check, too, that the car starts at once even with a hot engine (later – after your test run). After you've given the engine a chance to warm up, check that it's idling smoothly and that its tick-over speed isn't too high (it may have been adjusted to run fast to cover up poor slow-speed running and lumpiness). When the choke's fully in (ie you're not using the choke at all), the exhaust shouldn't smoke: black or *clear* blue smoke is usually a sign of faulty carburation. If you can be bothered to take out the sparking plugs, they should all look the same, with none seeming crusted with white deposits or black soot, looking oily, or having their inner white insulators burned brown. A dry pale brown is ideal. Although any faults here could be cleared up by a tune-up, that would cost you say from about £11 to £25 – and *Motoring Which?* tests of the results of tuner's work show that by and large it's very unreliable. And although trouble may simply be the result of maladjustment, it could be the sign of a more serious ignition or fuel system fault (spares example: £10 to £20 for a replacement fuel pump). So obviously, a clean bill of health from your tests here is best.

Cooling system troubles are much easier to spot: it's largely a matter of looking out for leaks and the stains that leaks have left. Also, check that the hoses, particularly where they join metal parts, or touch them, aren't at all worn. Hoses themselves are cheap to replace, but a worn one could leave you stranded expensively. A bad sign of trouble would be leaks or stains on the radiator itself (a new one might cost from £35 to over £100, depending on the car and whether it was a reconditioned exchange unit or brand new – and that's before fitting charges). Water pumps can be expensive, too.

Transmission faults are quite likely on older cars. Look underneath for oil leaks from clutch and gearbox housing, and from the back axle. If it's the back wheels that are driven, you'll see a flexible joint in the propellor shaft. Holding the shaft firmly on each side, twist the two parts in opposite directions – they shouldn't shift

at all; and if you can shift the whole shaft more than a fraction of an inch, there could be wear too. This is an important test on cars more than just two or three years old. Having the flexible joint replaced might cost around £25 to £33 – but if the whole propellor shaft had to be replaced it could be £65 or more. If the car's driven through the front wheels, check that the rubber gaiters protecting the point where the drive shaft goes into the wheel hubs are intact – any sign of wear and tear could herald serious damage. With the engine running and your foot on the clutch, and with the handbrake and footbrake firmly on, get into third or top gear and very gently let the clutch back in. The engine should stall: if it doesn't the clutch is very badly worn or faulty (a new clutch assembly could cost you £30 to £70 or more, with fitting maybe doubling that).

Steering and suspension faults can be quite easy to spot. Steering linkages get worn on cars more than two or three years old, and replacing worn parts could cost say £15 to £30. You can spot wear by standing by the car and stretching in to turn the steering wheel a bit – the car's front wheel should start to turn visibly when you've moved the steering wheel by two or three inches. If when the car's moving very gently, as if for parking, the steering feels slightly jerky or notchy when you move the wheel from full lock to full lock, the steering box itself could be worn – maybe £80 or more. Check too for visible signs of wear, particularly in the rubber flexible housings round steering joints. Shock absorbers often need replacement after four or five years – maybe £12 to £25 each, fitting perhaps up to double that. Check by bouncing hard down on each corner of the car in turn, letting it spring back up: if it rocks up and down more than once or twice there's probably too much wear in the shock absorber – certainly, if one corner behaves quite differently to the others. Wheel bearing trouble is uncommon except with some makes: to check you've got to jack the car up and then try to wiggle each front wheel about its axis, pushing and pulling at top and bottom – it should stay quite firm and not slop around. Look at the tyres: an uneven wear pattern may mean faulty wheel alignment (that coupled with extensive body respraying would strongly suggest that the car's structure had been warped by an accident – virtually unrepairable). Check that there are no obvious tyre defects – bulges, scuffs, splits. It's a nice bonus if they're radial-ply, and if there's plenty of tread on the tyres (including the spare) – illegal if there's under 1 mm over a quarter or more of the tread's width. Make sure that the tyres on the different wheels, including the spare, are all of the same type.

Brakes should be cheap to put right if they're simply out of adjustment – maybe £5 to £10. But a complete overhaul with new pads and linings would cost maybe £80. First try the handbrake. If it pulls up a long way it probably needs adjustment; if it doesn't feel as if it's doing any work as you pull it on, and just flops down when you let it off, the linkage may need overhaul. A really stiff handbrake may just mean the linkage needs greasing. Then the footbrake: with the car standing level, let the handbrake off and push down hard on the brake pedal. If it squishes softly down to the floor, the brakes could be worn and need replacement – almost certainly, if the same thing happens when you try it a second time. But if the second time the pedal feels much firmer and doesn't go down so far, the brake fluid has air in it and the whole system needs bleeding (maybe £5 to £10). A few physical checks are worth while: is the fluid in the brake cylinder up to its level-mark? are the unions of the brake pipes with the cylinder clean and leak-free? are the brake hoses leading into the wheels in good condition?

Engine faults are potentially disastrously expensive, and difficult to spot in good time; fortunately, they're not common. Look out for oil leaks (messy and trouble-some to locate, rather than costly). Open the bonnet and check the oil dipstick: beware of really thick black sludge (a sign that the oil hasn't been changed at the right time), and a creamy pale scum or little watery bubbles (a sign of potential engine damage). See that the oil is reasonably thin. If it's so thick that it only oozes very slowly down the dipstick the dealer may have put in a much thicker oil than usual to disguise faults – and you won't be able to trust the results of the pressure test which follows next. With the bonnet still open, start the engine: any oil pressure warning light should go out virtually at once, and an oil pressure gauge should immediately after a cold start give a reading close to its maximum. When the engine's warm, the pressure warning light shouldn't flicker on while it's idling, and the pressure gauge if there is one shouldn't drop right back to zero. If the light or gauge doesn't work in that way, the engine might well be worn – and you can start thinking in terms of £250 garage bills. Anyway, first, before letting the engine get warm, listen carefully: any rattling in the first few seconds after starting means that the oil pump hasn't got the oil circulating instantly, and the engine, turning un-lubricated, could have damaged the bearings – again, very expensively. Still while the engine's running cold just after starting, look in the radiator (hold the cap carefully in a cloth as you take it off, to protect you in case it's already developed a bit of pressure): any oil film, or air bubbles, are danger-signs – at the least a blown cylinder head gasket, but maybe a crack in the engine itself. Take off the oil filler cap, again with the engine still running but before it's warmed up (though it may stall when you do), and check that there are no wisps of smoke: signs of engine wear, yet again. Finally, when the engine's got fairly warm after five minutes or so, rev it several times, watching the exhaust: a blast of greyish blue or milky-blue smoke may again mean trouble.

Finally, the road test. You may want to check some of the points suggested for new-car buyers (see page 23), but for you the chief point of the road test is to confirm what you've found so far about the car's mechanical condition.

At very low speed, in the garage forecourt say, turn the car on full lock with your door open so that you can lean out to listen (or get your accomplice to do this): this shows up worn drive shafts or joints on front-wheel-drive cars – you can hear ticking noises. Any other scraping or squeaking noises in this test need investigation, too. This is the best time to swing the wheel from full lock to full lock, to check for wear in the steering box (see above, under steering and suspension faults); but bear this in mind too, throughout the test.

At about 30 mph in top, on a level road that doesn't dip down at the edges, leave the steering wheel to itself. If the car swings to one side, there might be a flattish tyre; otherwise, it's faulty steering or suspension alignment, or a binding brake: listen carefully for any whistle or scraping noise suggesting that one brake is partly on. Then, checking behind that the road's clear, brake gently, holding your foot steadily on the pedal. This should stop the car smoothly, without your having to increase your pressure on the pedal: if you do have to, there's a fault in the brake hydraulics. Again from about 30 mph – and this time warn your passengers, as well as checking behind – brake fiercely, as if for a panic stop. The car should stop sharp, without pulling to either side: if not, the brakes probably need adjustment – but there could be a more expensive fault, so get the garage to say whether or not they'd put the trouble right. If the car had inertia-reel safety belts, they should have held you firmly in place when you did the panic stop.

Get back up to your 30 mph, and change down to third gear. Then jab and release the accelerator suddenly and repeatedly: the car will certainly lurch back and forth, that's nothing to worry about, but listen carefully for any dull clonking noise – that's a sign of transmission wear. Another check on this is to get up to about 40 mph in top, ideally going down a gentle slope, then listen hard for a whining noise – again, differential wear. Check that there's no whine when you take your foot right off the accelerator, no thump or clunk when you press the accelerator down again.

Again on a level straight road, get up a good speed in a low gear so that the engine's really working hard, then take your foot off the accelerator. A knocking noise from the engine can be a sign of big end bearing wear (very expensive). If the car jumps out of gear when you do this, it's due for costly gear selector repairs – true if it tries to jump out of gear at any time. Not being able to get the car into gear easily is also usually a sign

of gear selector faults, but may be a fault of the gearbox itself.

On as steep a hill as you can find, try a hill start – check that the clutch doesn't slip as you move away. Accelerating as fast as you can up the hill, change as briskly as possible from bottom gear into second: again, the clutch mustn't slip. Was the handbrake happy at holding the car on the hill? Going down the hill, let the engine do the braking without help from you: any backfiring could mean trouble.

Throughout the test, make sure everything's working smoothly, particularly steering, gearlever and pedals. Listen for and try to locate any odd noises. Besides those already mentioned, a slack ticking noise from the engine could just mean that the valve clearances weren't adjusted properly (very common), but might mean the more expensive trouble of a worn-out timing chain. A nerve-racking knocking noise especially if it's only in one gear can mean a broken gear sprocket – jolly expensive. Noisy whine from the gearbox, again generally more obtrusive in some gears than others, may be a sign of wear – not in such urgent need of repair, but just as costly eventually.

Ideally, the test should give you a chance of getting up to a good cruising speed. Once above say 40 mph, increase the speed very gradually to the limit. This gives you a chance to check for any hesitation or missing (maybe just a sign of tired sparking plugs, but maybe some deeper-seated carburation or ignition fault); if you keep noticing a lack of power when you want to accelerate, the trouble's likely to be a faulty fuel pump. But most important, this test will show up any unbalanced wheels – you may be able to feel vibration through the steering wheel, and see the mirror vibrating, when the car's going at a particular speed. If you feel vibration not just at one speed but over quite a range, the trouble's more serious: probably faulty or worn wheel bearings.

The opposite page gives a check-list.

What price used?

The simplest way of getting an idea of roughly what the price should be is to look at one of the used-car price guides first. *Motoring Which?* has found that the monthly *Motorists Guide to new & used car prices* tends to be the most useful for this. You'll probably find that a lot of dealers will ask for a price higher than the top price suggested in the price guides. But most will bring their price down by 5% to 10% if you haggle firmly, which should bring it into the range of prices suggested by the guides. So don't agree to pay more than the top guide price, and expect to pay a bit less. Even then, a good dealer will under pressure put right at least some of the faults you've found, and give you a guarantee.

With a private owner, you can lean heavily on the fact that if he was selling to a garage, the price they paid him would be around 10% less than what they finally charged for even a highly saleable car – and could be 20% less on an older, tattier one. And you almost certainly won't get a guarantee of any sort from the private owner, though there's a slim chance he might agree at least to share the cost of putting right some faults you've found. That means that your haggling target can be much more ambitious than with a garage, even though you'll find his first asking price will tend to be rather lower than a garage's would have been. A fair price rule of thumb might be to try for around 5% lower than the guides' suggestions for a good-condition very recent model, and around 10% lower for an older one.

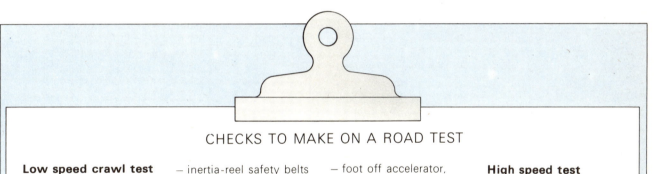

CHECKS TO MAKE ON A ROAD TEST

Low speed crawl test
— ticking noise at full lock
— other scrapes and squeaks
— lumpy or jerky steering

30 mph, level road
— no deviation when steering left to itself
— whistle or scraping noise from brakes
— gentle braking, steady pedal pressure
— smooth straight stop in panic braking

— inertia-reel safety belts work in panic braking
— 3rd gear, accelerator pumping to check transmission wear
— low gear, engine revving hard, then foot off accelerator to check for engine bearing knock

40 mph, ideally down a slope
— top gear, listen for differential whine

— foot off accelerator, check for whine
— accelerate again, check for clunk

Steep hill test
— hill start
— snappy gear change accelerating up hill
— going downhill with foot off accelerator in low gear, listen for backfires

High speed test
— hesitation, misfiring
— vibration at several speeds
— vibration at one critical speed

General
— steering smooth
— gearchanging smooth, easy to find gears, get into gear, no jumping out of gear
— pedals work smoothly
— other noises

3. MONEY, MONEY, MONEY

If you can afford it, paying cash is generally the cheapest way of buying a car. This is because the interest you could have otherwise got by investing your money is generally less than the amount of interest you'd have to pay, borrowing instead. It's very simple: the financial institutions which make their living by borrowing money (ultimately, *from* people like you) and lending it (*to* people like you) have to charge more when they lend than they borrow – or they'd go bust.

The amount you actually save, buying with your own money instead of borrowing, can be quite considerable – maybe up to around 10% of the price you pay. Under Borrowing on page 76 and later, you can see exactly how costs compare – because we've used the cost of using your own money as a yardstick, to measure how much borrowing really costs in each case.

Here, though, we're concerned with getting the best value if you do decide to pay cash.

First, there's a chance that you may be able to get a slightly better discount off the price the dealer's asking, if you pay cash. But the finance companies depend on private car buyers for the great bulk of the business they do with consumers, and indeed for about half of the total volume of their instalment credit trade – including their business and industrial lending. The fact that they depend so very much on car sales means that they can't afford much of a drop in car HP. So – although this is not generally known – they pay garages commission to encourage them to sell on HP. (See page 71, under Borrowing, for how this works.)

This means that although a car salesman may sometimes give you the impression that he's doing you a favour by fixing up HP for you, that's not true – it's you that's doing him the favour, earning the garage a bit of extra commission.

So, when you pay cash, certainly expect to get a discount – but you'll be lucky if it's any more than you'd have got buying on HP.

The amount of discount you can expect is discussed in more detail on page 53.

With a small dealer you may occasionally get a much better price than you'd expected, paying cash for a used car. There could be three reasons for this. The first would be if the dealer saw a way of using the money profitably right away – an opportunity for profit that he'd miss if he waited till finance company money came through, say. The second might be that for some reason that dealer didn't have a commission-based relationship with a finance company. And there could at least be the sneaking suspicion of a third reason: if the dealer reckoned to keep at least part of the transaction out of his accounts, so that he wouldn't be paying tax on the full amount – simpler without the careful and detailed paperwork that goes with an HP transaction. But of course, you can't imagine that just because you do find a good price the dealer must be on the fiddle!

POINT TO REMEMBER
Using savings to buy a car is cheaper than a bank loan – which is cheaper than HP.

Borrowing on HP

Nearly one in three used cars and about one in five new are bought on HP. But the majority of new cars are bought under the wing of a business. So the proportion of genuinely private buyers getting new cars on HP is probably higher than one in five.

Strictly speaking, 'HP' tends not to be HP at all. With true hire purchase, the dealer sells the car to the finance company, which then makes the contract with the buyer. While you're paying off each month, for say two years, the car remains the property of the finance company, though at the end of your monthly payments it becomes yours (maybe after a nominal 'purchase fee' of 1p). That used to be the most common form of finance company agreement. It has the theoretical advantage for the company that if you fall behind with your payments and haven't yet paid one-third of the HP price, they can repossess the car automatically. But in practice that advantage now no longer exists. With a compulsory minimum deposit of one-third, you'd be over the repossession limit almost at once.

In practice, most 'HP' car agreements are now for credit sale or even personal loan agreements. The difference scarcely matters (except that the car is truly yours right away): the Consumer Credit Act 1974 was based on the principle that differences in the way a loan is named or described should not make any difference to the legal position.

Most garages are agents for or at least associated with one finance company. If you want HP, they'll automatically make the arrangements with that company, because that's the company they get commission from. You don't have to use that firm, though. You can instead use any HP firm that accepts you. This is a valuable possibility for savings.

First, another company may advertise better rates – variations that could easily mean a difference of £2 or £3 in each of your monthly payments. Secondly, the way in which the HP firms give commission to the garages could encourage the garage to offer you a better deal as soon as you say you'd rather use a different, cheaper firm. Sometimes the commission is simply a direct percentage of the credit charge, the interest

you'll be paying – that's no help to you. But sometimes instead the HP firm lays down the rate which it has to be paid, letting the garage add on to that rate whatever it likes, up to some overall limit set by the HP firm. This obviously makes it attractive to the dealer to charge you the top rate – unless that means he'll lose his commission altogether, because you turn him down in favour of another, cheaper company.

POINT TO REMEMBER

Buying on HP, try to get a lower interest rate than the one which the dealer quotes first.

So – whether or not you've actually got another company in mind – always try to get the dealer to cut the interest rate by a few per cent. A cut of 2% means about £1 off your monthly payments for each £1,000 you borrow on a two-year agreement. If you belong to a motoring organisation, ask if that gets you a special lower rate, too.

The HP firm may charge about 2% extra on a used car rather than a new one – maybe up to 6% or so extra on a used car that's more than about three years old. And they tend to pay garages lower commission rates on older cars – maybe nothing at all on cars that are really getting on in years. This means that if your monthly payments were say £150 on a new car, for the same total loan they could be a bit over £152 on a one-year-old one; nearly £157 on a four-year-old car.

When you do decide on a particular HP arrangement, you'll have to give various details about yourself. Often, whether or not you get the loan depends on your answers to these questions. Although not all finance companies use the 'credit scoring' system, it has become widespread. What happens is that depending on the answers you give to each of about 10 questions on a proposal form, you get a 'score' for each question, the higher the better. If you're over a certain limit, you'll definitely get the loan; under another much lower limit, you almost certainly won't; in between, they may check you out more carefully.

The scoring is a sort of shorthand for credit companies' experience of previous borrowers: in each question, a low score means that they've found that characteristic a worse risk than the answer getting a high score. So, for example, you might get a score of 30 if you're between 30 and 49 years old, but only 10 if you're under 30. If your occupation is classed as skilled, you might score 20, instead of say 5 if it's unskilled. If you own your own home, you'd get a higher score than if you're a furnished tenant. And so on.

This can help a dealer to give you a very quick answer. He can ring the HP company while you're there in his office; or many finance companies delegate the job of deciding on credit-worthiness to the dealers that they trust. As a matter of routine, the HP company may ring one of two credit reference bureaux (called UAPT and Credit Data) which keep files of court debt records and so forth, as a check that there isn't some worrying black mark against you. Both these bureaux, too, can reply instantly.

So you should know right away whether or not you can get a loan. If you can't – if they turn you down – you have the legal right to ask if a credit reference bureau was consulted, and they have to tell you its name. You can then write to the bureau asking for details of what if anything is on file with them about you. You have to send a fee of 25p, and they have to answer: if there's a mistake on the file (which is claimed to be very rare indeed) they have to put it right.

One snag that can crop up is that if you've got a fairly common name, and don't give a very precise address, you may be confused with someone quite different who's run up a string of bad debts. So always give your name in full, and your address in precise detail.

A potentially useful thing about getting HP is that under the Consumer Credit Act the finance company is jointly and severally liable with the garage. What this legal jargon means in practice is that if there's something seriously wrong with the car, you've got a case not just against the garage itself but also against the finance company.

When it comes to signing, you might ask whether you can take the agreement home to show your family, your close friend and adviser, or whatever. Your legal rights will become rather better if you sign an HP agreement away from business premises, as it will then become subject to the regulations for 'doorstep sales'. Under these, you will have to be sent a second copy of the agreement by post – and you will be allowed to cancel the agreement without any forfeit at any time up to the end of the fifth day after getting that second copy. So if the car turned out to be an absolute disaster immediately you'd got it, you'd be able to get rid of it again without any loss or fuss. But as this certainly wasn't the original intention of sections 67 to 73 of the Consumer Credit Act, the garage might well think that this wasn't fair play – and so it might veto you taking the agreement away to sign!

If you buy on 'true' HP, the length of time allowed for repayment and amount you put down as a deposit is usually regulated by government Terms Control Orders. These vary the compulsory minimum for deposits from time to time, in an attempt to influence the national economy (in the long run it tends not to have the desired effect, though it does cause consumers problems – not to mention the motor industry itself). Although strictly speaking current types of car HP may be outside the legal scope of the Orders, the finance companies have a gentleman's agreement with the Bank of England to treat the Orders as if they were valid for all car HP. But occasionally dealers themselves may try to wriggle out of them. One trick is the false part-exchange dodge. Say you want to buy a used car priced at £2,100, and all you've got to put down as a deposit is an older car which the dealer's prepared to give you £500 for. If the minimum deposit is currently one-third, you're £200 short. But the dealer doesn't want to lose the sale. So he *increases* the price of the car you want to buy to £2,400, and to compensate says he'll allow you £800 on your old car. Effectively you're left having to borrow exactly the same as before – £1,600 – to make up the full price. But the difference is that your part-exchange allowance is now equal to one-third of the car's price, so that the dealer can meet the requirements of the Terms Control Order in arranging an HP deal for you.

This practice is severely frowned on by the finance

companies themselves: if they suspect that a dealer's doing it they may check the 'proper' prices of the cars in the trade price guide, *Glass's Guide*, and warn him off. But there's no denying that it's a convenience to those poorer car buyers least able to stump up a deposit, most severely affected by the way that in general car prices have been rising even faster than other prices, and therefore most discriminated against by the Government's interference in car HP – an interference which has been roundly condemned by every single official independent inquiry which has considered the matter over the last 15 years or so. So if you have trouble meeting the deposit requirements, why not suggest to the dealer that he helps you by charging *more* – not less – for the car you want to buy?

Probably the most important aspect of the HP deal to you is the size of your monthly payments. Assuming that the total length of time you're borrowing for and the total sum you're borrowing is the same, monthly payment size is also the best way of comparing the various different sources of loan. This is a lot easier than interpreting the effect of different rates of interest: but you should at least know about the way that these are worked out, for any loan agreement.

In the old days, an interest rate of say 15% meant quite different things to different lenders. Now, if an advertisement or an agreement quotes a rate of interest, it will be the 'APR': that's the *annual percentage rate* of charge for credit, worked out in a standard way and including not just the interest you pay the lender but any additional arrangement fees. You can use this as a rough and ready guide to the 'expensiveness' of different ways of borrowing money – an APR of 26% means that you'll be paying more for your loan than an APR of 12%. But it's very difficult to do the sums which convert those figures into what you really need to know – the size of your monthly outgoings. Indeed, as the later note on 'free HP' shows, even doing the sums may leave you with a wrong idea about the true cost.

The chart below shows how monthly repayments compare, for a range of APRs, over each £1,000 borrowed and repaid in one, two or three years (though Terms Control may set a two-year limit on car HP).

SIZE OF MONTHLY REPAYMENTS FOR EACH £1,000 BORROWED (£ per month)

For an interest rate of:														
0%	5%	6%	7%	8%	9%	10%	12½%	15%	17½%	20%	22½%	25%	27½%	30%

For a loan period of 1 year

83	86	86	86	87	87	88	89	90	91	92	93	94	95	96

For a loan period of 2 years

42	44	44	45	45	46	46	47	48	49	50	51	52	53	54

For a loan period of 3 years

28	30	30	31	31	32	32	33	34	35	36	37	38	40	41

As you can see, differences in the length of the repayment period are the crucial factor in setting the size of your monthly repayments – they quite outweigh the relatively small differences produced by higher or lower APRs. It's true that the longer you borrow money for, the more you end up having paid to the lender. But for most people this won't matter nearly so much as the easier budgeting allowed by a longer repayment period. For example, borrowing £1,000 at 20% for two years instead of one year adds about £100 to the total cost of the loan – but over two years the monthly payments are only about £50, against over £90 over one year.

So, when you compare different loan rates, be realistic and practical about it. Don't be swayed by small differences in APR into borrowing in a way that would mean bigger monthly outgoings (if that's what matters most in your budgeting) – but *do* use APR as a quick guide to comparative expensiveness of different loans, assuming you'll be able to keep other things like total number of repayments needed equal.

This brings us to the next important point to check, in your HP agreement. What arrangements does it make if you want to pay off early? Government regulations controlling this were expected when this book went to press, but had not been agreed in detail. In any event, you can be sure that you won't gain much by paying off early – and you could lose quite a lot. This isn't because the finance company is taking you for a ride. It's because of the way that the proportion of your monthly repayment which actually represents the loan itself being paid back, and the proportion which is interest, changes as the repayments build up. At the beginning, much more of the repayment represents interest – so you're not actually paying back much of the loan. There are various different ways of calculating how much of the loan is still outstanding at any given moment, but they all tend to give much the same result (and may shortly be standardised by government regulation).

Here's an example of how early repayment might work out, on £667 borrowed at 26% on a three-year HP contract (that is, the loan part of an HP deal on a £1,000 car, after paying a one-third deposit). Paying off the loan after two years would mean that you had about £275 still owing – because your montly payments of just under £26 each would by then have been devoted to paying some £230-worth of interest, leaving only some £390-worth for paying off the loan. So, altogether, you'd end up paying something just under £900 (almost as much as you'd have paid if you'd kept the agreement going until the end of the three years). By contrast, if you'd arranged the loan, at the same interest rate, for just two years to start with, you'd have ended up paying only about £840.

So paying off earlier than you'd originally intended means that you lose money, by comparison with what you would have paid over the same period – fixing that period from the start. In fact, the penalty of arranging the wrong loan-period to start with, and having to pay off early, is so great that by and large it completely swamps any differences between the cost of relatively expensive loans and relatively cheap loans.

POINT TO REMEMBER

Paying an HP agreement off early can cost much more than an agreement set for exactly that period – so don't fix a longer loan period than you're really going to need.

'Free HP' is sometimes advertised, usually for particular makes of car. It *is* genuinely free, in terms of APR – say you borrow £1,000 for 24 months, your monthly repayments would be £41.67, which multiplied by 24 comes to £1,000.08. But, given the same car, that doesn't actually mean that your monthly payments are lower than they'd have been if you'd borrowed the money in some different way. The paradox is this. When 'free HP' is advertised, it's usually as part of a special scheme arranged by the manufacturer or importer. Dealers don't get their usual HP commission – what they'd have earned from a finance company if they'd fixed up a non-free HP deal for you. Moreover, the scheme as a whole has to produce the money to pay for capital locked up in all that 'free HP' advanced to car buyers – and the only source of that money has to be the mark-up on the car, the difference between the cost of producing it and the price the buyers pay. So dealers have less room to manœuvre, in fixing a price for you, than usual. With 'free HP', they are therefore much less likely to give you a discount on the list price of the car.

So, when you see 'free HP' advertised, by all means check it out with dealers. But be sure to find out:

1. will the dealer give you a discount off the car's list price, using 'free HP'?

2. for his best price, what monthly instalments would you pay, with the 'free HP'?

3. what's the keenest price you could get, NOT using the free HP?

4. at that price, how would monthly instalments work out, for the cheapest loan you could arrange?

Don't be surprised if the answer to Question 1 is No – and if that means that you'd work out paying less per month, under Question 4, than with the so-called 'free HP' under Question 2.

POINT TO REMEMBER

Free HP may work out more expensive than a normal loan.

If you're slightly dubious about your job prospects – after a recent spate of redundancies in your firm, say – ask for an extra quote, for full insurance of the loan, for death, accident, sickness and unemployment. This is now beoming common in the United States but is still very rare here, so the garage may not have heard of it. However, most finance companies can arrange this extra insurance package for their loans. It's quite expensive – on a two-year HP agreement it could add around £3 or £4 per month to your payments, for each £1,000 you borrowed.

Borrowing in other ways

By and large, borrowing on HP is the most expensive way of borrowing to buy a car.

Bank loans are becoming more common as a source of money for buying cars. With some banks, over half of all personal loans granted are now for buying cars. There are two ways of borrowing for this from your bank. If you are a long-standing customer, perhaps with a standing overdraft facility which the bank is entirely happy about, there is a remote chance that you may be able to arrange with the manager that your overdraft limit is increased to let you buy the car. He'd want to know when and how you planned to pay off the loan, but wouldn't fix a set schedule of repayments. This might suit both you and the bank if for example the pattern of your earnings was slightly irregular though wholly reliable – perhaps a farmer depending on harvests, perhaps a shopkeeper with a lean period in summer, a fat one in the autumn, perhaps a worker with a regular but seasonal pattern of overtime earnings.

More likely, the bank manager will suggest a loan which you paid off in monthly instalments, probably over two years – just like HP, in fact. If possible, try and have the interest on this calculated at the overdraft or current account loan rate. This is slightly cheaper than the rate for personal loans.

Whatever sort of loan you hope for, be careful and thorough with your application. Write in advance, leaving plenty of time (a bank manager might play safe by saying no if he felt rushed). Say how much you want to borrow and how quickly you'd repay it (either in monthly instalments, or in less regular payments – but still within two years). If you don't want to pay in equal monthly instalments, give a good reason. It will help if you can make clear how the payments will fit into your budget – reflecting a pay rise, say, or the fact that you've stopped paying on some earlier HP deal. If the car will definitely be valuable to you (helping you to do a new job, for example, or saving on train fares), add that to your letter. Best of all, offer any security which the bank could hold, noting its value: life insurance policy, savings certificates, stocks and shares; even a guarantee from your firm or a rich relation, though banks are likely to be less impressed by your rich father-in-law than you are.

If the bank manager doesn't already know you well, he'll probably arrange an interview with you – maybe as much to get a good idea about your reliability, as to go through the detailed business of it. In any event, you're most likely to be able to get a bank loan for buying a car if the manager *does* know you or at least your account well enough to know that you do pay up and can manage money. (With this last point, the very fact that you know a bank loan is cheaper than HP is obviously a point in your favour.) But if money's tight, there's a chance that the bank will be setting such strict conditions on lending that it has to turn even good customers down.

Insurance companies might be another source. If you have a life insurance policy, it will probably entitle you to borrow up to the present guaranteed value of the policy. If your policy is very old, it would be worth looking carefully at the small print. Some old policies lay down a fixed rate of interest for loans, well below the present market rate. Otherwise, loans against an insurance policy are roughly comparable in cost with bank loans – perhaps a bit cheaper sometimes. If you are entitled to one, backed by a policy, there'll be no fuss whatsoever about arranging it – no interview, no scrutiny of your ability to repay – because the insurance company itself will be sitting not merely on a piece of paper but on the actual money already put into your life policy.

Some firms will lend their employees money, usually at very low rates of interest. This is a 'fringe benefit' which helps them to offer employees material advantages – in this case, means to buy a car – without attracting income tax. So it's a relatively effective way for them to bump up their employees' remuneration – a material advantage to you, costing the firm less than if you'd had a pay rise to pay for it. But the advantages for you and the firm are bigger if the firm actually buys the car for you instead – see below, page 78.

A relatively new and very cheap way of borrowing money to buy cars is the credit union. This is a save-and-lend club whose members are all linked by a 'common bond' (living in the same neighbourhood maybe, or working for the same firm). To belong, you save regularly with the credit union, which in turn then lends these savings to its members. In effect, it's just like a building society, even with tax-relief concessions for the savers – and, as it's run on a small scale by its unpaid members, it doesn't have the huge administrative expenses of a building society. In the United States, credit unions are the fastest-growing major source of credit, and nearly a third of what they lend is for car purchase. Here, they got a big boost from the Credit Unions Act in 1979, which for the first time sets out a sensible legal framework for them.

The maximum you can borrow from a credit union is £4,000: £2,000, plus the amount of your savings with it, which can go up to another £2,000. The Act sets a maximum rate of interest at 1% per month, on the amount you still owe – which would be under 13% a year, APR. You can get addresses of unions near you – and help, if you'd like to start one yourself – from the Credit Union League of Great Britain, Ecumenical Centre, Firbeck, Skelmersdale, Lancashire WN8 6PN.

How borrowing costs compare

The basic measure of the cost of loans is the banks' Minimum Lending Rate (MLR). The HP companies tend to follow this quite closely, with their own Finance House Base Rate (FHBR). The interest which you'll pay is always considerably higher than these rates. But the 'pecking order' is always the same: cheapest is a credit union or a very low-interest insurance policy loan; next is a bank or average insurance policy loan; most expensive is a finance company.

Swings in MLR and FHBR – the basic factors in loan costs – are very marked and swift. For example, in mid-1972 both were 5%: by the end of January 1974 FHBR had shot up to 16%. More recently, in January 1977 both were around 15%: by the end of that year they'd plummeted to around 5% – only to climb back up to around 12% during the next 12 months. These changes make a difference of around £5 a month to the cost of borrowing £1,000 over two years. So if interest rates are high – say, an MLR of 12% or more – at the moment you're thinking of buying a car, *don't* jump into a fixed-interest loan, either from a bank or from a finance company. If you do, and if interest rates come down, you'll be stranded there, at the top rate. When interest rates are high, you should either wait for them to come down, or – as you might have to wait for nine months or so – arrange a variable-interest loan: say, an ordinary bank loan, at overdraft rate. Conversely, if interest rates are relatively low – and nowadays that means an MLR under 8% – the advantages of an overdraft-rate ordinary bank loan over HP aren't quite so marked, though they're still definite. While you've got the loan, interest rates will probably jump up, adding to your loan costs with the bank, but not affecting a fixed-interest HP loan.

So check on MLR in the papers before you plan your final loan strategy.

Here is how borrowing costs might compare with each other, and with using your own money to buy, for a two-year deal on a £4,300 car which you paid a one-third deposit on. They are based on run-of-the-mill interest rates – neither extremely high, nor extremely low.

Monthly cost (inc hidden cost of lost interest on own money, paying deposit and then each instalment)

Using your own money	£28
Credit union, or very cheap insurance policy loan	£38
Average insurance or cheap bank loan	£48
Reasonable HP	£70

These are *not* monthly instalments: they're the actual cost of using or borrowing the money. So what the figures mean is that borrowing as cheaply as possible, with that car, would end up costing you about £10 a month more than using your own money would have done – a bank loan, maybe £20 more ... and HP, maybe £40 more. Part of these cost differences are hidden in

the interest you're losing on money that might have been invested – the money you're paying out on the monthly instalments. The actual differences you can see for yourself, in the level of your monthly instalments, are smaller. Monthly instalments with a credit union might be around £135; with a bank, about £140; with HP, perhaps around £150.

Get the best price for your old car

Trading in your old car, you need the same basic armament as for getting the best price on buying a second hand car – you need to know the general price level for it. Again, the most useful source is *Motorists Guide* (see previous chapter).

The obvious starting-point is the offer you get from the garage where you're buying the replacement. But this is unlikely to be the best offer you could get, shopping around – unless perhaps you're selling and buying cars of the same make. You may have slightly more leverage on the first-offer price from 'your' garage, though, because the salesman won't want to lose you as a customer for the new car you're getting. If you look very crestfallen, and talk in terms of trying for a complete package deal – part-exchange of the old car, hand-in-hand with buying the new one – somewhere else, you may be able to bump up his price slightly more than elsewhere. Whatever you are offered, you should ask for around 5% extra – £50 extra in each £1,000 – and certainly expect to see the dealer's original opening offer increased by around 2% – £20 in each £1,000.

That sort of improvement, though, is very small beer to what you can expect if you start shopping around more diligently. If the car is newish, and in good condition, you may well be able to get the best price of all selling privately. For convenience, try a few garages first – preferably distributors or main dealers for the make. If you get an offer appreciably higher than the so-called basic trade value given in, say, *Motorists Guide*, call it quits there, and feel reasonably pleased with yourself. Because the next stage is more effort.

To get a higher price for your old car than the best dealer's price, you'd have to sell it privately. You'll find this very trying indeed unless the car's in outstandingly good condition, and even then you'll have to be prepared for boring let-downs: an awful lot of people who arrange to come and see the car simply won't turn up. If you do want to try, we've found the most successful places to advertise have been local and evening papers (the London evenings are good but very expensive). Or you could try one or more of the car buyer/seller matching services, maybe computer-linked, already mentioned.

If you can put up with the delays and effort of selling privately, you're likely to get as good an offer, maybe better, than any you'd get even trying a great many garages. Again, that's if the car's a good one. The top private offer you get for it is likely to be only about 10% less than the so-called first-class-condition retail value given in the price guides. So, for every £1,000 of the price shown there, you should expect to get around £900.

To give a rough idea of the money you can make from putting a bit of effort into selling your car, here are prices you might reasonably expect for a typical three-year-old car (priced £4,300 new) which you're selling in good condition:

Typical garage opening offer:	£1,920
Same garage, after haggling:	£1,960
Worst garage offer:	£1,750
Best garage offer:	£2,200
Very best private sale:	£2,300

These examples, based on the margins which have been found by *Motoring Which?* trying a variety of ways to sell the same car, show that keen work at the *selling* stage is likely to be a lot more rewarding than hard bargain-hunting at the buying stage. On this typical car, the best offer could easily be £500 better than the worst.

If your car isn't an easy one to sell, then you can't expect such big gains. The easiest are cars which sell in large numbers, which are still in production in the form you've got, and which are in glisteningly good condition. Problems come with cars which are rare (because people don't want them much – not because they're Penny-Black-rare, like a connoisseur's early

Bentley or Hispano-Suiza); decrepit cars; cars replaced by genuinely improved versions; high-priced cars with a relatively restricted appeal; cars which have done an unusually high mileage for their age; and cars which simply have a bad reputation – say for reliability or high petrol consumption. Any of these factors even in moderation will make selling privately much more difficult – you'd be better to stick to a garage. And garages may turn down a car they'd find difficult to sell themselves. So, if there's a real difficulty – say, really tatty bodywork – then your best bet of a reasonable price might be an auction. We've found they can be a good way of getting a decent price for cars that are rather scruffy or long in the tooth. In particular, they save a lot of time – selling on the day you take the car along. Take it as early in the day as possible, and offer the auctioneer's assistant a £5 tip to bring it into the ring quickly, while there are still a lot of buyers.

However you sell, give your car a good chance of attracting a generous price. It's the surface appearance that makes most difference to the offers you'll get, so make sure the car's as smart as you can get it. Clean up the inside (you can have this done professionally, but a thorough job is expensive). Polish the bodywork (see page 111). If there's a worrying amount of rust on a car which in good condition would fetch over £1,000 or so, you might consider paying a bodywork specialist even £100 or so for a bit of a face-lift.

Help from the taxman – and from the boss
Because car prices have been rising much faster than prices in general, in the last few inflationary years, it's now difficult for people to buy a new car out of their taxed income. In the four years up to the beginning of 1979, for example, typical car prices had increased by nearly 110%, while prices in general had increased by only about 75%. On the basis of past history, this coming year car ownership costs will probably increase by more than 20%.

Because of all this, people have been relying more and more on outside help, to afford new cars. The two chief sources of help are the taxman, directly, and employers (which often again means the taxman, but indirectly). Even at the beginning of the 1970s, nearly three-quarters of those richer drivers who are most likely to have new cars got help on the cost of running them, from the taxman, their firm, or both. The trend to subsidised cars has accelerated, with the acceleration in the rise of car costs. Indeed, the proportion of new cars bought 'on the firm' has been increasing so fast that by 1985 or 1986 it is likely that the great bulk of new cars will be bought not by private owners but by businesses.

This fundamental change in the pattern of car buying has consequences of tremendous importance for the car buyer. It means that, nowadays, anyone who buys a car (new or secondhand) *without* the help – from firm or taxman – that most new-car buyers are now getting is condemning himself to a much lower standard of living than he'd otherwise enjoy. On average, people running cars now spend between a quarter and one-third of their total family outgoings on the car. With cars soaking up so much of their money – and car prices, and now petrol prices, fast outstripping other prices – people must get all the help they possibly can, from their firm and the taxman, to avoid their car becoming a tremendous budgetary albatross.

First, let's take the firm.

Something in the region of – or now probably slightly more than – two million cars, originally bought new by their present owners, were paid for by firms. This means that very roughly around one in ten of the country's working population now gets a new car more or less 'on the firm'. As a rough rule of thumb, you should therefore expect a new car from your firm if you manage your section or department – or, obviously, if your work clearly needs a car. In addition, if you're in a profession or self-employed you should now at least be able to claim most of the cost of running a car as a legitimate business expense.

This is a practical interpretation of the ownership figures – it's what happens in practice, not what the Inland Revenue's rules lay down. But it's the best guide to what you should do yourself, to cut the cost of car ownership. If your firm doesn't pay for your car at the moment, tot up roughly how many of your fellow-employees do get this important perk. In a typical firm, maybe the top 10% would be getting a car on the firm. So if you reckon that you're in that top 10%, you could well have a strong case for persuading the company to work this into your next pay review. If you belong to a union, check with the union on the general position in your industry. If you don't, consider getting together with your colleagues – people on the same level as you, or above, who *don't* have a car as part of their remuneration – to put forward a strong case for bringing your firm's car policy into line with what is now the general rule.

The benefit you get from having your car paid for by your firm is (if you want to run a new car) huge. One of the most attractive things about it is that it's not taxed much either. If you're not highly paid and the car genuinely goes with the job, you won't be taxed at all on the benefit you get from it. If you count as 'higher-paid' (with total earnings including the value of any fringe benefits coming to £8,500 a year or more), the value you get from the car will be taxed – but only in part.

This is the scale which the taxman uses for company cars under four years old at the end of the tax year (the figures are rather lower for older cars):

	assumed taxable value of the benefit you get from the car
Cost new up to £8,000:	
1,300 cc engine, or less	£190
1,301 cc to 1,800 cc	£250
over 1,800 cc	£380
Cost new £8,001 to £12,000:	£550
Cost new over £12,000	£880

So, if you run a company car, you pay tax on the assumption that that's what it's worth to you. If you pay tax at the basic 30% rate, this is how things would work out for you, on a typical car costing £4,300 new, and kept for two years. The comparison assumes that, with the company car, the firm pays insurance and tax, though not petrol or garage bills; with the wholly private car, it assumes that it's bought using own money, not a loan (which would cost a lot more).

Monthly pay needed:

To meet the taxman's cut on a company car	£9
To afford the same car as a private expense instead	£180

You can see from this that getting your firm to pay for the car is worth a lot to you. In effect, it's equivalent to a pay rise of over £2,000 a year.

But you probably shouldn't think of it in these simplistic terms. This is because in fact the company car brings you rather a complex pair of benefits. The first is the money saved by not having to run a car yourself. But, if you'd had to pay for this yourself, you'd probably have bought a cheaper car, say secondhand. To pay for that, you'd maybe have needed only half the £2,000. The second benefit – much harder to put a price on, and maybe one that's not important to you – is the material advantage of having a better car than you'd have paid for yourself.

These bare figures don't cover some points you might consider, if you're ever for instance comparing a job which does bring a car with one which doesn't. If you take a car instead of extra salary, you're losing pension rights that would have been attached to that. If the firm reimburses you for any running costs which you pay, you will probably be taxed on a proportion of that. If the firm insures your car, you won't be able to keep a no-claims discount running – so if you later had to insure a car yourself, your insurance could cost more.

On the other hand, the company car may bring you peace of mind you value – knowing that it wouldn't be you who paid for an expensive disaster. And of course, now that you've got the car, that part of your after-tax salary is index-linked – coping automatically with increases in motoring costs.

The advantage of a company car becomes even greater for people who pay tax at a higher rate – and, doubtless, run a posher car. Take a Rolls-Royce, for

example. A company which expected its chairman to fork out for one himself would have to spend around £24,000 a year extra on his salary or fees to compensate. With the old 83% higher tax rate, it would have been an extra £80,000 a year instead. Obviously, hardly anyone's been getting that sort of car money in their pay packets – yet there's at least a fair number of Rolls-Royces around. That's because the firm – to get a Rolls as a company car for its chairman – might need to find only about £10,000 a year, plus perhaps another £1,320 to add to his income so that he could meet the taxman's demand for £530 in respect of the £880-worth of benefit he's assumed to have had from the car.

If you're not employed by a firm which agrees to pay for your car, you may still be able to get substantial help from the taxman – even without changing your job to work with a company that has a salary policy more in line with present-day realities.

An employer may at least be ready to write you a note saying that you'll be expected to use your own car at least sometimes, for your job. The detail of how and what you can claim as an allowance, against your tax, if you use your car for your work is given in the annual *Money Which?* Tax-Saving Guide, each March. You'll need to keep careful records of what you spend on the car, and of how much of your mileage is for work purposes (just as you would with a company car, if you get any expenses reimbursed). You can't count the cost of driving to work – but you can for example count driving to clients and customers.

Keeping these careful records of your business mileage pays off handsomely. If you pay tax at the basic rate, even very occasional business use adds up to useful allowances. Say only one-tenth of your use of a typical new family saloon is for business: that could notch up allowances totalling maybe £180 in the car's first year. That would earn you a tax rebate of over £50.

If you're self-employed, you probably need a car for your work. Again, you'd need to be able to produce proper written records to back up any tax claim. But, most likely, and with a bit of hard, careful thinking, you'll find that 80% to 90% of your use of the car can be put down to essential business or professional purposes. Oddly enough, with a typical new car this would mean that the personal benefit you got from the car (as opposed to its necessary business value) was roughly in line with the scale of taxable benefit used for company cars!

If you pay tax at the standard rate, you'd score heavily by making sure you get the tax allowances on your car that you're entitled to – again, see *Money Which?* Tax-Saving Guide for details. With our typical new family saloon, and assuming you could claim 85% of your use of it as being for business, you could reckon on say £720 capital allowances and £630 other car expenses to offset against tax. That would cut your actual tax bill by over £400 a year.

OK, so you aren't self-employed – and you can't get your firm to help at all. Think carefully about your spare-time activities. You may find that something you think of as just a hobby – something you use your car a lot for – is really a little business. It doesn't have to make a profit. But so long as you can show that it was run on a commercial basis, and that you might reasonably have expected some sort of reward from it, the taxman will accept your accounts for it. Say for example that you sell some vegetables from your allotment to your friends, or are in river-fishing for the money, or have sold some snapshots to the local paper, or are struggling to be a writer: you'd need your car for all those businesses. After calculating in your car expenses you might well have a worthwhile business loss to offset against your normal income – and get a tax rebate. And of course as soon as you do have significant earnings from your spare-time efforts, you'll find it vital to get tax relief on all the business expenses you've incurred – especially on the use of your car. Again, see the *Money Which?* Tax-Saving Guide for help.

This book isn't the place to help you decide whether or not to register for VAT, if you have the choice. But, if you are registered, bear in mind that you *can't* claim back VAT that you've paid on the price of a car. You can claim the whole of VAT on repair and maintenance, even if the car's used partly for private purposes. And you can also claim VAT on accessories fitted to the car – so long as they're not included on the original order form (ie, they've got to be fitted and paid for separately, on a new car). Petrol carries VAT, so you can claim that VAT back; so does parking – but not street meters. Insurance and the road tax are exempt, so no claim there.

Leasing

Car leasing – different from hiring, which is discussed in the next sub-section – is an alternative to buying. It is almost entirely restricted to business users (companies and the self-employed), though finance companies might be prepared to arrange leasing for a private buyer who was particularly keen.

With leasing, the finance company buys the car. It then leases it to the customer for a long period, often two years, but maybe three. A common arrangement is for the customer to pay three months' rental in advance, then, three months later, to start regular monthly payments. At the end of the leasing period the car would go back to the finance company or could be kept by the customer. Either way, a settling-up arrangement is built into the contract. For example, after two years the customer might have to pay a 'balloon payment' of 55% of the car's original price to become its owner; after three years, 45%. If he wants to keep the car, that's that. But if it goes back to the leasing company, the money fetched by selling the car would be set against the balloon payment, to see whether the customer had to pay anything extra. The contract might for example say that 95% of the selling price would be offset against the balloon payment. Say that after two years a £4,300 car sold for around £2,480; 95% of that would be around £2,360 – virtually the same as the 55% 'balloon payment'. So there'd be nothing to settle. In practice, most cars – given continuing inflation – should fetch more than that, so it would be in the interests of the customer to 'keep' the car, making the balloon payment, and then sell it for the extra. But the Inland Revenue have made it clear that they would then tax any windfall profits that leasing customers made by doing this.

Leasing can work out a relatively cheap way of getting a car. This is because the finance company can claim capital allowances on the whole cost of the car, which in effect is the capital equipment they buy for their business. (Until the June 1979 budget, they could claim 100% of this in the first year; since, they've been able to claim it on a declining 25%-a-year basis – not so good for them, thus increasing the lease payments somewhat.) But then in turn the customer can offset the lease payments against *his* tax, as an allowable business expense. Moreover, people or firms registered for VAT can normally deduct the whole of the VAT part of the lease payments from their VAT liability. These benefits, added to the lower initial payment, can make leasing a better buy than finance company HP. Before the 1979 Budget changes it also worked out as generally better value than using money from other sources for car purchase. Since, the decision is less clear-cut, and needs careful consideration in the light of the customer's particular position and needs.

In 1976 leasing was equivalent to only about 2% of the total volume of new-car instalment credit. By 1977 it had jumped to over 20%, and this has been increasing sharply since. In the United States, somewhat ahead of this country in trends of credit use, the motor industry expects that more than half of all new cars produced in 1980 will be leased, not sold in the old way.

Hiring

Hiring is not a cheap alternative to full-time ownership of a car. It works out more expensive. But careful analysis of how you use a car might convince you that you're really only a part-time owner. If the car does stand idle for most of the time – or, during that time, if you simply use it 'because it's there', not because you need it – then you might be better off without a car of your own: instead, just hiring one for the times when you really need it. Or you might buy a smaller, cheaper car than otherwise, hiring a bigger one just for the occasions when you need the extra space.

First, though, what about long-term contract hire?

A contract covering two years – unless you drive a very high mileage indeed – tends to work out considerably more expensive than buying yourself. The one advantage is that the hire contracts are pretty comprehensive. Typical contracts include in the cost of the hire the car's annual licence disc, tyre replacement costs, maintenance and repair, and provision of a replacement car if yours is off the road for say two days or more.

Short term hire is usually what people mean when they talk about hiring cars, conjuring up the familiar names like Avis, Godfrey Davis and Hertz. In fact, Budget, Europcar, Kenning and Swan also have national hiring networks, and there are many local firms which might tend to work out cheaper.

Hiring a car is generally easy. You can book in advance, even by telephone (though few companies will guarantee to let you have exactly the car you want, they will guarantee a car from that price range). You can usually pick up the car at any time of the day that the firm is open, and return it similarly at any time of the day – extra hours may be charged at around one-fifth or one-sixth of the daily rate, if you're late returning it. If it's inconvenient for you to get to the firm's office, you can generally arrange to have the car delivered and collected for you, perhaps for an extra few pounds. Also, with the national firms you can usually pick up the car from one office and leave it at another, so long as you arrange this at the start.

You need to have had a full driving licence for at least a year, without any serious endorsements on it (speeding doesn't usually matter). A bad accident record might stop you getting a car. And you almost always have to be over 21 – sometimes 23 or 25.

The only expense that you have to pay for is petrol. You're also responsible for crash damage perhaps up to around £250, unless when you sign for the car you agree to pay extra for 'collision damage waiver', usually up to around £2 a day.

When you take the car out, you theoretically have to pay a deposit – quite hefty, usually the likely hire charges in advance plus something extra. In practice, though, the firms don't like getting this in cash, as that wouldn't help them trace you if you ran off with their car. In effect you don't leave a deposit at all if you use a credit card; or you can use a cheque.

Rates vary quite widely from firm to firm. Usually they are quoted for groups of similar cars, starting say with cars like Ford Escorts, Austin Allegros, Vauxhall Chevettes; then maybe Avengers, Marinas, Cavaliers, Cortinas; then Granadas, Rovers, Volvos and the like. Depending on the firm, there might be subtle cost graduations within these groups. As a very rough guide, you might find rates for an Escort or similar car around £6 a day, with an extra 7p for each mile you covered; for a Cortina or similar, around £7.50 a day, plus 9p a mile; for an automatic Granada or similar, maybe £16 a day plus 16p a mile, or more.

Especially for longer rentals (say, over three days), you can usually get an 'unlimited mileage' rate, which doesn't have an extra charge for the miles you drive. A full week's unlimited mileage might be charged at around £70 for the Escort, £90 for the Cortina, £150 or often more for the Granada. Hiring at weekends can also work out cheaper: often three weekend days are charged at the rate for two normal days.

Whether hiring works out cheaper than buying for a car you use only occasionally depends on the exact pattern of the way you'd use it. As a very rough guide, you'd probably find the cost of buying and the cost of hiring broadly comparable, if say you drove only at weekends and used the car for between 30 and 40 weekends in the year – or, say, took it on a fortnight's holiday and also used it for maybe 25 weekends in the year. But using it every weekend would be more expensive.

And of course, if you hire a car you don't have to bother about its mechanical condition . . . or do you?

Sadly, yes you do. Repeated spot-checks by *Motoring Which?* on hire cars have shown that only about one in six were in good condition, and about two-thirds had more or less serious faults – including quite a few safety faults that would fail an MoT test. So if you do hire, at least check the following points:

● tyres, including spare, OK, with jack etc there
● lights all working properly, also horn
● wipers, washer OK
● radio works
● doors, bonnet and boot open and shut (and lock)
● windows work
● under the bonnet, brake fluid and engine oil topped up.

In a round-the-block test drive, check that the engine idles smoothly (after starting easily). Look out for squishy or swerving brakes, a weak clutch, shaky steering, noisy exhaust, or a great many rattles and squeaks – ask for another if it 'fails' your spot-check.

An interesting way of cashing in on the hire firms' trading practices is to keep an eye on their calendar year. Often, they set their rates for a whole year, starting in maybe January, February or March. As motoring costs increase by maybe 20% over the year, a hire tariff that's been in force for several months may slightly lag behind true motoring costs. So you could find hiring a better bargain late in the year than early.

Another point to consider, of course, is hiring *in addition to* running your own car. For instance you may not need to compromise between something economical and nippy for the bulk of your driving, in town say, and something which cruises fast and comfortably for occasional long-distance excursions. You might find it cheaper just to buy the basic little nippy car and forget about the high-speed comfort side of things – simply hiring a bigger, smoother car for those long runs. The same sort of thing goes if for instance you need four full seats only occasionally, or the big luggage-carrying capacity of an estate car. And for holidays it can pay to hire a car at the other end, instead of driving all the way there.

Can you escape tax altogether?
In certain circumstances you may be able to get a car entirely tax-free. This would mean a saving of over £800 on a £4,300 car. The person buying the car would have to establish that they were normally resident abroad, or that they were shortly going to be based abroad for their work. They would then probably be allowed to keep the car in this country for up to a year, but at the end of that time they'd have to export it or pay the tax they'd been excused.

If you think there's even a chance that you may qualify for these savings, get in touch with the Export Sales Department of the maker or importer of the car you're interested in.

4. NEW CARS: THE FIRST YEAR

It's already been made clear that you may save money by having extras fitted to a new car *after* you take delivery of it. This is so as to avoid paying car tax on things that aren't part of the basic car; and, if you're entitled to recover VAT, to make sure that you can get it back on the extras, radio etc (you can't, if they're fitted as part of the new car when you first take delivery of it).

Beyond this, when the car you've ordered turns up you may have to be very strong-minded indeed to avoid paying extra for things you don't want.

First, you will have to pay extra for number plates (maybe £10 extra) and delivery (varies with where you live and the car itself – allow at least £30), on most cars: not Alfa Romeo, Bristol, Colt; delivery only on Mercedes and Lancia. Car makers often leave it up to dealers exactly what they'll charge for delivery, but its worth checking with the maker's or importer's head office what would be about right for your area: we've found individual dealers charging £5 to £10 over the odds.

Second, refuse to pay anything like a 'preparation charge' or 'pre-delivery inspection fee'. The cost of the dealer's pre-delivery work is included in his mark-up on the car. But some dealers have pretended to need separate payment for this.

Third, the car may turn up with some extra that you didn't want – metallic paint, say, or special wheels. That's when you've got to be strong-minded about not accepting, because it could mean a long wait until you can get the car in exactly the form you've wanted.

In any agreement with the garage about hidden extras, you could find it useful to quote section 11 (2) of the Trade Descriptions Act. This says:

If any person offering to supply any goods gives, by whatever means, any indication likely to be taken as an indication that the goods are being offered at a price less than that at which they are in fact being offered he shall, subject to the provisions of this Act, be guilty of an offence.

Checking your new car
When you collect your new car from the garage, don't rely fully on the pre-delivery inspection which will have been done on it for you. *Motoring Which?*, in all its years of testing, has never yet found a new car without faults. Some are preposterous: over 40 defects in a single new car, for instance, or obvious things like wipers not working, wheels of odd sizes, parts of the car simply missing altogether. So do your own checks, and insist on getting the faults put right.

POINT TO REMEMBER
All new cars have faults. A careful check now saves trouble later.

Under the Code of Practice used by garages in the main trade associations, you should be given a copy of the dealer's pre-delivery inspection check-list. If you're lucky, it may be the very one used for your car, showing what jobs have been done. Most likely, though, it'll be just a blank specimen. To check your car, you'd do better to follow the list below, which is based on the likelihood of there being a fault.

In addition to these common faults, engine faults are quite likely. Valve clearances may be set wrong, carburation may be wrongly adjusted, the contact-breaker gap may be wrongly set, and the ignition timing may be wrong. Although you might notice faults from difficult starting, rough engine running and idling, poor performance, maybe exhaust fumes, these faults need special equipment to check. And it's not really fair to judge on engine adjustment until the car's been running for a while – say, until after its first free service.

Another fault which crops up fairly often, and which you can try to spot using the check suggested on page 66, is wheel bearing trouble. But again, it really needs special equipment to spot this.

With any or all of these faults – and with a thorough check you're likely to find over a dozen – make sure the garage puts them right promptly. Don't be fobbed off with some excuse about waiting for the car to settle down. A problem you may find is that the dealer may correctly claim that the guarantee doesn't cover 'adjustments', and that that's what you're asking for. (Ford have been particularly sticky about this.) Well, whether it does nor not, all the faults described above *are* faults – things which a new car fit for sale would not suffer from. So the dealer does have a legal obligation to put them right: be polite but firm about that. Above all, the sooner you check for these faults, the harder it would be for a self-respecting garage to wriggle out of putting them right, free.

Underbody sealing
Extras you might want added to your car are mostly discussed in the next chapter. After all, there's no hurry about any of them. But there's one thing which you should make your mind up about right away – and that's underbody sealing. If you're going to have it done, now's the time: right at the start of the car's life.

If your car anyway has a very good reputation for resisting rust (because its makers take more care than usual to build in rust protection), then you're lucky – you don't need to worry about the decision of whether or not to pay for extra rust protection. Mercedes go to great lengths to fight rust, as do some very expensive cars. Volvo used to have a good record, but recently has no longer been outstanding. Saab, too, used to be clearly above-average – they've retained their lead, though less clearly recently. Recently, larger Renaults have tended to be better than average; Audis and Volkswagens, much better.

With the rest, the idea is that extra rust protection should help to do the anti-rust job that the maker should have done properly in the first place. Generally, maybe around 20 lb of a thick gunge is coated over the underside of the car, and a waxy film spread into hollow body places. The object is to coat the metal, to stop water sitting there and rusting it. It now costs close on £100. Previous *Motoring Which?* tests show that, well applied, these coatings do work. And most – but not all – people who've had it done to their cars have said that they're satisfied: but they still found signs of rust eventually.

Bad application can actually be worse than no application at all. If the sealer leaves a crack or pocket against the metal surface, it's quite likely that water, or salt even, will find its way in. Once there, the flap of waterproof compound will act like a little pressure-cooker almost, creating the humid atmosphere which rust just loves.

Motoring Which? has been developing ways of testing how well anti-rust treatments work in practice. This could eventually give a clear answer on whether they're worth while.

Anti-rust treatments come with a guarantee, for even up to 10 years. The firms generally say they'll make good rust coming through from *underneath*, or buy the car. You will almost certainly have to put the car in for regular inspections (paying for any work that's needed), and get it treated after any body damage – the merest scratch left untreated might invalidate the guarantee. Some car makers now offer a broadly similar guarantee.

CHANCES OF FINDING A FAULT WITH YOUR NEW CAR

On new cars, some faults are much more likely to turn up than others. The following lists show which have been found most often in the past by the *Motoring Which?* test unit. Their searching three-day inspection gives the full picture — and the odds shown below are based on that. But even a very much more superficial check is likely to show up quite a few of these 'Top Thirty' faults.

Even chance of a fault
external trim — may be loose or faulty
wheel balance — check for vibration as described on
p 68

Two to one against a fault
paintwork chips and scratches
poorly-applied paint — variable thickness, an 'orange
   peel' look, dull lack of gloss
door and boot locks — may be stiff or loose
inside trim fastenings — may be loose, screws may be
   missing
water leaks — check by spraying doors and windows
   with hose or in automatic car-wash
exhaust mountings and connections — may be loose:
   check by tapping and manhandling
engine and cooling system clips, bolts, etc — may be
   loose (but hard to check thoroughly without special
   equipment — do your best)
wheel alignment — may be wrong, but impossible to
   check without special equipment
windscreen washer — jets loose or aimed wrong

Three to one against a fault
doors fitting — check for gaps, draughts, wind noise
door, bonnet, boot opening — may be stiff to open or
   shut

Four to one against a fault
bodywork actually dented
safety belt mountings — may be loose

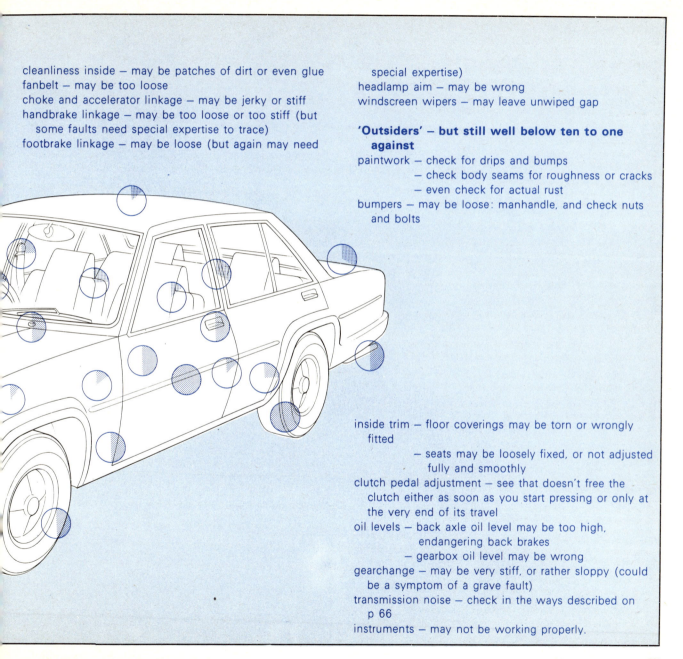

cleanliness inside — may be patches of dirt or even glue
fanbelt — may be too loose
choke and accelerator linkage — may be jerky or stiff
handbrake linkage — may be too loose or too stiff (but some faults need special expertise to trace)
footbrake linkage — may be loose (but again may need special expertise)
headlamp aim — may be wrong
windscreen wipers — may leave unwiped gap

'Outsiders' — but still well below ten to one against
paintwork — check for drips and bumps
— check body seams for roughness or cracks
— even check for actual rust
bumpers — may be loose: manhandle, and check nuts and bolts

inside trim — floor coverings may be torn or wrongly fitted
— seats may be loosely fixed, or not adjusted fully and smoothly
clutch pedal adjustment — see that doesn't free the clutch either as soon as you start pressing or only at the very end of its travel
oil levels — back axle oil level may be too high, endangering back brakes
— gearbox oil level may be wrong
gearchange — may be very stiff, or rather sloppy (could be a symptom of a grave fault)
transmission noise — check in the ways described on p 66
instruments — may not be working properly.

A small but valuable extra is a set of mudflaps: they're a real help in preventing underbody rust.

Running in

Running in is far less of a chore than it used to be. If the car's handbook recommends you not to go faster than set speeds in each gear, follow that advice. But much more important is to give the engine an easy time in its first few hundred miles – and that's not quite the same as driving slowly.

The trick here is to keep the lightest touch possible on the accelerator pedal. When you want to go faster, just gently press it down, always letting the car keep pace with you as it were. You know that feeling when you push right down on the accelerator – and the car seems for a moment to be almost gasping for breath. That's something you should avoid. Another familiar feeling is when you press the accelerator and the car doesn't seem to want to go any faster – you press a bit more and it feels sort of labouring. Usually, that's when you're in top gear and going quite slowly, maybe even going up a slope. Try not to let that happen in your new car. At the slightest hint, change down to a lower gear so that the car feels as if it's running more easily, almost as if there's a weight been lifted from it.

Another useful way of making things easy for the engine is never to have your foot the whole way down on the accelerator, even if the engine does seem to be responding easily. Maybe halfway down – even less, in the car's very first few hundred miles – would be a good limit.

POINT TO REMEMBER

Running in isn't so much going slowly as driving gently – really quite different.

In this first period, too, a few longer runs are better for the car than lots of starting and stopping. Gentle steady cruising, changing the speed very slightly from time to time, is ideal.

Whatever the handbook says, don't feel that as soon as you've done 1,000 miles you can jump straight from being a docile Dr Jekyll driver into a maniac Mr Hyde racer. It's much better to be gradual. Drive as you did before – but gradually accelerate more briskly, drive a bit faster.

The light-footed approach you've been using will be a help, too, in driving economically – see page 128.

The first service

The car's first service, usually free, is the time for putting right the many problems which are likely to have cropped up. Beforehand, it pays to keep a log of faults or peculiarities – even keeping a pad handy in the car, so that you can write things down the moment you spot them.

It's particularly important to keep your ears open for anything that doesn't sound quite right. Squeaking brakes (although worth mentioning to the garage) are probably all right – just settling in. But any other noises need attention. Especially, whines from gearbox or axle could be heralds of serious trouble. The dealer may say that such noises are nothing to worry about – that they'll disappear after a few thousand miles. If he does, make sure he gives a written undertaking to correct the fault free under guarantee if it persists.

Before you take the car in for the service, give it a good inspection. Repeat the checks you made when it was brand new. Add to these the checks for water or oil leaks, and for loose connections and fastenings, suggested for used-car buyers on page 65. And give the car a road test, as described on page 67.

End of the guarantee

As the car comes up to the end of the guarantee, it again pays to put it through a thorough check, so that you can have faults put right free before the guarantee runs out. It's best to do this maybe a couple of months before the expiry date, so that there's plenty of time to chase up elusive problems.

POINTS TO REMEMBER

Check the car thoroughly a month or two before *the guarantee runs out.*

Once again, you'll find the used-car checks on pages

62 to 68 useful. Check specially carefully for rust or paintwork weakness – the merest trace now could mean crippling expense later. And look at the tyres very carefully. Uneven patterns of wear, most likely on the front wheels, betray suspension and steering faults which are difficult to spot in other ways.

With some cars, you can opt to extend the guarantee to a second year, when you buy them. On average, the cost of this is broadly comparable to the repair cost total that's likely for the car's second year. But of course the average car repair bill includes some cars which have been virtually trouble-free, and others which have had a lot of trouble. Obviously the guarantee extension wouldn't be worth while for the 'good' car, but would be a real money-saver for the 'bad' one. Equally obviously, you can't tell in advance which your car is going to be, good or bad. On balance, extension schemes seem a good idea for the relative peace of mind they can bring.

A point to bear in mind is that even if the car is out of guarantee, you may be able to have faults put right free. No car makers reject this sort of claim out of hand – about half are met in full, and another quarter at least partly. The basis of any claim should be that the fault has been developing all along, or at least that it stems from some manufacturing defect or material weakness which was there when the car was new. Although the guarantee is the maker's, your legal rights are actually against the dealer who sold you the car, and if some weakness in the car that's been there all along finally shows itself in a serious fault, what the guarantee says makes no theoretical difference to the dealer's duty to put it right. But of course, that 'theoretical' is important. Even if you could persuade a court that your out-of-guarantee claim was valid – and that means that you'd have to *prove* that the underlying weakness had been there all along – it would be much cheaper and simpler in practice to rely on the maker's good will. So never fall back on your basic legal rights against the dealer unless you're driven to it – for example, by some really expensive fault which quite clearly has been there all along, just waiting until the moment the car's out of guarantee to erupt finally.

Serious trouble with a new car

If your new car breaks down, and the repairs take several days, you could be seriously put out by losing the use of it. This is called 'consequential loss', and legally the seller might have a duty to make good your loss – in this case, most obviously by providing another car for you while yours was off the road. But you'd probably find it very difficult to win a court case based on this argument. You'd have to prove that, buying the car, you had a right to expect more reliable service from it. You'd be able to show that more easily if you'd made clear to the dealer that you depended on using the car every day, before you bought it. But you'd probably also have to prove that your car had spent an unreasonably long time off the road. In practice cars even in their first year spend an average of four or five days off the road needing servicing and repair. So you'd probably have to show a repair history much worse than that. And if it came to fighting a court case, the dealer and perhaps manufacturer would no doubt field a formidable force of technical witnesses to show that they'd done everything possible to fix things – and that really a replacement car wasn't part of the deal at all.

However, makers say that they look at any claim under guarantee for a replacement car on its merits. A friendly approach to the dealer is probably best. Bearing in mind that four-to-five-day average for off-the-road time for new cars, you might feel justified in needing a replacement car if, over the year, yours went in for a total of more than say ten days' repairs; or if, for any one job, it looked as if you were going to lose the use of it for more than just two or three days on the trot.

A much more serious problem is the so-called 'Friday Car', the real 'lemon'. That's a car which starts with a long string of delivery faults, then has to go back to the garage again and again for repair. You're entitled to press for a replacement, or your money back, on the grounds that the car is not of merchantable quality, nor fit for the purpose for which it was sold to you (because of its poor quality). See *The Buyer's Right* and perhaps *How to sue in the county court*, both published by Consumers' Association, for an action plan.

SECTION THREE

RUNNING YOUR CAR

Which way to get the most out of your car, for the
least money; how to avoid trouble, and how to
face it if it comes

1. CHEERING UP YOUR CAR

Things you can have fitted to your car fall into four main categories: safety; anti-theft; performance (not just going faster, but economy and general efficiency too); and luxury or appearance. On new cars, have them fitted *after* you've bought the car. This makes sure that they won't be included, as original fittings, in the basic price of the car. So they won't have to carry car tax as well as VAT – which saves about 9 or 10%.

Particular extras many come cheaper if you get them from garages or dealers specialising in those extras. Some may be fitted free, others may bring good price cuts. This can bring their cost well below what you'd pay if you got them from your regular garage. Always get a quotation from your usual garage – but check to see whether you can get the same thing cheaper from a specialist. If it's something you can fit yourself, try one of the many cut-price car accessory shops, too. Finally, don't turn up your nose at car breakers and dismantlers (listed under that description in telephone directory Yellow Pages; or you can get a list of members of the Motor Vehicle Dismantlers' Association from its Secretary, R J Charles, Britannia Road, Eleanor Cross Road, Waltham Cross, Herts). As well as the scrap-type ageing cars they deal with, they dismantle many newer cars which have been irreparably damaged in a crash. However bad the crash, it could have left unscratched just the thing you want: high-powered foglamps, a special horn, maybe even seats from a luxury car which with a little ingenuity and perhaps a lot of work you could fit into your own.

Safety extras
Only very few cars come with safety belts fitted to the back seats. In a crash, people in the back are to some extent protected by the backs of the front seats – much better to smash into than the windscreen and dashboard. And the back part of the body compartment tends to be less damaged in crashes than the front part. However, safety belts are an added safety factor even for people in the back. And in a really bad accident there's even the risk that someone in the back, hurtling forward, will undo all the protection from someone safely strapped into the front – a safety belt for them would have stopped that risk, too.

POINT TO REMEMBER

Back-seat safety belts – and special restraints for children – save lives.

So back-seat safety belts are a potential life-saver.

With estate cars and hatchbacks you may well find you need special versions of the belts, to fit in the back. And you might find that the belts are annoying, when you fold the back seat flat – and sometimes, that they get in the way of the luggage space.

Ordinary safety belts can let children weighing under about $5\frac{1}{2}$ stone slip out in a crash, so are virtually no use for small children. It's very dangerous, incidentally, to try and put an ordinary safety belt round both yourself and a child: in a crash your greater weight would kill the child by crushing. Without safety belts, children are much safer in the back than the front – even holding one in your lap in the front would be no good, as the tremendous force of a crash would certainly break your grip.

So, if you've small children, special safety restraints for them are virtually essential.

Carrycot restraints have lengths of webbing to hold the cot on the back seat, and keep its cover firmly on in a crash. For safety, you'd have to pack the baby securely and snugly into the cot, as it's the cot, not the baby itself, which is kept in place.

Child safety seats generally do for children from about nine months to $4\frac{1}{2}$ years old. The child has a full safety harness holding it into a special child-sized seat strapped on to the back seat – children usually find them comfortable, and get a better view out as they sit higher up. If you just have one fitted, a good place would be on the left side of the back seat, that is diagonally opposite the driver.

Children's safety harnesses are again full shoulder-and-waist harnesses: for children between around four or five years old, and the age when they're big enough for a full adult belt. You might find it best to adjust them so that the child can sit on a cushion – to see out better. As with any safety restraint it's crucial to have them buckled up tight.

In April 1977 *Motoring Which?* published a brand comparison test of all these restraints. To make choice easy for you, brands which had the British Standard approval kitemark were always among the best (but there was no standard for carrycot restraints).

For children of the four-and-upwards age range, there are some newer alternatives: an energy-absorbing block, such as the Britax Playsafe, which fits between a child and a normal safety belt; or a belt specially designed to cope with children as well as adults, such as the Kangol Generation.

Do-it-yourself fitting, which may involve drilling through bodywork, can be a problem as children's safety restraints usually need four mounting points – cars usually provide only three. It may be beyond you, if for example the petrol tank is in the way. So if the in-

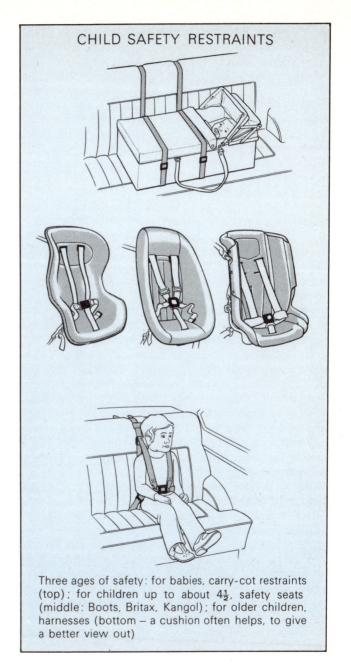

CHILD SAFETY RESTRAINTS

Three ages of safety: for babies, carry-cot restraints (top); for children up to about $4\frac{1}{2}$, safety seats (middle: Boots, Britax, Kangol); for older children, harnesses (bottom – a cushion often helps, to give a better view out)

structions aren't crystal-clear (most are good) check with the maker of the restraint or your car. And do this even if the restraints are being fitted by a garage – correct fitting is absolutely crucial, and garages may get it wrong.

Lighting is the next area for safety improvement. Even on clear nights some car headlamps seem patchy and dim, particularly on dipped beam. A close look may show that the lamps are of a standard size, especially if they're sensible round ones. You might then be able to replace them with a brighter set.

If your lamps have separate bulbs, instead of being single sealed units, don't be tempted just to shove in a bright tungsten-halogen bulb. It's unlikely to match. You'd do better to think of replacing the entire unit – perhaps, if you can get it, with a one-piece sealed beam unit, which is anyway likely to give a better beam pattern and to last longer without dimming than a separate bulb. Tungsten-halogen, incidentally, is a type of lamp or bulb where the filament is held in a sliver of quartz instead of the relatively big gas envelope of a conventional bulb: it can be much brighter.

If you do want to change lamps, the wattage of the new ones may be higher than the old ones: you can check, because the wattage is always given on the lamps themselves. If there's a big difference, you should get your garage to check that the output of your car's generator is high enough to cope with the extra load – changing to a higher-rated generator as well would be too expensive to be worth while. But normally the generator should be able to cope.

An alternative way of getting more light on to the road is to fit extra lamps. Unless you use them only in fog or falling snow, you have to have their centres mounted more than two feet above the ground. If you have a pair of lamps fitted, they've got to be mounted symmetrically, and the outer edge of each lamp must be within 400 mm – that's a bit more than 1 ft 3 in – of the outside edge of the car. It's vital to fit them very securely, so that they don't wobble and disconcert other drivers.

If you do fit extra lamps and you want them to be helpful in fog, you really have to fit a pair of foglamps (rather than say one foglamp and one spot or driving lamp with a longer beam). This is because, in fog, you have to have a pair of lamps on – so you couldn't switch off the headlamps and just have the one foglamp on its own. The important thing in fog is to have a very flat cut-off at the top of the lamp's beam, with no shafts of stray light above it – then, the foglamps can cut underneath the fog. A spotlamp wouldn't be much use for that. A possible compromise is a foglamp mounted on the near side and a spotlamp with a very 'clean' narrow beam on the offside. For clear nights you could have the spotlamp aimed straight ahead, perhaps wired so that it and the foglamp came on when you went on to main beam. But, for this, you'd have to have a good, bright dipped beam – or the contrast could leave you feeling rather in the dark. A separate fog switch would cut out the normal headlamps, and you could then in fog reset the spotlamp so that it was aimed across the front of the car, to pick up the nearside verge some 30 ft ahead – maybe farther in thinner fog.

That might be the best compromise for a car with headlamps which you needed to supplement even for ordinary driving. But it wouldn't be so good for driving in fog as a pair of pure foglamps. One reason is that, if you use them only in fog, you can mount the lamps at any height – lower than the usual 2ft limit. The lower they are, the better they'll be at cutting under the fog. Then, for thick fog, they should be aimed so that the brightest part of the beam lights the road some 25 to 30 ft ahead.

Choosing foglamps, you want a wide beam, with the brightest part up near the top of the beam, and – as noted above – a very sharp flat cut-off with no stray light. If you live in a foggy part of the country (and that's probably the only circumstance in which you'd find foglamps worth while), you can easily see for yourself how well different lamps work, on a foggy night. It's then very easy to see whether the beam is truly flat and 'clean' – so with foglamps you can often rely on friends' recommendations (if you really cross-question them about stray light and so forth).

One of the worst dangers in fog is people piling into you from behind. Especially on motorways, people cling to each others' tail-lights. The dimmer the tail-light, the closer people get. You can get a special back fog lamp, red and much brighter than conventional tail-lights. Cars made since 1979 have to have them, by law. Cars with these fitted show up to about twice as far away in mist or fog. So they're a good protection against being rammed from behind in fog. The danger, of course, is that they're so bright that when you put your brakes on someone behind might not notice the extra brightness – so might not slow down.

Don't use the back foglamp except in fog or falling snow – it's dazzling for other drivers in normal conditions.

Reversing lights aren't strictly a safety feature. But of course they make it much simpler to back your car at night without fuss. If you have reversing lights added, you'll probably have to have a switch with a built-in warning light fitted: the law demands either a warning light, or a switch built into the gearlever so that the lights come on only when you're in reverse. It's illegal to have white lights showing at the back of your car when you're going ahead.

Depending on where you live, you may have to leave lights on if you're parked by the roadside at night. The drain on the battery of side and tail-lights overnight could well run it down. A small parking lamp showing red behind and white in front, which you can clip into the off-side window of your car for night parking, is allowed instead.

Mirrors are vital to safe driving. External mirrors are essential for estate cars or hatchbacks in which the view through the inside mirror may be blocked by a load in the back. But in all cars there's a blindspot outside the range of the inside mirror, where a car overtaking you could take you by surprise. On recently-made cars, an outside mirror the driver can adjust is mandatory. Although convex mirrors give the widest view of all, they distort angles and speeds. You'll find it best if the mirror's the sort that, when bumped, springs back into place without needing readjustment.

For normal driving, mirrors fitted on the car's near side are much less use for normal driving, but may be handy for parking, driving in cities, and if you're driv-ing abroad.

In cold or wet weather, the back window can get steamed up badly. Almost all modern cars now have a heated back window, with wires buried unobtrusively in the glass to clear mist from the inside, and even ice or snow from the outside. If you've got a car without, having a heated back window of that sort fitted is expensive. You can get electrical substitutes, either little heaters or transparent warming pads. But in fact plain transparent stick-on panels can work well and are much cheaper. The sort that keeps in direct contact with the glass, breaking any mist droplets down into a see-through film of water, tends to work better than the 'double-glazing' sort that leaves an air gap between plastic and glass.

Although a wipe with an ordinary cloth or chamois leather will clear mist off side windows, in really muggy conditions – if you've got in with wet clothes, say – the mist will come back. Although you can get impregnated anti-mist cloths which keep the windows clear for some hours, cans of anti-mist liquid to use with just an ordinary cloth work out as better value.

In really severe weather de-icing aerosols are extremely convenient and effective: they clear quite thick ice in moments, and are harmless to paintwork and wiper blades.

POINT TO REMEMBER

Buy cold-weather things like deicers and antifreeze before the cold weather starts.

On a motorway say, the driver of a noisy lorry won't be able to hear an ordinary car horn. A louder horn is very much the sort of thing you could get most cheaply from a car breaker. Besides horns which are simply louder versions of ordinary ones – glorified buzzers, really – you can get air horns. These work more like trumpets, powered by a little air compressor. Loudest of all are the klaxons which you can get from marine suppliers and which are used by lorries and buses in mountainous countries with really bad roads – where they need to give warning miles away.

Some cars now have head restraints fitted as standard. They protect you against 'whiplash' neck injury if your car is rammed behind. Many people dislike them because they can make it less easy to look round over your shoulder, and can seem rather claustrophobic for people in the back.

Fires in cars are rare. Car fire extinguishers can be useful in the rare event of a fire – if the fire's small and if you act really quickly to catch it before it gets hold. But in practical terms, bearing in mind the fact that insurance normally covers fire damage and that if you had enough time to use an extinguisher you'd have enough time to get safely clear of a car fire, they're probably not worth while for normal drivers. If you do think one would bring you peace of mind, get the biggest you can fit, mount it so that it's really handy, and have it checked once a year by the maker to see that it hasn't lost weight. There is now a British Standard for portable fire extinguishers, with a 'kitemark' approval scheme.

Anti-theft extras

Theft, like fire, is covered by most people's car insurance. But, unlike fire, it's now so common that you will find it worth buying special protection against it. In its ten-year-life, there's now nearly an even chance that a car will one day be stolen or broken into.

Car makers generally use pathetically inadequate locks. The *Motoring Which?* test unit locks expert can – without causing any damage – get into about four out of ten cars *within about five seconds*. Half the rest take him only about ten seconds, and very few indeed keep him out for long. A professional car thief might find a locked boot more trouble, but would generally sail through a locked glovebox.

Alarm systems usually involve a compromise. If they're the sort which sound only *after* a door's been opened, the thief – already inside the car – can generally quickly immobilise them. On the other hand, the sort which sound when the car's tampered with or rocked – to warn *before* the thief gets the door open – generally go off accidentally with the slightest knock, or even the car being swayed by wind. In July 1977 tests, *Motoring*

Which? found one alarm which did go off if the car was tampered with, but not if it was simply swayed or rocked: the Simba Inertialarm, from Simba Security, 2 Occupation Road, London SE17 – but it's expensive. It would be worth while if you can't avoid leaving papers or valuable things in your car (and should stop at least a joyrider, if not a professional thief).

Most modern cars have steering-column locks, which defeat the typical car thief – a weekend joyrider, usually a teenager. To defeat or deter one of these in an older car without a steering lock, almost any anti-theft device would work. A simple, visible one perhaps costing only a couple of pounds, should at least put off joyriders.

Professionals, though, could probably get past most anti-theft devices – and would, to steal a car they'd earmarked. The 1977 tests reckoned that the Autosafe (which locks ignition and brakes, and would need careful professional installation) should give even a pro a very tough time.

Kits which etch the car's registration number on all the windows and the windscreen would annoy and might deter a professional – he'd have to get all the glass changed before he could sell the car. (But the usual amateur probably wouldn't even notice them.) In any event, some form of special identity marking is useful, as a pro would get all the usual markings, and even the car's colour, changed. An alternative to window-etching is a secret mark of your own, hidden somewhere like under the boot covering or carpet.

Petrol thefts may well get more common as the stuff gets scarcer. If your car doesn't already have one, you can get special locking filler caps.

Performance extras

In theory, much the most useful performance extra is the sort which helps you to save fuel. These are now widely advertised. Sadly, in practice they don't seem to work. Careful tests on five, reported in January 1978 by *Motoring Which?*, showed no consistent or significant improvement with any.

Making the car go faster tends to be rather an expensive undertaking. Some car makers sell kits to modify their own engines. Ford, for example, have 'Group 1' replacement engines which are very much more powerful than the basic engines, but very much more expensive. Even if you are considering performance equipment *not* designed or approved by the car maker, consult his technical service department first. This is particularly important if the car's still under guarantee: the guarantee might be invalidated if the maker disapproves of the equipment. And any significant change should also be reported to your insurance company.

Advising on the detail of performance equipment is beyond the scope of this book. If you don't know anything about it, you need a complete education before you start, reading some of the very many specialist magazines and books. And if you do know something about it, whatever we added would seem pretty slim.

There are however one or two general tips which might be a help.

A small but appreciable part of the engine's power is normally soaked up by the cooling fan. In practice the radiator needs help from the fan for only part of the time – when the car's running very slowly for a longish time, say. For the rest of the time, the airflow created by the movement of the car itself is enough. So fitting a thermostatically-controlled fan instead is a help (though most modern cars' fans are thermostatically controlled).

People often choose an exhaust other than the maker's own in the hope of getting more power out of their engine. The theory behind this is that a specially 'tuned' exhaust can be better at clearing the exhaust gases quickly. But choice of exhaust can be a long-term moneysaving question, too. If you fit the maker's own exhaust again, it'll rust through just as quickly as the first one. Although a 'stainless' exhaust costs perhaps twice as much, it should last much longer.

A common reason for cars losing power, and becoming less economical, is poor maintenance – especially, faulty ignition adjustment. Although special ignition systems, electronic and so forth, are often advertised as giving more power their only real advantage for the ordinary motorist is that they should be less affected by wear, therefore need adjustment less often.

Comfort extras
The most important comfort extra is sound equipment – radio, perhaps cassette player.

With the spread of local radio, car radios are increasingly useful in warning of bad road conditions or blocks. The cheapest sets just have long and medium wave. This gets you all the local stations, and most of the national ones, at least in most places. VHF, which costs more, gives less interference at night, and better sound quality (it's also the only way of getting stereo radio). Now, you also need it as well as long and medium wave to get the full range of the BBC's programmes, as they've developed the nasty habit of carving up their programmes between wavelengths – if you want classical music on Radio 3, for instance, you might have to tune to VHF to avoid getting cricket all day; and then retune to medium wave to avoid getting the Open University in the evening. In radio only, VHF sets cost nearly twice as much as medium/long-wave sets of similar quality. And in many parts of the country VHF reception in cars is not good. Even when it's ok, you have to retune as you go from area to area.

Push-button tuning, where you can just press a button to get the station you want instead of twiddling a knob, is certainly worth the extra. It's very much more convenient. Although the price difference seems quite large on paper, in practice you can usually get such big discounts on the popular sets – which tend to be push-button – that the difference rather fades away.

POINT TO REMEMBER

In spite of the higher price, push-button tuning is good value.

A less cumbersome, and generally less costly, alternative to having a separate cassette player as well as a radio is to have the two combined (see *Motoring Which?* brand test, April 1979). But it's now difficult to get a stereo VHF combination with push-button tuning for much less than £200, though you can get a manual tuning set much more cheaply – reasonable performance for less than half the price.

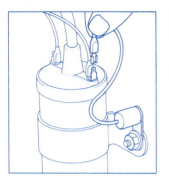

First step in suppression is to fit a 2 μF capacitor between the ignition coil's low tension connection and 'earth'

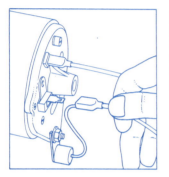

Electric motors, generator, etc may also need a 1 or 2 μF suppressor, fitted in the same way between the supply lead and 'earth' – an alternator needs 3 μF

If your car doesn't have built-in mounting panels for stereo speakers, you can get *much* better sound by having holes cut to mount them firmly, say in the back parcel shelf, than by simply fixing the speaker-boxes on top.

If you live in a town, you'd find a power-operated aerial a worthwhile investment. Many sets now have connections for these: they normally stay recessed within the car bodywork, extending only when the set's on. Aerials on parked cars now seem virtually irresistible to vandals, and however careful you are with an ordinary aerial you're bound to forget to push it down on the night that it's destined to become the neighbourhood maypole. Besides, power-operated aerials are rather fun in a rude sort of way.

Whatever sound equipment you decide on, be sure to go discount-hunting – you can get up to nearly a third off recommended prices.

The sound quality you get can be improved quite a lot by using just slightly more expensive loudspeakers. But the most likely way of getting better sound is to eliminate interference. If the set sounds more crackly when the engine's running, it probably means that the ignition system's to blame – especially if the crackle or buzz gets worse as the engine speeds up. Check that there's a suppressor capacitor fitted to the lead between the ignition coil and the car's ignition switch: if not, fit one rated 2 μF. Another possibility is just one electrical accessory causing the trouble. Check each in turn by switching it on and off. When you've found the culprit, you may need to fit a suppressor choke in the supply lead to the component. When you're checking, you may find that the interference actually decreases when you try the brakes. This is one pointer to an unusual type of interference, where the non-driven wheels build up static electricity. To cure it you have to fit sliding hub contacts; or with independent rear suspension, you may have to fit bonding straps between the suspension arms and the bodywork.

If the interference is rather sporadic, and if you hear distinct clicks and crackles when the car goes over bumps, it's probably a poor aerial connection. Make sure it's bolted securely to the car's bodywork, on to bright unrusted metal.

Car sound equipment is a prime target for thieves. See above for protection against them. Also, check your insurance policy: if you'd lose your no-claims bonus by having your radio stolen, you might find it worth insuring separately for a few pounds a year.

The reverse of sound, of course, is silence. There's a lot you can do to most cars to make them quieter. First search out holes between the body compartment and the engine, and seal them by squeezing in rubberised sealing compound. Do the same with floor and bulkhead holes (but *not* the very small drainage holes). Thick felt under the floor carpets and against the bulkheads is easy to fit. Sound insulating felt or foam fixed to the bonnet and to the engine side of the bulkhead is also good, and fairly easy to fit. Although a heavy layer of felt over the gearbox cover and transmission tunnel will usually help, you can't really cure noise

from this source without getting at the underneath of the cover, to coat it with sound-absorbing material – again, rather a beastly job. If you do feel like embarking on the harder jobs, you'd also find sound-absorbent linings deadened noise from the door panels – but beware of fitting anything that could trap water, and start rust. Linings would be worth putting under the back parcel shelf – and often in the boot, too. Cutting down body-panel booms is difficult, though you might even find that efforts to stiffen them made them noisier.

You can get ready-made kits to 'silence' individual cars – the makers advertise in the car magazines – for around £30.

If your car has slightly inconvenient controls you may be able to do something about it, cheaply. You can get an extension to screw to the top of a distant gear-lever, for example.

Extra instruments can be fun. If you fit a clock, you'll probably wonder in the end how you ever managed

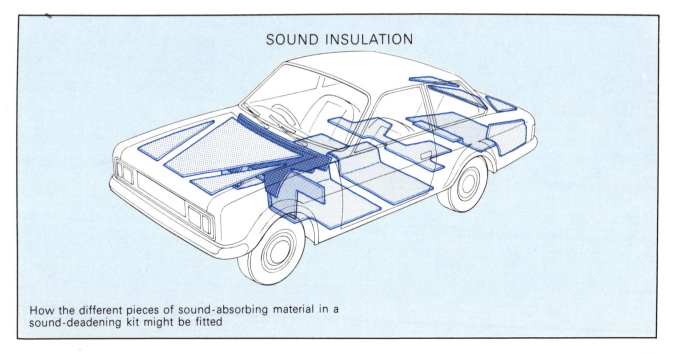

SOUND INSULATION

How the different pieces of sound-absorbing material in a sound-deadening kit might be fitted

without it. But you might enjoy knowing how fast your battery's charging (an ammeter), how well charged it is (a voltmeter), what the oil temperature or pressure's doing, or the water temperature, or how fast the engine's turning (rev counter, or tachometer). Really, unless you're going in for competition driving and therefore need to know how your engine's behaving at the extreme limits of its performance, all these instruments are more a matter of amusement than practical value. Good, big warning lights are probably better at drawing your attention to something that's amiss.

Some people find that a vacuum gauge, which measures the pull with which the petrol-and-air mixture is sucked into the engine, helps them to drive economically – but you have to have a real feel for the way engines work to use this information effectively. (And if you have that feel, your right foot will do the job automatically, without help from a dial.) Now, you can get mpg-meters which give a continuous reading of how much fuel you're using. And there are trip computers, which you can use to calculate things like estimated time of arrival, or average mpg.

Luggage racks (recent brand test comparison in *Motoring Which?*, April 1978) are much more of a practical extra. They let you carry about an extra 100 lb of luggage – more on many cars with strong roofs – and maybe more awkwardly-shaped things than you'd get in the boot. Most are pretty tough, but tend to look a bit rusty, and howl a bit at speed. They do obstruct the airflow enough to increase fuel consumption – so don't leave one on when you're not using it.

Extra-special car seats used to be worth thinking about, but car makers have devoted much more attention to making sure their basic seats fit people well in the last decade or so, so they're now much less likely

to be rewarding. If the car has seat coverings which get hot and sticky, you might like a backrest panel which leaves an air gap between you and the seat.

Perhaps the most exclusive extra – more than TV (which has to be installed so that only people in the back can see it) or even the cocktail cabinet in your Rolls – is now a communication system. The cheapest of these are message relay systems, where someone wanting to get in touch with you contacts a central relay post, which then 'buzzes' you in your car. You can pass a message back through the controller, or stop at a callbox to ring back. A service of that sort might cost around £50 a year, with an extra deposit for the equipment in your car. A full-scale car radio-telephone, with your own number so that people can ring you, or you ring from your car, costs around £1,200, with £50 fitting charge; or, including the £15 licence you need, about £150 each quarter if you lease it. But you are usually restricted to say 30 miles round one of the transmitters (now in most big cities). And at the moment there's a very long waiting list indeed for the London area, though not elsewhere.

Once you start moving into that league, though, maybe you should start thinking about the ultimate – the bullet-proof, bomb-proof car that every true plutocrat now needs. Be sure what level of protection you want. The best, giving protection against even high-velocity heavy machine-gun fire – say, top-specification armoured glass and body panels, a mine-proofed floor, crash-proof heavy door bolts, bullet-resistant tyres, and a direction-of-fire readout to tell your bodyguards where the hostiles were firing from – would probably cost over £100,000 on your Rolls. But you could penny-pinch and have it done on a smaller, cheaper car: on a Mercedes it shouldn't cost more than about £80,000.

2. INSURANCE

Car insurance is one of the biggest costs you meet, running a car. But your scope for cutting the expense to a minimum is limited. First, although different companies' rates vary so much that one might charge two or three times as much for the same car as another, the best car insurance may be the most expensive. Second, the best you can do to cut costs, once you've chosen a company, is very much a gamble: paying out less for a cheaper type of policy, for instance, carries the risk that eventually you'll be caught out by extra repair costs.

Even so, it's very much worth taking the trouble to understand the ins and outs of car insurance, so that you can get the most possible out of it.

Finding a company
You can either approach an insurance company direct, or go through an insurance broker. For ordinary drivers, insurance brokers are not very useful. People who deal with them on average have been less satisfied with the general service they get than people who deal direct with an insurance company. Because insurance companies pay them commission, using brokers could tend to push up insurance costs in the long run. And the basic idea of going to a broker – to get a better deal, by having a wider choice of companies – can be a bit

POINT TO REMEMBER
To get good value from an insurance broker, do your homework first—and get quotes from more than one

of an illusion: one broker's best-value deal can cost at least 20% more than another's, even for the same type of cover. In special cases, though, brokers can be an important help.

If you want to insure with a Lloyd's syndicate (see below), you have to go through a broker. And if you're a difficult case (again, see below) a good broker should be able to do a lot better than you could on your own. If you do decide to use a broker you should be able to get a very wide range of quotations by going to one who subscribes to Quotel or a similar subscription service giving the broker instant up-to-date details on many different companies. Trying more than just one broker for quotations will probably be more rewarding than just sticking to a single one.

Lloyd's syndicates are groups of underwriters – that is, people who club together to provide insurance. About three dozen syndicates do car policies. There are no fundamental differences between Lloyd's policies and those with companies, though of course there are individual differences between policies.

In the 1960s and early 1970s, over two million motorists found themselves in trouble because their insurance companies collapsed. There is no risk of this with Lloyd's syndicates, which are protected by a general compensation fund. And the Policyholders Protection Act now gives quite wide protection against failure, with insurance companies. Claims against you for death or personal injury would still be met even if your company had failed, and so would most of the cost of damage (including damage to you own car, under a comprehensive policy). But you'd still have to meet 10%of the cost of damage, and you'd lose your premium.

So you might still want to be ultra-cautious, and go either for a Lloyd's syndicate or for a very big company which does a lot of general insurance and isn't just a car-insurance specialist, which has been doing car insurance for a good long time, and which hasn't suddenly expanded its car-insurance side a lot. These include Commercial Union, Eagle Star, General Accident, Guardian Royal Exchange, Legal & General, Municipal Mutual, National Employers' Mutual, NFU Mutual, Norwich Union, Pearl, Phoenix, Provincial, Prudential, Royal, South British, Sun Alliance & London, and Zurich.

Money Which? compares policies every few years, reporting in particular on the important point of how satisfied people are with their company. The most recent report was in December 1979.

Choosing a policy
Most people get a Comprehensive policy. It covers injury to other people (with some very limited cover for yourself), damage – including fire or accident damage to your own car, theft of your car, and a limited amount of theft from it.

Third Party, Fire and Theft policies don't cover accident damage to your own car, and may not cover you for things stolen out of it – notably car radios. Less importantly, you lose the scanty compensation for injury to yourself.

Third Party policies also exclude fire and theft.

Road Traffic Act policies are the minimum the law demands: they cover only claims for injury to other people, and only on public roads. This may be the only cover you can get if you're a really bad risk (see below). If you've a choice, get something better – to avoid being saddled with hefty repair bills not just for your own car but maybe for someone else's.

If you're getting the car on HP, the finance company will probably insist on your having a Comprehensive policy. Otherwise, the choice really boils down to Com-

prehensive, and Third Party, Fire and Theft (because this costs only a little more than pure Third Party, the extra cover you get against the significant theft risk is worth while).

In theory, in the long run you're likely to be better off with just Third Party, Fire and Theft. There are two reasons for this. First, the no-claims discount system (see below) means that even with a Comprehensive policy you might not claim for damage to your own car. Secondly, only two-thirds or less of the premium money paid in to insurance companies is actually paid out again to meet claims. If you decide instead to pay for your own accident repairs, in the long run you'll cut the cost by that one-third or more that would otherwise have been soaked up by insurance companies' or brokers' overheads and expenses.

Sadly, though, few people can afford to make long-run calculations of that sort. That's because the long-run ideal has a nasty habit of turning suddenly into the short-run crunch – say, your new car written off in a few months' time, costing thousands to replace. Only if you could find that money easily from other reserves, should you think of 'insuring yourself' for damage to an expensive car. But if your car's older, costing only a few hundred pounds to replace, Comprehensive cover is a less worthwhile protection. Commonly, it costs about £100 more than Third Party, Fire and Theft for a typical saloon, before no-claims discounts; and could be £200 or £300 more in London, say, for a fast car. If the car itself is worth only a few hundred pounds, you could have easily paid out more than its replacement value in just two or three years – obviously not worth while.

Some policies have special features which you might need. A few, for example, let you pay your premiums in instalments, instead of just once a year. One or two pay for a hire car if yours is stolen or out of action after a crash, and a few others pay a small allowance towards this. Many will replace a newish car with a brand-new one if it's stolen or badly damaged, or will at least set an agreed value in advance (instead of surprising you with a fair but low valuation when disaster strikes). Many – but not all – let you authorise repairs after a crash yourself, without waiting for the company to come and check. Many let you cover the windscreen separately against breakage without forfeiting your no-claims bonus. If any of these features would be valuable to you, you should check the policy carefully for it before you buy – or set it as a requirement for a broker, if you decide to put one to work for you.

No-claims discount

Each year that passes without a claim, your insurance premium is cut by a discount – the no-claims discount. Typically, one year brings a 30% discount, two years 40%, three years 50%, and four years 60%. (If you've never insured a car before, you may get an 'introductory' discount of, say, 25% in the first year.) After that, the discount stops growing. Any claim normally pushes you back down the ladder by two rungs. If for example you were on a 50% no-claims discount, after three claim-free years, a claim would mean that when your policy came up for renewal you'd drop back to a 30% discount. Another claim in the same year would put you back to zero discount at renewal time (and you'd obviously end up back at zero too if you had a claim in the year following your first one). With some companies, once you've built up a full no-claims discount you can shift to a policy which lets you have at least one claim before the premium goes up, though there may be restrictions on whether you qualify for one of these 'protected bonus' schemes, and you may have to pay extra. These schemes save many headaches.

POINT TO REMEMBER

Comprehensive Insurance doesn't necessarily mean you should sit back and let the insurers pay for damage—you may save a lot, paying yourself and thus protecting your no-claims discount

The discount system means that you have to think carefully before claiming on your policy. A claim doesn't just mean you'd be paying more the next year. The effects ripple on for between two and four years, depending on where you are on the no-claims ladder.

For each £100 of *pre-discount* premium paid now, this is what you lose by claiming, with the typical 30/40/50/60% system:

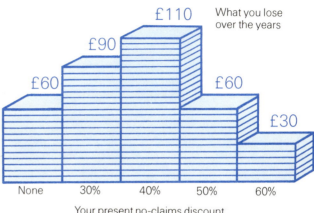

LOSS BY CLAIMING

£110

£90

£60

£60

£30

What you lose over the years

None   30%   40%   50%   60%

Your present no-claims discount

It might seem odd that you'd lose, claiming even without a no-claims discount. But that's because the claim stops you getting one next year – and for the three years after that you'd be one rung lower on the ladder than if you hadn't claimed. These figures don't allow for inflation. In practice you'd lose even more, because premiums tend to go up each year. But the figures in the chart are the ones to consider, when you're thinking about making a claim. If you know that your parking mishap is going to cost £85, say, and your gross premium is £150, check off the figures in the chart. What percentage is your present no-claims discount? Multiply the figure against that by 1.5 to get your cost of claiming. As you can see, it's pretty marginal if you haven't got a discount or if you're on 50% (claims cost is £60 × 1.5 = £90 – that is, not much more than the repair cost). But you'd save by claiming on a full no-claims discount (£30 × 1.5 = £45 – saving about £40). And you'd certainly lose by claiming on a 30% discount

($£90 \times 1.5 = £135$) or a 40% discount ($£110 \times 1.5 = £165$); in both cases the cost of claiming is much more than the repairs cost.

Use the same system to work it out for other premiums. If your present premium is £50, for instance, multiply the chart figures by 50/100, ie .5. If it's £125, multiply them by 125/100, ie 1.25. Whenever the answer comes out much higher than paying for the damage yourself, it's not worth claiming. A factor to consider – but impossible to work into the sums – is whether you think you're likely to have another accident soon! This doesn't make much odds if you're on a 50% or 60% no-claims discount. But with a lower no-claims discount, claiming on a later accident would land you back at zero the next year – whether or not you'd claimed on the first one. So, if you hadn't claimed, and then had another accident where the costs were so much that you simply had to claim, you'd feel a bit of a fool missing out on the first one.

Claiming – what to do
The section on page 146 tells you what to do if you're in an accident.

After any accident (whether or not you want to claim), and of course if you want to claim for theft, you have to tell your insurers, right away. When you fill in the accident report form they send you, make absolutely clear whether this is for a claim on your policy, or whether you hope not to claim. If you are claiming, you'll probably lose any no-claims discount whether or not the accident (or theft) was your own fault. But you then just send everything involved (estimates, bills, cross letters) straight to your insurers.

Most insurers have a 'knock-for-knock' agreement among themselves. To save the cost of working out exactly who is to blame in an accident, each insurance company will normally pay the claims of their own policy-holders, without regard to blame. In an expensive accident, say one that involves serious personal injury where a court might award substantial damages, the insurance companies may prefer to go to the cost of sorting out who is to blame.

The moment when you first make contact with your insurers is the moment to check carefully on the detail of your policy. If your car needs repairs, the insurance company may set out some procedure you've got to follow – letting them have an estimate in advance, say. If you're definitely going to claim on your policy, or if you're going to fall back on it if you find a claim against someone else doesn't work, then check that you're not doing anything which might stop you being able to claim.

If someone else was to blame, send them a recorded delivery letter asking for confirmation that they'll pay, with an estimate of the repair costs and of any additional costs that the accident caused you. That's usually the point at which the person who was so nice at the scene of the accident changes his mind about paying up. If you don't get the answer you want in a fortnight or so, write again saying that you'll be forced to take legal action unless you get satisfaction promptly.

The next step is the one that could start costing you money, if you lose. If the amount involved is up to £200, you can use the small claims procedure which is simple and virtually free (though there's a small risk of having to pay legal costs if you lose and the amount involved is between £100 and £200). Up to £2,000, you can use the normal county court procedure: here, you are likely to have to pay legal costs if you lose. So with the county court, and if any substantial sum is involved, you should probably consult a solicitor before getting in too deep. And of course, a letter from your solicitor might well get satisfaction before you have the bother of going to court. See *How to sue in the county court* (Consumers' Association), and the notes on *Small claims in the county court* which you can get from your county court.

Special points when you insure
Always tell the truth on the proposal form which you fill in to apply for insurance. Your contract with the insurers is based on the assumption that it *was* the truth, and if it's not your insurance may be invalid. 'The truth' means the whole truth – things you might have left unsaid, as well as answers to direct questions. So for example if you've got a country cottage in a cheap

insurance area (see below) as well as a flat in expensive London – and spend most of the time up in the flat – tell the company. Insurance just based on the country cottage alone might fall through if your car was stolen from outside the London flat.

This principal holds if anything happens after you've got the policy, which you think might affect the insurers' attitude to you or your car.

These are things which insurers would expect to be told about:

- an inexperienced, very young, or very old driver regularly using your car
- someone with a bad driving record using it
- medical trouble
- motoring convictions (though not for parking offences)
- and of course, change of address or change of car.

Small savings when you insure

Check with your firm or union on whether your employment or membership entitles you to a discount, perhaps with a particular insurer. Think about any insurer that's actually *only* for you, like the NFU Mutual for farmers and the like, or Municipal Mutual for civil and some public servants: they may be specially good for you.

Agreeing not to let anyone else drive, or maybe just one (or even two) other named drivers, may get you a discount of around 10%. With most companies, you'd still be insured if garage staff were driving your car – but check for this.

On a Comprehensive policy, you can usually get a discount of 10% to 20% by agreeing to pay the first whack of damage to your car – say, 10% if you agree to pay the first £50, 20% for £100.

If you've got more than one car, you may get a discount of 10% or so by including them all on one policy.

Keeping the car in a garage might get you a small discount.

What it all costs

The three things which insurers consider in fixing a premium are your car, where you live, and your driving record – including whether you use the car for business.

Cars are put into seven or eight groups. Not all insurers agree about the detail, but the groups might include the following examples:

Group 1 (cheapest): Sunbeam 1000 cc; Citroën 2CV; Fiat 126; Ford Fiesta 900 cc, Escort Popular; Mini; Renault 4.
Group 2: Austin Allegro (up to 1300); Sunbeam 1300; Avenger (up to 1300 cc); Fiat 127 900; Ford Fiesta 1100, most Escorts, Cortina 1300; Morris Marina 1300; Vauxhall Chevette, most Vivas; VW Polo.

Group 3: Austin Allegro 1500, basic Maxi; Citroën GS; Sunbeam 1600, Horizon 1100, Avenger 1600, Hunter; Datsun Cherry; Fiat 128, most 127s, and Mirafiori 1300; most Ford Cortinas and cheapest Capri; most Ladas; more expensive Morris Marinas; Opel Kadett; Peugeot 304; Renault 5TL, 12; Simca 1100; Skoda; Toyota Starlet, Corolla; cheaper Triumph Dolomites; VW Derby
Group 4: Alpine 1300; Datsun Sunny; Ford Capri 1600; Honda Civic; small Mazdas; Opel Ascona; Peugeot 104SL, 305; Polski-Fiat; Princess; Renault 14, 16; Vauxhall Cavalier; VW Golf.

Group 5: Alfasud; Audi 80; Colt Lancer; Datsun Bluebird; Ford Cortina 2000, Granada up to 2300; Honda Accord; MG Midget; Opel Rekord, Manta; Peugeot 504; Renault 18; Range Rover; Saab 99; Subaru; Toyota Carina; Triumph Spitfire; Vauxhall Carlton; VW Passat; Volvo 343.

Group 6: Alfa Giulietta; Citroën CX; Daimler Sovereign; Datsun 240; Fiat 132; Ford Granada 2800; Jaguar 3.4 or 4.2; Lancia Beta; Mercedes-Benz 200 or 240 diesel; Morgan 4/4; MGB; Renault 20, 30; Rover; Toyota Celica; Triumph TR7; Vauxhall Royale; Volvo 244.

Group 7: Alfetta; Audi 100; BMW 320; Daimler Double-Six 5.3; Ford Mustang; Lancia Gamma, most Mercedes-Benz; Morgan Plus 8; Peugeot 604; Reliant Scimitar; Saab 900; Volvo 264.
Group 8: BMW 525; Bentley; Ferrari; Jaguar XJS; Lotus; Porsche 924; Rolls-Royce.

Roughly, Group 7 cars cost about three times as much as Group 1 to insure comprehensively, and nearly two-and-a-half times as much for Third Party, Fire and Theft. With Group 8, you'd probably have to meet special terms such as a hefty 'excess' (when you pay the first part of a claim for damage to your own car), though the rates might not be much higher than for Group 7 – that is, if you had the excellent record that would be virtually essential, before you could even persuade an insurer to consider you.

Another way of looking at the difference in costs is that each step up to a higher group adds roughly 20% to insurance premiums. So if you paid say £140 for a Group 3 car (likely to be quite common in 1980), you might pay roughly £170 for Group 4; £200 for Group 5; £240 for Group 6; £290 for Group 7. Or, dropping down, maybe £115 for Group 2, a bit under £100 for Group 1.

Insurance companies may use 7 groups for areas, too. Again with variations, they might go like chart opposite.

Here, there's less difference between areas, at first. Steps between areas are more like 5% up to say Area 4. But Area 6 is 15 or 20% more expensive than Area 5, and Area 7 15 or 20% more than Area 6.

The company will rate you as extra risky if you're young (maybe 50% extra if you're under 21, double under 18); if you've a physical defect (and you'll have to get a doctor's certificate saying you're able to drive – which you probably won't be able to get under the NHS, but will have to pay for privately); if you're new to driving here; if you've been convicted of driving offences – especially drunken driving; and if you've had many accidents.

Some jobs are frowned on by insurers – including journalism, entertainment, sports, bookmaking, market trading, keeping a pub. Students may do badly, too.

If you fall into any of these black-mark categories, you may have to pay extra for your insurance; you're quite likely to have to pay a part of any claim for damage to your own car; and you – or a broker – may have to hunt hard just to find a company which will accept you at all.

INSURANCE AREAS

Area 1 (cheapest): remote countryside like the Western Isles, maybe West Country, Lincolnshire.

Area 2: most of Scotland and Wales; English countryside.

Area 3: busier countryside like Sussex, Oxfordshire, West Midlands rural areas; medium-sized towns like Norwich, York.

Area 4: busy countryside like Kent, Buckinghamshire, Essex; Cheshire, Lancashire; Merseyside; biggish cities like Oxford, Bristol, Dundee.

Area 5: Birmingham conurbation, Edinburgh, outer London, Greater Manchester, Blackpool.

Area 6: Liverpool, outer Glasgow.

Area 7: London postal districts, central Glasgow (central Glasgow can now be more expensive than central London).

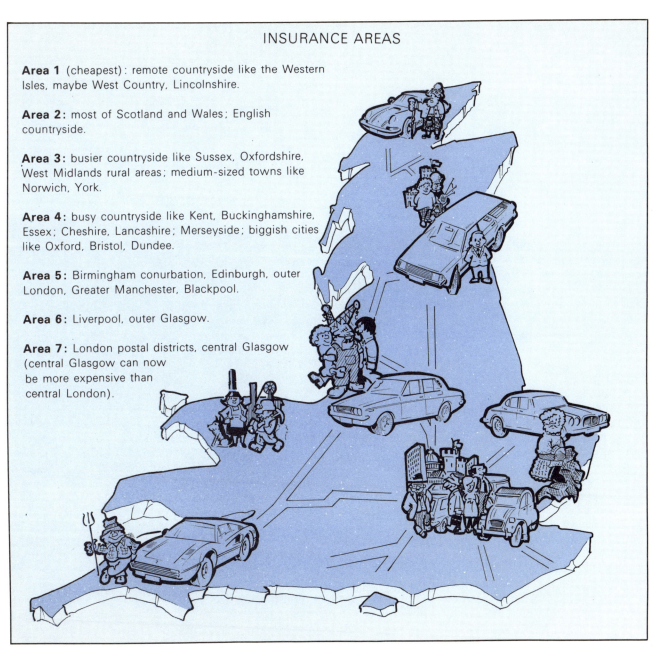

3. LOOKING AFTER IT

Modern cars virtually look after themselves. The checks that were virtually daily essentials even 20 years ago, on water levels and so forth, are now rare events. Routine services used to be a thousand-mile chore even more recently – now, some makers spin them out to an annual event. Yet, like a sensitive friend or relation, even the most up-to-date car will be much less likely to cause you some embarrassing scene if you do give it regular attention – something more than just an annual birthday treat.

Topping up
Cars vary in the rate they use oil. Generally, old cars use more than new ones. Cars driven fast or for long journeys use it more quickly. As it comes up to a routine oil change a car's more likely to get through oil slightly more quickly than just after one. Very slight differences in the way individual cars' engines are put together can make one car use oil five times as fast as another of exactly the same make and model.

A few cars, at least in their first year or so, hardly ever need topping up – Volkswagens very rarely use much oil, and recently large-engined Fords have tended to be good too. Mostly, others might typically get through a pint of oil every two or three thousand miles or so, at least while they're fairly new. But one in six or so needs a top-up every seven or eight hundred miles. Obviously, if you left this to a routine service the engine could easily get damaged through lack of oil.

So check your dipstick every so often – even with a VW a routine oil-level check would give early warning of some engine trouble.

Don't worry if the oil on the dipstick looks dirty – it will, if it's doing its job properly. But actual lumps of dirt are a sign that the oil needs changing – in modern oils, chemical additives help to keep dirt broken down into minute harmless particles, and if these start clotting together it may mean that the additives aren't up to their job any more. A creamy pale scum on the dipstick, or watery-looking bubbles in the oil, could be a sign of trouble; worth getting the garage to check for a blown cylinder head gasket.

It's not necessary to stick to the same brand of oil when you top up. And although some car handbooks name particular brands, you don't need to stick to these. There are some notes on brand choice under 'Oil changes', on page 117.

Cooling systems in recently-made cars shouldn't normally need topping up with water. If they do, there's probably a leak. Many are sealed, with an overflow reservoir, so that they should never need topping up at all – the handbook will tell you if yours is like this. And anyway, cooling systems are pressure-tight so that the water can heat up to a higher temperature before boiling, and they don't normally 'boil over' like old-fashioned ones.

Antifreeze is best left in all the year round. It contains chemical additives which stop corrosion – water on its own might corrode the cooling system. If you do have to top up the water much – say, more often than between services – you should try to keep the proportion of antifreeze constant. That's to say, add antifreeze to the topping-up water, at the concentration recommended in the car's handbook. If there's no particular recommendation, one part of antifreeze to three of water would do. Ideally, use the same brand.

If after a period a blue antifreeze has turned green, it may well mean that the water in your cooling system has become acid (and some red antifreezes have an indicator in them which turns yellow if this happens). That would be a good moment to flush the old out, and refill with new (see page 131 – which also discusses basic types of antifreeze for different cars).

Check the brake fluid reservoir from time to time. Again, it shouldn't normally need topping up between services – if it does, the brake pads may be wearing markedly, or there may even be a leak. So get your garage to check.

The battery may need topping up from time to time. The hotter it gets, the more likely this is – a battery just above a very hard-working engine in summer will need more frequent attention than one well insulated from engine heat. Some batteries are transparent, or have a transparent plastic top with floats inside to show whether the level's OK. Usually, you have to take off the top – jolly boring when there's a separate screw-top for each separate cell, but usually just one or two pull-off lids. The level of fluid inside should cover the metal battery plates, or a horizontal plate above them if there is one. If it doesn't, you have to top up with *distilled* water – which you can buy cheaply from chemists and motor accessory shops. Although garages usually provide it free, in a convenient spouted container, there's the horrid fear that one day it might turn out to be just tap water instead of distilled.

It's well worth adding a screenwash chemical to the windscreen washer reservoir when you top that up. You probably wouldn't use plain water to get ordinary dirt off your clothes – your wipers could do with a bit of help, dealing with the smeary film of grease, tyre rubber, engine fume deposits, tar, insect remains and so on that coats your windscreen. Plain washing-up liquid works perfectly well, but tends to foam a lot when you

Checking the oil dipstick, make sure the car's standing flat, and give the oil time to drain down into the sump

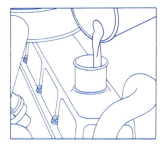

Though it's handiest to buy a small top-up tin whenever you need it, you may make big savings by keeping a large-size economy can at home, instead

Some cars may have brake and clutch fluid cylinders side by side: don't confuse them

Remember that each of the battery's six cells may need topping up separately

fill the bottle. Also, the branded screen cleaners have the advantage that they help to stop the washer water freezing in bad weather. In really cold weather you can stop freezing by using a double dose of cleaner, or adding some methylated spirits. If your car's handbook says that meths would be bad for the paint, use surgical spirit or iso-propyl alcohol instead.

It's worth checking your tyres weekly. Do it when the car's been standing still for a while, if you've got a tyre pressure gauge of your own – most are reasonably accurate . . . and in the past tests of the automatic garage pressure gauges have shown that at least a few of those may be really inaccurate. If you do check at a garage, after you've been driving, hold your hand against the tyres' sidewalls first. If they feel at all warm, rather than distinctly cool to the touch, the reading will be mislead-ing – with driving, tyres tend to heat up, which increases the pressure of the air inside above its normal level.

As a general rule, it's safer to have the tyres inflated to too high a pressure, than too low. If anything, this will tend to improve the car's handling and roadhold-ing, though reducing the ride comfort. Pressures too low may increase the risk of a burst tyre, because they'll let the tyres' sidewalls flex more than usual which could overheat them.

POINT TO REMEMBER

Don't check your tyres when they're warm to the touch (say, on a long run): the pressure will have risen.

When you check tyre pressures, it's a good idea just to look over the tyres themselves, for any cuts or bulges. And always do that if you scuff the kerb or hit a really bad stone or pothole. It's probably worth get-ting the wheel alignment checked if you really clout something badly.

Keeping your car clean
Frequent washing is good for cars. Although dirt on its own doesn't do much harm, salt from the roads does – it can speed up rust. Chemicals in polluted air, especi-ally in industrial areas, may damage paintwork. And bird droppings can make some sorts of paintwork shrivel.

Washing by hand is usually the most thorough, for getting the bodywork clean. Use lots of water, with ordinary household washing-up liquid – it seems to work just as well as the special car shampoo liquids. Start at the top, and soak everything well before you take a cloth or sponge to it. Don't swab too vigorously at really dirty bodywork – bits of sand or grit in it could scratch the paint. And rinse out the cloth or sponge very frequently. A rinse afterwards, either with a hose (if you're allowed) or swilling it down with a bucket of plain water, will get rid of any soap smears. You might feel like drying it off with a damp chamois leather, for a glossier finish.

Very few car-wash machines get bodywork as clean. Most have blindspots round the bumpers, and the simple ones tend to leave a lot of dirt on the wheels. In big cities there are a very few much bigger and more elaborate car-washes – obvious not just by their size but often by the long queues of cars waiting for them at weekends. One advantage of a powerful car-wash machine over handwashing is that underbody water jets may flush away mud-and-salt deposits from hidden nooks and crannies which you'd be unlikely to get at yourself.

Car washes do tend to gobble up aerials, if you leave them out. And they can damage wing mirrors, bend wiper arms, and knock number plates around. Machine washing can produce a web of tiny surface scratches all over the paintwork, too. Complain about this if it happens, or go to another car wash: it's probably the result of poor machine maintenance.

If you can avoid it, don't park under trees, particu-larly lime trees. In summer they leave thousands of tiny sticky droplets over the car, which attract grime – and which can be very difficult to get off if they're left for long.

On new cars, polishing won't bring up much more of a shine than simply buffing down with a clean soft cloth. But if the bodywork is scratched rust can be held at bay for a short while by polish or wax. For corrosion protection, you have to work the wax or polish well into places where rust is likely to start – that's to say, body seams and joints, rather than the main body panels. But it washes off much more readily than the adverts suggest. In July 1978 *Motoring Which?* reported that Simoniz GT Wax (solid or liquid), Shell Whipped Wax and Vauxhall Car Clean Cream lasted reasonably well.

POINT TO FORGET

Polishing new cars.

On older cars, paintwork can lose its gloss. Ordinary wax or polish isn't the best way of getting it back. Use instead a paint restorer such as T-Cut, which you rub in (hard) like a polish. Use a circular rubbing action – just a small patch at a time. If that doesn't seem to bring up a shine on a really grubby old car, try 'rubbing compound' – really hard work, but so potent that it can cut right through the colour (even down to the undercoat, if you're too heavy-fisted). Then follow with an ordinary wax or polish – either the longer-lasting ones mentioned above, or perhaps for extra corrosion resistance (but less lasting power) Autobrite Liquid or Super Turtle Solid Wax.

As has been said, waxes and polishes don't help much on newish cars – if all you want is high gloss, an ordinary soft cloth will do. But you can get some improvement if you match the make of polish carefully to your car's paintwork type. This was discussed in detail in the 1978 *Motoring Which?* report. To summarise, here are liquid polishes you might consider, just for high gloss (liquid's easier to use than solid):

For Alfasud, Citroën, Ford, Peugeot, Talbot, Toyota and most metallic finishes:

Simoniz GT

For Audi, BMW, Datsun, Honda, Lada, Lancia, Leyland (but not Rover), Mazda, Polski-Fiat, Renault, Saab, Skoda, Volvo:

Vauxhall Car Clean Cream

For Rolls-Royce, Rover, Vauxhall, and metallic Alfa Romeos or open Lancia Betas:

Motorcraft Liquid
Porzelack Brilliant.

Whatever polish you use, it'll do too for the car's brightwork – you don't need a special chrome cleaner for that.

If you get tar spots on the bodywork, you should be able to get them off with petrol or paint-brush cleaner, washing it off with water as soon as possible afterwards (try it on an inconspicuous area first). If you've got none handy, the special tar removers you can get from motor accessory shops work just as well.

Don't get wax or polish on the car's windscreen: it'll smears in rain. Even getting it on the side and back windows is a bad idea, as you might then wipe some on to the screen. You can get stubborn dirt off the screen or windows by rubbing them down with methylated or surgical spirit. You'll also find a big difference in the clarity of your view out if you clean *inside* the windows (again, not out – to avoid wet-weather smearing) with an ordinary household window-cleaning cream.

Much the best thing for cleaning inside the car is a vacuum cleaner. Unless you live at the top of a block of flats, getting an extension power lead for your household vacuum cleaner is better than buying a little battery-operated car one – but of course, use it only in absolutely dry weather. Some people might like one of the 'new car smell' products from a motor accessory shop as a finishing touch.

4. BASIC SERVICING

In repeated tests of how well individual garages do their job, *Motoring Which?* has found virtually no difference between using a garage which is a dealer for the make of car and using one which isn't; between garages approved by the AA or RAC and garages not approved; between garages that belong to the MAA (Motor Agents Association) and those that don't; between big garages and small ones. But on average people tend to be a little more satisfied with the service they get from garages that aren't franchised dealers for any make of car – maybe because these tend to be smaller, and so may give the impression of giving more personal attention. Moreover, these garages are more likely to give an accurate and firm estimate of costs in advance, though they tend not to do the actual work any better.

Generally, the more reliable people's cars are, the more satisfied they are with the service they get from their garages. It's obviously hardly surprising that if your car keeps going wrong, your garage finds it more difficult to keep you happy. But some franchised dealers have caused more dissatisfaction because of poor workmanship than you might have expected from the reliability records of the cars they deal with. These have tended to include dealers for Citroën, Fiat, Ford, French Talbot cars, and Vauxhall. That's to say, owners of these cars have been quite a bit more likely than average to find the dealers' workmanship unsatisfactory. This may not be the garages' fault: it may reflect difficulty in working on the cars concerned – specially likely with Citroëns, which tend to be tricky to

fix when they go wrong.

All this makes it very hard indeed to choose the best garage for your routine servicing. And the trouble is that it's far from being a question of choosing among a whole lot of good garages. In general, garage servicing standards have been dreadfully low. Over the years, of 127 garages tested carefully by *Motoring Which?* to check how well they've done a routine service or a tune-up, only two have done an entirely acceptable job. In these tests, many garages have replaced parts which were in perfectly good condition. Some have charged for parts they've never even fitted. Others have overcharged. Most have made adjustments wrongly or haven't made them at all. Safety checks have rarely been done properly. In 21 out of 127 cases, very little of the job's been done at all, or very serious mistakes have been made.

Your best hope – as mentioned on page 52 – is to know the work of a garage so well that you can trust it. Failing that, there are some pointers to success.

The garage should look clean, and have an efficient atmosphere. Get to know the service manager – or the owner if it's a small one. Without being unpleasantly pernickety, show that you care about how well the service is done. Make sure the garage uses the proper service schedule for your car. If the garage belongs to the MAA or its Scottish equivalent the SMTA, make sure it will follow the Code of Practice agreed between these trade associations and the Office of Fair Trading. In particular, you should be given an estimate of costs –

in writing, if you want. If – as is quite common – the service schedule lays down exactly what needs to be done, the garage should give you not just an estimate but a binding cost quotation. Even if you've just had an estimate, the garage should get in touch with you if, doing the work, it comes across anything which would put the price up: so leave a phone number. Say that you'll expect to see any parts which the garage has replaced.

Next, check on the bill. Some manufacturers lay down prices for the service and may quote 'menu prices' for common repair or overhaul jobs. Others say how many hours of labour should be involved. This probably won't be given in your handbook, but you should be able to find out from the maker's service department. The garage will tell you what its hourly labour rate is. Make sure the bill itemises the cost of any parts. You can easily tell from this if you've been overcharged – by comparing the cost given in the manufacturer's parts catalogue, which any parts distributor for the make will have (you can usually get a parts price quotation over the phone).

Finally, make at least a superficial check to see what's been done.

● engine oil should look clean, and be at the correct level

● grease nipples (on older cars – few recent ones have them) and parts needing greasing or oiling should have had muck wiped away, and there should be at least some trace of clean oil or grease there

● sparking plugs that you've been charged for should look new and shiny

● the mileage recorder will show whether there's been a road test

● wheel nuts, and the nuts and bolts on the engine's rocker box cover, should show signs of having been undone and done up again (easiest to check if you've marked them surreptitiously beforehand, maybe with tiny scratches or paint blobs)

fanbelt tension should have been set right (the handbook should show how to check this).

If you're unhappy, see 'Rows with your garage', on page 137. But the basic idea of special vigilance isn't to catch your garage out – it's much more to show the garage you're a customer it should treat much better than garages usually do.

Doing it yourself

About one in five people now do their own servicing, at least sometimes. One in ten do all their own. Basic servicing can be much simpler than you might imagine, though the rule-of-thumb must be never to do anything you're not confident about.

Some cars are rather tricky to work on – most notably, Citroëns. Audi, Volvo and VW tend to discourage private owners from doing their own work, though Volvos are actually easier cars than many to work on. Jaguars, smaller Peugeots, the Renault 14 and the Volkswagen Beetle tend to be more difficult than average; though the Fiat 128 is easy enough, cramped underbonnet space can be a problem.

Japanese cars generally tend to be easier than average to work on – especially the Datsun Bluebird and Toyota Corolla. Chryslers (though not the Alpine), the Lada and the Morris Marina are also good for do-it-yourself, with helpful handbooks; the Lada's got a good tool-

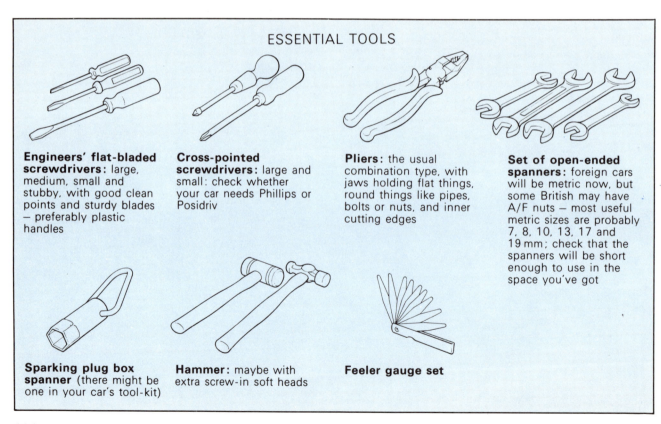

ESSENTIAL TOOLS

Engineers' flat-bladed screwdrivers: large, medium, small and stubby, with good clean points and sturdy blades – preferably plastic handles

Cross-pointed screwdrivers: large and small: check whether your car needs Phillips or Posidriv

Pliers: the usual combination type, with jaws holding flat things, round things like pipes, bolts or nuts, and inner cutting edges

Set of open-ended spanners: foreign cars will be metric now, but some British may have A/F nuts – most useful metric sizes are probably 7, 8, 10, 13, 17 and 19 mm; check that the spanners will be short enough to use in the space you've got

Sparking plug box spanner (there might be one in your car's tool-kit)

Hammer: maybe with extra screw-in soft heads

Feeler gauge set

kit, too. The Ford Fiesta and Escort are also good, but their handbooks are largely unhelpful. Independent publishers produce handbooks for individual makes and models which help out well on routine servicing. 'Handybooks' are specially good for beginners: clear, and based on the assumption that you don't know much to start with. If you're more ambitious, and reckon to have the expertise you'd need for tackling more complicated repairs, the independent publishers' workshop manuals are a good buy. They're often more helpful and almost always much cheaper than the ones produced by the car makers themselves. The 'Haynes' series are very clear indeed, and perhaps best if you're not very expert. 'Autobooks' and 'Intereurope' are also

good, though probably more rewarding for the more experienced: 'Intereurope' manuals are specially good on routine servicing.

For routine servicing, you'll need a basic tool-kit costing around £20. Below are the essentials (notes on each, and references to brand test reports, in *Motoring Which?*, April 1979):

Learning about servicing

You'd learn a lot, just tackling simple servicing jobs with the help of a good car handbook – those mentioned above would steer you through basic servicing, even if you had very little experience.

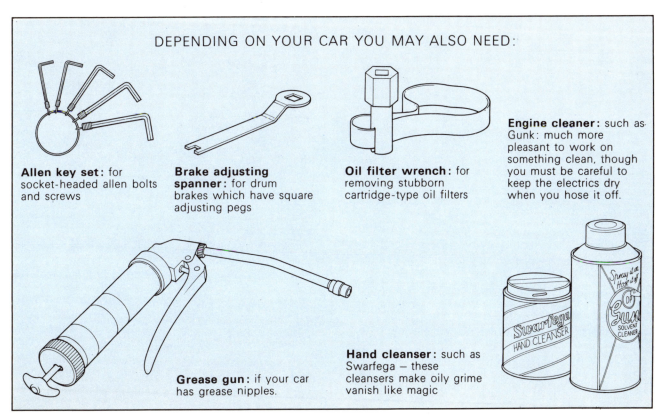

DEPENDING ON YOUR CAR YOU MAY ALSO NEED:

Allen key set: for socket-headed allen bolts and screws

Brake adjusting spanner: for drum brakes which have square adjusting pegs

Oil filter wrench: for removing stubborn cartridge-type oil filters

Engine cleaner: such as Gunk: much more pleasant to work on something clean, though you must be careful to keep the electrics dry when you hose it off.

Grease gun: if your car has grease nipples.

Hand cleanser: such as Swarfega – these cleansers make oily grime vanish like magic

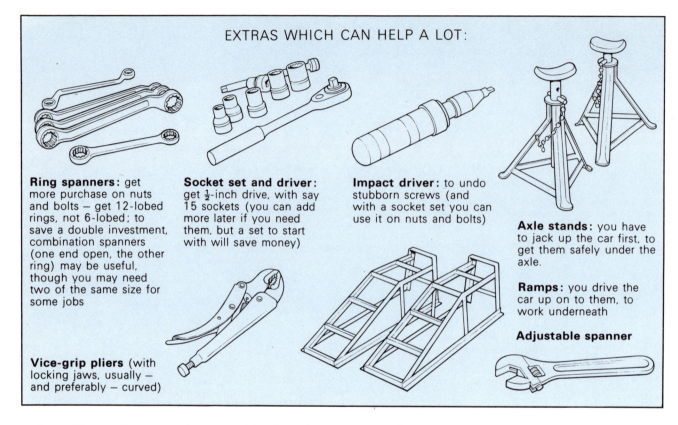

EXTRAS WHICH CAN HELP A LOT:

Ring spanners: get more purchase on nuts and bolts — get 12-lobed rings, not 6-lobed; to save a double investment, combination spanners (one end open, the other ring) may be useful, though you may need two of the same size for some jobs

Socket set and driver: get ½-inch drive, with say 15 sockets (you can add more later if you need them, but a set to start with will save money)

Impact driver: to undo stubborn screws (and with a socket set you can use it on nuts and bolts)

Axle stands: you have to jack up the car first, to get them safely under the axle.

Ramps: you drive the car up on to them, to work underneath

Adjustable spanner

Vice-grip pliers (with locking jaws, usually — and preferably — curved)

A good but rather expensive general book on how cars work, and the basics of servicing them, is the *AA Book of the Car*.

Car maintenance classes are an excellent way of picking up knowledge and confidence, even if you're a complete beginner. They're run all over the country by local education authorities – especially in big towns. As with other classes, you have to enrol in the autumn at the start of the 'evening class year'. Usually there are about a dozen two-hour lessons in each of three terms. The best are those which include quite a lot of practical work, on cars – rather than just classroom theory.

At the end of this chapter there's guidance on three jobs you might consider starting with – oil and filter changing, fanbelt replacement, and minor bodywork restoration.

Safety with tools

Careless do-it-yourself can produce anything from lots of painfully grazed knuckles to serious casualty-department injuries. There are some simple rules which you must follow.

Never do a job that you're not confident about; you must always know exactly what you're doing.

Always use the right tool for the job. A bodge-up or makeshift substitute could slip disastrously. If the tool's worn, replace it. Make sure it's not slippery with grease or oil – and that your hands, using it, are clean and dry.

Don't support something from behind with your

hand when you use a screwdriver on it: you'll gash yourself when it slips.

Pull spanners, don't push them – or you'll bash your hand when the spanner slips.

Keep a bright light on what you're doing.

Take off rings, bracelets, watch-straps: they catch on things, and a metal watch-strap shorting a battery terminal, say, would burn you. Always disconnect the battery earth lead (the one to the car's bodywork), anyway.

No smoking – and no distractions like the puppy or your children.

Don't overtighten nuts and bolts – even worse than leaving them loose.

Easy guide to oil changing

A basic servicing job is changing your engine oil. Doing this and changing the filter will take you under an hour, and will save you up to £5 on garage labour charges, and another £1 or £2 on the cost of the oil itself.

First, buy the oil, a spare sealing ring for the sump plug, and either a new filter cartridge with sealing ring (if your car uses the throw-away type) or filter element (if it has the replaceable type), again with sealing ring.

Get the oil grade recommended in your car's handbook. It'll most likely be a multigrade, say 10W-40 or 20W-50.

Oils are graded by their thickness at different temperatures, on the SAE viscosity scale (devised by the American Society of Automotive Engineers). The higher the number of its grade, the thicker (more viscous) the oil. Ideally, you want an oil which isn't too thick when its cold (that would make winter starting difficult, and would spoil fuel economy), but which stays at least thick enough to keep a lubricating film between moving engine parts when it gets hot. The 'W' number rates the oil's cold performance, and the second number its performance when hot.

In a 'straight' oil, a non-multigrade, one rated 10W would flow much more easily than one rated 40 when cold: at 0°F, it would take less than one-tenth of the time to trickle down a tube, say. But at 210°F, the 40 oil would still be at least twice as thick as the 10W one.

Multigrades add viscosity improvers to a relatively thin straight oil, which don't make it much thicker at low temperatures, but keep it reasonably thick at high ones. So a multigrade 10W/40 oil combines the cold-weather thinness advantage of the 10W oil with the hot-running thickness advantage of the 40 oil. A minor problem is that the polymerised multigrade oil loses thickness as it gets older: after 6,000 miles a 10W/40 tends to thin to nearer 10W/30, for example. But this tendency doesn't counteract the basic tremendous advantage of the multigrade, combining economy and appropriate viscosity in cold weather with good lubrication when it's hot.

In practice, the advantage of a 10W multigrade over a 20W, in cold-weather starting, is very great. At the other end of the scale, the higher the 'summer' rating the less oil you'll use. Using a 10W/40 oil instead of a 10W/30, for example, you might save a few pounds a year in an oil-thirsty car – perhaps over £10 a year in a really thirsty car, if you used a 20W/50 instead of a 10W/30 and were prepared to sacrifice the cold-starting advantages of the 10W rating. The thicker oils result in slightly higher petrol consumption, but generally this would make very little difference even to someone who used their car only for short trips in which it never really got warmed up. The oil doesn't warm up properly until long after the engine's warm.

So on balance the 10W/40 rating seems best for most people – with heavy oil-drinkers going for a 20W/50 unless they face starting problems in very cold weather.

Even when the car's handbook recommends a particular brand, car makers have said that they'd never normally consider invalidating a guarantee on a new car because it used a different oil (so long as it was of equivalent specification). Tests over 12 years ago by *Motoring Which?* showed that virtually all multigrades including cut-price brands gave excellent protection against engine wear, even after serious abuse. So look for the cheapest.

So you've got your oil, and the other supplies you need. You'll need a spanner to fit the oil sump plug, and maybe another for the oil filter. A small screwdriver will get its rubber sealing ring out. Have a drain tin

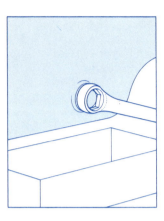

DRAINING THE OIL
Remember to have the drain tin in place before you unscrew the sump drain plug

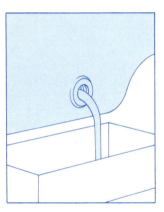

The oil will run out much more quickly if you've warmed it first, by running the engine

Get the sump plug really clean before you screw it back in – and check that the sealing ring's flawless

handy (anything with low sides, and big enough to hold all the oil from the sump, will do). And arm yourself in advance with a way of getting rid of the old oil. Many garages will accept used engine oil – one that's sold you the new oil may be most willing. Failing that, your local authority should have disposal arrangements. But don't just pour it down a drain.

When you've checked where everything is, and what to do, in the car's handbook, you're ready to start.

First, warm up the engine, so that the oil will run out more easily. Switch it off and disconnect the battery. Undo the oil filler cap on top of the engine. Clean round the sump plug with a rag. Put the drain tin ready underneath it, and start cautiously loosening it (once it's open the dirty oil will pour out, and you want it to go in the tin, not over you. As soon as the oil starts dribbling out, twist the plug out as quickly as possible with your fingers, pushing up on it to stop the dribbles as you do. Then leave the oil draining into the tin.

Clean the sump plug (paraffin's ideal for this), and check that its sealing ring isn't gashed. If it is, replace it with the spare you've bought. When all the oil's drained out, screw the plug back in by hand, making sure it's going in smoothly – it should screw in very easily. When it's home, tighten it with the spanner, but not too much.

Now for the oil filter. Try and get the drain tin under it, and put a lot of newspaper on the ground round about. What you do next depends on whether it's a throwaway cartridge, or a replaceable element inside a permanent metal container (the 'filter bowl').

If it's a throwaway cartridge:

Unscrew the filter. It should come, just turning by hand. If it won't you can get a stronger grip on it by pulling a leather belt or strap tight round it, or twisting a fanbelt round it. If a garage has previously tightened it so much that you still can't shift it, you can get a special oil-filter-removing tool to grip it really strongly – it shouldn't cost much more than a pound or so.

As it comes loose, put it down carefully, as it'll still have oil in it. Check that the old sealing ring came away with it, and if it didn't pull it away from the sealing face on the engine. Clean that sealing face with a non-fluffy rag, taking care not to get dirt into any of the oil holes.

Smear some clean oil on the sealing ring of the new filter cartridge, then screw the cartridge on. Just tighten it by hand. Once you can feel that the sealing ring is up against the sealing face, don't turn it more than half or three-quarters of a turn, and certainly don't pull it fiercely tight (if you do, it won't just be hard to get off but will probably leak).

If it's a replaceable element:

Loosen the fixing bolt – it usually comes out at the bottom, sometimes at the top of the filter bowl instead. Undo the bolt by hand, so that once it's free you can keep it held inside the filter bowl (this is important). If the bowl won't come off when the bolt's free, give the bowl a sharp tap with a soft-faced hammer or mallet.

Holding the filter bowl over the drain tin, and keeping the fixing bolt and element held in place, tip out the oil. Then pull out the old filter element. Do this carefully, so that you can check the order of the washers and spring inside, as you take them off – again, important. If they don't come off very easily, don't pull at them. On some cars (obvious from the way they're fitted) they aren't supposed to come off.

Wash out the filter bowl, using paraffin.

Put back its bolt, washers and spring in the right order, then put the new filter element in.

On the engine sealing face where the filter bowl fits, you'll find a sealing ring. Get this out. If it's recalcitrant, don't worry about breaking it. A small screwdriver or something pointed should do the trick. Then clean the recess.

Fit the new sealing ring in its place. A smear of grease will help to hold it in its place. If the filter element came with more than one ring, use the one which matches the old ring. Be gentle – this one you *mustn't* break. So anything you use to push it in mustn't be sharp or pointed.

Push the filter bowl, with its new element in place, into the sealing ring. You may have to push hard to

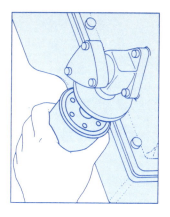

REPLACING A FILTER
Taking off the filter – looks clean enough here, but in real life you'll need a drain tin under it

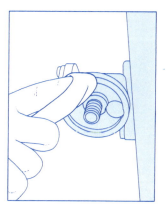

The sealing face on the engine, where the filter fits, needs careful cleaning: make sure the rag's not fluffy

Use your finger to smear some clean oil on the sealing ring of the new cartridge

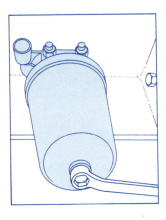

REPLACING A FILTER

Replaceable oil filter holders have a fixing bolt — usually at the bottom like this, sometimes at the top

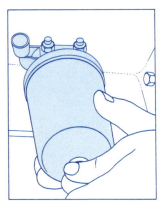

Hold the bolt in place as you remove the filter bowl

Take out the filter element *carefully,* so that you can keep tabs on exactly how the innards fit together

pictures continued opposite

get it into its groove. Hold it in firmly while you start doing up the bolt, by hand. Tighten the bolt with a **spanner, making sure** that the bowl is still in the groove. Finally, check carefully that the filter bowl is now fitted neatly and snugly into the groove with the sealing ring.

Now, the new oil.

Pour in the new oil through the filler hole, and replace the filler cap. Check the oil level. If it's too low, make sure there's no leak, and top up with more oil. Reconnect the battery, and start the engine. If the oil pressure warning light stays on for more than ten seconds or so, switch off. Did you remember to put back the oil filler cap? Are there any leaks, from sump plug or oil filter? If there are, it's much more likely that they're caused by a broken or damaged sealing ring than by the plug or filter being too loose. You'll have to go back to the stage where you're taking out the offending part to start with, to check (but if you've done things carefully there shouldn't be any risk of having to do this).

If the oil pressure warning light goes off as it should, leave the engine idling for a while, and have a look for leaks as it runs (take care to keep well clear of any moving parts, and remember that though you probably won't be able to see the cooling fan it'll be spinning fast enough to chop you up). Once it's warm, switch off, and let the car stand for a few minutes. Then, check the oil level on the dipstick, with the car standing level, and add oil if the level's low.

For the next few days, keep an eye open for leaks.

Get rid of the old oil, as suggested above. Congratulations! In less than an hour, you've probably saved yourself a good £5. And you may have saved trouble that a garage would have caused you. Out of 95 oil and filter changes tested by *Motoring Which?* 2 garages didn't even change the oil at all, 2 didn't change the filter, 4 damaged, dirtied or lost crucial parts, 7 overfilled the oil (which could harm the engine). And many left the car dirty.

Fanbelt replacement

The fanbelt is a key component of your car. It usually

drives the water pump and the car's generator. So if it breaks the battery stops charging and the engine stops being cooled: either or both will bring you to a stop. So always keep a spare in your car (spares, if the car uses more than one belt). But more important, regular checks (say, once a month) should save breakdown. Any splits or frayed bits do call for replacement. And the tension must be right. If the belt's too tight the water pump or generator might be damaged. If it's too loose, the cooling system may not be working properly, and the battery may get run down – moreover, the belt, slipping on its pulleys, is more likely to get frayed and break.

The handbook for your car will show how much tension there should be. There should usually be about half an inch of free play when you press the belt firmly at the centre of its longest run between pulleys.

If replacement's needed, you need the new fanbelt, two spanners of the right size for the nuts and bolts holding the generator in place, and a screwdriver. To change the tension, you need the same equipment, but not of course the new belt.

NB: the following notes don't apply to the few cars like the VW Beetle where the fanbelt is tightened by altering the number of washers in a pull-apart pulley on the generator.

First, disconnect the battery earth lead.

Check that the spanners are a really secure fit on the nuts and bolts holding the generator in place. There should be two bolts, and may be three. You need to loosen those holding the generator to the slotted arm, and the slotted arm to the engine. Loosen them one by one – this may need a really strong pull on the spanners.

If you're fitting a new belt, tilt the generator towards the engine. You may have to loosen the bolts more before you can move it. When the fanbelt is really slack, slip it over the pulleys and the fan so that you can get it off. On some cars there may be a cover over the fanbelt: on these, you've got to work the belt through the

The new filter element should pop into the bowl in exactly the way that the old one fitted

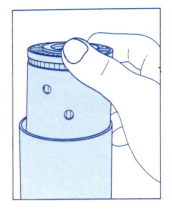

Though you can use a screwdriver to get out the *old* sealing ring, use something blunt to push the new one into place – it mustn't break

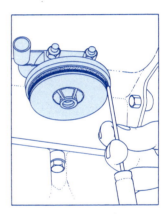

Be sure to hold the filter bowl assembly very firmly in place while you're screwing it up

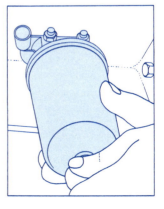

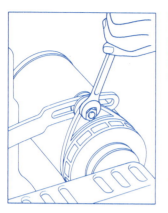

FANBELT TENSION
Make sure the spanner fits perfectly before you loosen the generator mounting bolts — they may be really tight

It's far better to pull the generator out with your bare hands, to get the right tension on the belt — if you really *have* to use a lever, make sure it's wood, not metal

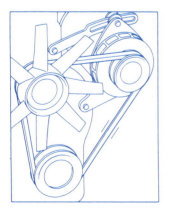

The car's handbook should show how much slack to leave in the longest part of the belt, when you give it a firm push

gap in this cover. Then reverse the process, to get the new fanbelt over the pulleys. Doing this, tug the fanbelt if necessary, but don't be tempted to force it into place by tugging at the fan itself.

Now pull the generator away from the engine, until the fanbelt has the right amount of free play. If you really can't get enough tension on the belt, just using your bare hands, you'll have to use a lever. If you have to do this — and you should avoid it if possible — use wood, not metal. And work it against the mounting plate at the end of the generator, not the middle of the thing.

Holding the generator firm so that the belt stays tight, do up the bolt holding the generator on to the slotted arm. Then, still keeping the generator firmly held, do up the other bolts. Although they should be firmly tightened, don't try any Tarzan stuff.

Reconnect the battery.

Recheck the tension of the fanbelt after a day or two, and retighten it if necessary.

This time, you won't have saved as much money as with an oil change. But you will have staved off the risk of a breakdown. And in 34 of the 95 tested garage services garages missed a slack fanbelt, or adjusted it wrongly: one even stripped the thread of a mounting bolt.

Paint faults and rust
Although dealing with these shouldn't really be a matter of normal servicing, it is in practice — partly because even new cars are much more rust-prone than they should be, partly because even careful drivers seem to attract scrapes and scratches which demand early attention if they're not going to turn into bad rust.

Simple scratches that don't go down to the bare metal, or marks on your bodywork from — say — the paint on another car or a lamppost, can be rubbed off with a paint restorer like T-Cut (see page 111). If you don't have that, try ordinary household metal polish. Rub firmly, using a soft cloth and a good dollop of cleaner — but stop if there's any suggestion of colour change in the bodywork. Then buff up the patch with another soft cloth, or perhaps with polish or wax.

If the scratch goes down to the metal, or the body-work's so marked that you're going to have to paint anyway, keep it smeared with grease (colourless Vaseline is ideal) until you can do it – and with aerosol spray cans particularly, that needs really dry warm weather, or a garage you can heat up to at least living-room temperature.

If the scratch is very small, a little phial of touch-in paint the right shade for your car, with its own built-in applicator, will do. Otherwise, you'll need fine rubbing-down paper – 'wet and dry' paper of at least 600 grade or finer (1000 grade is best); and spray tins of undercoat and topcoat. If the damage goes down to bare metal, you'll also need metal primer.

For the small scratch or mark, shake up the paint applicator for at least two minutes, very vigorously. Touch in the scratch after cleaning and drying it really thoroughly – you'll have needed plenty of detergent to get rid of the grease that even fingermarks leave, let alone Vaseline. Use the applicator deftly and smoothly. As it dries really fast, don't try to work it in: you'll only spoil the surface. Letting it dry for half an hour or so (longer, if the instructions say), lightly touch in a second coat. This time, give it at least 24 hours to dry really hard. Then rub it down hard with paint restorer, like T-Cut, until it's smoothed well into the surrounding bodywork.

For the larger damage, you'll get much better results by working in good warm conditions – say, at least 67°F or 20°C. Again, thoroughly clean the area with detergent. Then rub it down with the wet and dry paper. Dip this often into soapy water, and keep it quite flat against the body surface – a sanding block behind it will help doing this, except on sharpish bits like door edges. What you want is a perfectly smooth matt finish, looking entirely flat, with no bumps or dips. It doesn't matter if you haven't got down to bare metal – in fact if you can avoid that it's better not to, as it saves you having to use a primer coat. *Don't* feel for smoothness with your fingers – even a trace of grease will spoil the eventual finish.

Dry the patch thoroughly, and touch in any primer needed for bare metal. Let that dry for say half an hour,

RETOUCHING PAINTWORK
Touch-up paint phials usually have their own integral brush

To prepare bigger patches for repainting, rub down with fine wet and dry paper, using lots of soapy water – on smooth body areas, a firm sanding block should help you get an even finish

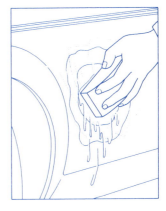

Aerosol sprays generally work best when really warm, and *must* be very well shaken first

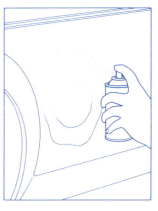

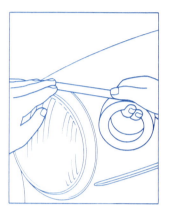

To mask a very small area, tape on its own will do: otherwise, use the tape to fasten paper or polythene sheet in place

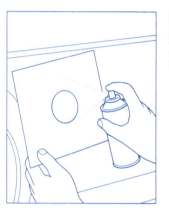

A cut-out card held between the spray and the bodywork helps to get a smooth edge, merging into the old paintwork

A brisk rub with "haze remover" or "paint restorer" is best, before you polish the finished paint job

then put on a second coat. Rub down gently until you've got a good smooth matt surface. Then make sure everything's really clean and dry.

You want to make sure that no paint goes where it shouldn't. As a precaution, you can mask off any nearby glass, brightwork or rubber, using masking tape and paper or polythene. You want to confine paint to the area you're working on, too, so that you don't get blobs of 'overspray' on the rest of the bodywork. Don't use tape for that, though: it would leave an obvious hard edge round your newly-painted patch. Instead, cut out a hole in stiff card, the shape of the patch that you'll be covering but a tiny bit smaller, so that you can hold it between the spray can and the body surface to get a smoothly graduated edge round the new patch.

Meanwhile, the spray cans should have been warming up in a basin of hot water – a half-hour hot bath for them will make them do their work much more enthusiastically. When everything's ready, you can start – but *not* on the bodywork! Practise with your cut-out mask on some scrap surface to start with – say, an old biscuit tin. Again, you'll need to shake the can first for a good couple of minutes, as hard as you can. Start at the top, going smoothly from side to side, and work down to the bottom. Once you're sure you can get a smooth even result, you're ready to start in earnest.

After the first coat of undercoat, let it dry according to the instructions – probably for half an hour or so. Then spray on a second coat of undercoat. If the results don't look perfectly solid, use a third coat after that. Then leave it for at least 24 hours, until it's really hard, and rub it down as described above, really thoroughly. Once the area's perfectly smooth and flat – and quite dry again, of course – you can put on the top coat. It, too, should have been in its warm bath, and needs a really tough shake-up. Spray it on in just the same way, using the same cut-out mask. Again, you'll need two coats. After letting that last coat dry for 24 hours – or a week if you've now reached the end of your weekend – rub it down hard with the paint restorer, and finish the job off with a normal wax or polish (see page 111).

Metallic finishes can be much beastlier to touch up. You can get single-coat aerosols for touching up. Even these need more care than plain paint. Getting the right lustre and depth of colour depends on the angle and distance you spray from. But some metallic processes need instead a lower silvery coat glistening through a thin top colour coat. Although the basic painting process is the same, a perfect match depends on the balance between the two layers. The thicker the top layer, the darker the colour. With the bottom layer, spray just as described above. But for the top layer, spray from farther off – up to a couple of feet. This gets a lighter, more brilliant finish. After the first coat of top layer is dry, look critically at how well it matches the rest of the paintwork. If it's *too* lustrous, spray the next coat from closer in: that should give a rather duller result. But if it's simply that the colour itself isn't rich enough, just put on another coat from the same distance – that should deepen the colour without making it too dull. Finish off as before.

If the damaged paintwork has rust under it, you've a choice between using rust remover, and using rust 'converters', 'stabilisers' or 'inhibitors'. All are powerful chemicals, so be extra careful about storing and using them.

The strongly acid rust removers have to be worked into the rust, after you've thoroughly cleaned the area and got rid of any loose rust or paint flakes. Once you've got clear, bright metal, you can go through the full painting process, with primer and top paint coats as above. Check the body panel *underneath*, too. If there's rust on that side it'll eat through, however clean you've got the top. Treat that side in just the same way – if anything, it needs even more protection than the top side.

Rust converters leave the rust there, but bond it into an inert metal which should not go on corroding. You then paint over this, as if it were steel.

Most, properly used with really careful attention to their instructions, and thorough painting afterwards, go a long way towards keeping rust at bay.

One thing should have been obvious to you from all this. Attention to bodywork – whether rust's involved or not – is really time-consuming. Moreover, it's the sort of job where extra care and attention really scores. So, although you do need to be a perfectionist over it, it's something where do-it-yourself can save enormously, avoiding high garage labour charges and ensuring high quality results. Above all, thorough bodywork care can add literally hundreds of pounds to your car's resale value.

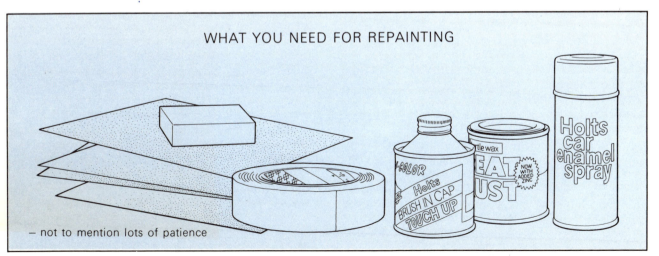

WHAT YOU NEED FOR REPAINTING

– not to mention lots of patience

5. SAVING ON PETROL

Recent petrol price increases have in fact more or less put petrol prices back where they belong – in the few previous years they'd been increasing more slowly than other motoring costs. But that certainly doesn't take the sting out of buying petrol. And it seems probable that in the long run petrol prices will rise faster than prices in general – say, by an extra 15 or 16% over five years.

So fuel economy is increasingly important.

As was explained on page 37, quite small differences in fuel economy may make a big difference to the running costs of a relatively thirsty car. But if a car's got good mpg to start with – say, better than 30 mpg – the change in fuel economy has to be more substantial to make a worthwhile saving.

The obvious place to start is with gadgets advertised to cut petrol consumption.

Motoring Which? tested some of these in January 1978. They didn't seem to work. Although one might in one careful test appear to give slightly better mpg, in another test under identical conditions that gadget might give slightly worse. None gave a consistent or significant improvement.

The *Motoring Which?* test on electronic ignition systems, in July 1979, showed that they can keep ignition up to scratch for longer than the traditional system. Although poor ignition tuning causes higher fuel consumption, if your car is serviced well (not something you can always rely on a garage for), the small savings which you might get are unlikely to compensate for the cost of installing electronic ignition.

Thermostatically-controlled cooling fans save power, by ensuring that the fan works only when the engine needs its help to keep cool (usually, for only quite a small part of the time). They also let the engine warm up a bit more quickly, perhaps letting you dispense with the choke sooner. But although in theory this saving could be worth up to around £10 a year, in practice you might not save as much.

Tuning

As you can't use the magic wand of a petrol-saving gadget to make your car more economical, it's important to keep its engine well in tune. In a typical car – almost certainly poorly tuned – this could save easily £30 a year on petrol bills.

The big snag is that if you take your car to a garage for a tune-up, it will probably do the job badly. In tune-up tests on 32 garages (*Motoring Which?*, January 1977), most failed to check valve clearances, often no attempt was made to put right incorrect carburettor adjustments or ignition timing, and even when adjustments were made they were rarely put exactly right, and sometime made things actually worse.

Those tests included four mobile tuners. Three of the four did at least a fair job (and one was best of all 32 places tried). At least with a mobile tuner which comes to your own home you can see that *something's* being done. And some fraternisation (at least tea and biscuits) may make the mobile tuners more sympathetic to your car. They're usually listed in telephone directories Yellow Pages under Engine Tuning and Reconditioning.

Tuning yourself

More and more cars are being designed with carburettors that don't need to be adjusted – in fact, can't easily be. Even with those, you can however make sure that the ignition system is working perfectly. And on other cars you may well be able to keep the carburation set right, too.

The spark which ignites the fuel in the engine is produced by the ignition coil, and its timing is controlled by the contact-breaker points in the distributor. The 'dwell angle' defines for how much of the engine's rotation the contact-breaker points stay closed.

You can get quite a good approximation to the right 'dwell angle' by making sure that the gap between the contact-breaker points at its widest moment is exactly as specified by the car's handbook. The handbook should show how to do this. It usually means removing the sparking plugs so that you can turn the engine freely, by nudging the car gently along in top gear, or jacking it up and turning a driven wheel by hand. Then, when the points are at their widest, check the gap with the specified size of feeler gauge. It should be a tight sliding fit. The gap's adjusted by loosening one or two screws so that you can move the plate on which the points are mounted. As you tighten the screws, recheck the gap: it often changes.

To improve on that, you need an electronic 'dwell meter'. In July 1977 *Motoring Which?* reported that these made it easier, and maybe gave less scope for mistakes. Out of the small selection tested, the best was the expensive RAC Maxitune. It, like others, had an extra scale which you could use to see how good a contact the points made. If they don't meet cleanly (or if they look dirty or pitted) it's best to replace them. Or you can try rubbing some contact cleaner on to them, and work a piece of white card between them till the card comes out clean.

Ignition timing is set either when the engine's not running ('static setting') or when it is running ('dynamic timing'). The handbook will give the correct

CHECKING CONTACT BREAKER

Inside the distributor, you usually find a rotor arm, a stubby spinning arm with a brass contact on its end – you can simply pull this off, and, exposing this underneath . . .

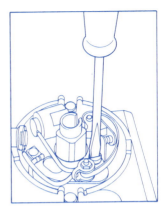

You can loosen the screw or screws which hold the works in place, so as to adjust the gap between the contact-breaker points, checking the exact width of the gap with a feeler gauge

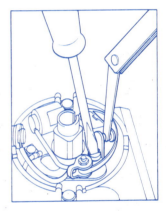

settings – for example, 10° BTDC. That means 'ten degrees before top dead centre': when the rotation of the engine is ten degrees before the point at which the Number 1 piston reaches the top of its stroke. That would be the moment when the contact-breaker points should open, to create the spark. The handbook will give settings for either static or dynamic timing – maybe both.

To set static ignition timing on a car with conventional ignition, connect a light bulb (car sidelight bulb, say) so that one of its terminals is wired to the circuit on one side of the contact-breaker points, the other terminal on the other side. With the ignition key switched on (but not pressing the starter), again turn the engine slowly, until the timing marks engraved on the flywheel or crankshaft pulley (see the car's handbook) coincide. The bulb should light up at this point. If it doesn't (or if it lit too soon), the timing can be adjusted quite simply – perhaps by turning a small wheel under the distributor.

The dynamic setting is checked with a 'timing light'. The best take power from the car's battery (they have leads which clip to its terminals), and also connect to one of the sparking plugs so that they give a quick, bright flash each time that plug sparks. When the engine's running, these flashes – one for each full engine cycle – 'freeze' moving engine parts. So you point the light at the timing marks to 'freeze' them at the exact moment the spark occurs. You can then adjust the timing so that the marks coincide, if they don't. The 1977 tests found these worked well, and recommended the RAC 523.

You need a rev counter, to use one of these timing lights, as dynamic ignition settings are given for particular engine speeds. Even if your car has a rev counter itself, you probably won't be able to use it to set the engine speed as accurately as you need. For accurate results, you'd probably need a separate rev counter, preferably with a low speed range. Dwell meters such as the RAC Maxitune have rev counter scales, so if you'd decided to go in for tuning in a big way and were getting a dwell meter too, you could use that with the timing light for checking ignition timing.

With an adjustable carburettor, the rev counter also lets you set the engine idling speed to the handbook specification. Again, a simple adjustment: usually a screw which you turn while the engine's running – you should do this when the engine's properly warm.

The most important carburation fault, from the economy point of view, is a faulty mixture of air and petrol: what the engine burns is mainly air – say, more than 15 parts of air to one of petrol when the car's cruising. The car's handbook may suggest simple checks for the carburettor if it's an adjustable one. But a neat and fairly cheap gadget called the Colourtune helps quite a lot. Basically a sort of transparent sparking plug, it

lets you look into the combustion chamber while the engine's running. The instructions describe how you can adjust the carburettor to get correct mixture, by watching the colour of the burning petrol/air mixture.

With twin carburettors, you have to get the flow of air equalised between them. There's again a simple and fairly cheap gadget which helps a lot with this – the Carbalancer. Holding its mouth against the carburettor air inlet, you can read the suction of the air off a little scale; doing this with each carburettor in turn helps you to balance the pair.

Buying these gadgets would set you back well over £50, even if you didn't need the Carbalancer. That's more than you'd save on petrol in a year. But in the longer run they could save you a great deal of money – as well as keeping your car running more smoothly than you'd be likely to get at many garages.

Further tuning that you *don't* need gadgets for include setting the valve clearances (quite simple at least on engines which don't have overhead camshafts – using feeler gauges, following handbook instructions); checking that the carburettor air cleaner is clean enough to do its job (very simple); and adjusting the sparking plug gaps (again very simple – but if you have to alter the gap, don't press against the central electrode as you could crack its insulator). If the sparking plugs are dirty you may be able to get them clean with a wire brush, but it's usually best to replace them if they've been in for long.

Driving for economy
Besides keeping the car's engine in tune, you should keep the tyres at the correct pressure, and make sure that the linkage of the accelerator pedal to the carburettor works smoothly and easily.

If you do a lot of long runs, you can gain significantly by cutting your top speed. This is especially true with small-engined low-powered cars. On a two-hundred-mile motorway trip in a Mini, say, you could save over £1.50 in petrol costs by cutting your speed from 70 mph to 60 mph. On a more powerful car (one which would normally use more fuel than the Mini, but would take more easily to high-speed cruising), you'd still save by making that top-speed cut, but you'd save less.

The next important thing is to try to keep your speed as steady as possible (except letting the car speed up to go downhill, so that the build-up of speed gets you up the next hill more smoothly). With this trick, the more powerful the car the more you'll save. It means thinking ahead a lot. Try to moderate your speed in advance so that you don't need to use the brakes. Each time you use the brakes is petrol wasted: the petrol you used to keep up speed just before you braked, instead of slowing naturally to avoid using the brakes. When you accelerate, don't push your foot right down, but nurse the accelerator so that the engine's never burning more fuel than it really needs for that speed. When you're going up hills, don't stick in a high gear until the labouring engine's forced you to hold the accelerator right down: change down to whatever gear lets you keep the lightest pressure on the accelerator. But otherwise – when you're not having to go up a hill or increase speed – the more you can keep in top gear the better.

A typical overall average speed for cars might be around 40 mph. Equally typically, a car's average fuel consumption might be 30 mpg. If by careful driving the driver of that car could convert his 40 mph average (made up of stops, starts, braking, accelerating and so forth) into a truly *constant* 40 mph, he'd be likely to improve that car's fuel consumption to around 50 mpg. Over a year's driving, that could save £160-worth of petrol. Obviously, it's an impossible ideal. But, for any given journey, it gives you an idea of the saving that's possible by using the light-footed approach to steady-speed driving.

POINTS TO REMEMBER
Keep your car in tune. Cut your top speed. Drive steadily. Don't carry more than you need – even an empty roofrack may waste fuel.

Town driving is murder to fuel economy. Aside from the ideal of avoiding it altogether – using public trans-port in towns, or maybe even a bicycle or moped – you can still save. Try to plan to avoid multiple stops and starts. Never accelerate furiously away from a stand-still. In traffic jams, don't rev your engine, and try to balance your speed with the way the queue seems to be moving, so that rather than starting up and slowing down you can crawl at an even gentle speed.

If you have to drive to work, say, see if you can get someone to share your petrol money with you. This is now allowed. But take money only as a share of your costs: any profit element could invalidate your insurance.

If there's something heavy in your car that you carry around almost out of habit – turf it out. The less weight you carry, the better economy you'll get (though the saving'll be very small – unless it was an elephantine mother-in-law, say, and even then there are greater savings in life than financial ones). The same goes for a roofrack, only more so. Keep it on your car only if you're actually using it, because aerodynamic drag from even an empty rack can drastically increase your fuel bill at speed.

Petrol brands
You won't get better results, choosing any one brand of petrol instead of another. In general cut-price brands, or brands coming from only a few petrol stations in restricted areas of the country, work just as well as the household names.

So the important thing is to choose the cheapest brand you can find, regardless of what it's called.

You should also make sure that you're using the lowest grade of petrol which your car will run on without 'knocking', or 'pinking', which you get when the grade *is* too low. You can hear it best if you are going up a slope in a high gear so that the engine is having to labour a bit – so that you're having to push the accelerator down without getting more speed.

When you're on a motorway run, you can almost always get worthwhile savings by turning off the motorway to fill up, instead of using the service areas. You can often find a garage with lower petrol prices, within just a mile of your turn off – maybe much closer.

129

6. REPAIRS

Careful routine attention – see Looking After It – will avoid most car trouble. But even the best-behaved car eventually breaks its routine (and yours). If it doesn't actually break down, it's going to need repair. What can you do, to minimise the chance of being stranded by the roadside? How can you get repairs done best? What do you do, if things are really bad?

Prevention
Regular checks on the most 'wear-outable' parts are essential. Besides the fanbelt (see page 120), check hoses and their clips carefully for signs of wear, or the slightest leak. Watch carefully for oil leaks. Every few months, you might check the level of oil in the gearbox and back axle (unless your handbook shows that your car doesn't have oil to top up there), as well as your more frequent checks on all other levels. You can treat the inspection procedure suggested on page 62), for secondhand cars as an early-warning system on your own car – worth doing the mechanical checks every six months or so. And pay special attention to odd noises, as described in that procedure – whenever they crop up, they need investigation.

Keep a lookout for one or two other signs of trouble ahead.

Louder-than-usual exhaust noise will almost certainly get worse: often, suddenly much worse. So have it dealt with early on.

A light rather clattery noise from the engine usually means that the valve clearances need adjusting. If it's particularly noticeable as a rattle when the engine's running slowly, the timing chain may need adjustment or even replacement. But in any event, this needs investigation by a garage.

Squeaks from under the bonnet, when the engine's running, need investigation. If it's coming from the water pump (usually by the cooling fan), it's usually nothing to worry about. Motor accessory shops sell anti-squeak which you can add to the cooling water. But if it comes from the distributor or the generator, the bearings probably need lubrication (simple enough on the distributor, but probably a pricey garage job with the generator).

Poor running usually means the ignition's out of adjustment, with contact-breaker points the main culprit. It's essential for best performance and economy to keep the points gap at the setting in the handbook – too small, and advanced ignition will lead to rough running, pinking, maybe engine damage; too big, and retarded ignition means hesitation, poor performance and mpg.

Old, badly-adjusted sparking plugs take the edge off performance, too. But really bad hesitation under hard acceleration could be caused by breakdown of ignition coil or condenser – needing early replacement. Or it could be fuel starvation. If the car is elderly and fitted with an electric petrol pump, that's the prime suspect. Give it a sharp tap to get it ticking again, and replace it at the earliest opportunity. Other causes of fuel starvation are blocked filters and fuel lines – it's unlikely that the carburettor itself is faulty.

If the engine seems to take longer than usual to warm up, and you get very little heat from the heater for a long time after starting, the cooling thermostat needs checking. Gingerly, feel the top of the radiator after the car's been running for quarter of an hour or so. Unless it's so hot that you feel you'd get burnt if you left your hand there for longer than a moment, you should get a garage to check the thermostat properly, and replace it if it's faulty.

If you smell petrol, check at once for leaks (but it may be that you've just overfilled the tank a bit).

Steering vibration and wobbles, gear changing problems, and trouble with the clutch on hills, as described on pages 67 to 68, all need attention before they get worse or lead to serious trouble. So do the brakes if they pull to one side, feel much squishier than usual, or make a nasty scraping noise (a high-pitched squeak, though irritating, might cure itself). More unusually, the brakes may stick on slightly when they shouldn't: you'd notice this as a drag on the car so that it seemed to labour more than usual, and didn't accelerate so briskly. This needs garage attention, too.

Keep an eye on the oil dipstick. Suddenly increased oil consumption needs garage attention. So does any pale scum or water-bubbling on the dipstick: and an *increasing* oil level is a sure but rare sign of serious engine trouble.

When winter comes, you're likely to have problems with the electrics ... especially if your car fails the battery-power test outlined on page 64.

To prepare for winter, check that electric wiring and connections all look sound. Make sure the battery terminals are really tight, and smear them generously with Vaseline (you won't get a shock).

If starting is sluggish even in warmer weather, check the fanbelt tension (a likely culprit). If that's all right, and you've looked after the battery terminals as above, you may have a faulty generator or voltage regulator. More likely, and expecially if you've had it for a couple of years or more, it's the battery failing.

Any battery will get weak if it's left for a few weeks without the car being run. And a lot of idling and very slow running, or slow-speed journeys with lights, wipers and heater fan working furiously, will sap its strength. So if you suspect the battery, give it a chance by getting it fully recharged. If in just a very few days it's back down in the dumps again, you do need a replacement. In a *Motoring Which?* test report on batteries, January 1979, Basildon, Chloride, Crompton Golden, Dagenite Demon, Esso Voltpak Premium, Exide Supreme, Halfords, Lincon, Monza 5-Star, National GT Plus, QH Heavy Duty, Stolworthy and Tungstone 5-Star were rated good value.

A way of bolstering up a weedy battery for another winter (it then should be able to survive the summer) or to keep it coping till you sell the car – and that way you'll save the more-than-£20 replacement cost – is to use a battery charger. These plug into the mains, and have clips to attach to the battery terminals. Usually, they charge the battery gently overnight, but some have an arrangement for quicker charging – maybe a half-hour burst if you've drained the battery on a cold morning. Make sure it has a fuse or cut-out to prevent damage to the battery if it's faulty. Make sure that the basic charging rate is no more than about 1 amp (much more might harm the battery, if you left it charging once the battery was fully charged). An ammeter is a useful extra, as you can tell from the way that the charging rate drops when the battery is fully charged. And it's best if the charger has non-rust clips for the battery terminals, with good long leads both for them and for the mains.

The only pre-winter essential is antifreeze. If yours is one of the cars using a mainly light-alloy engine, the handbook may recommend 'Type A' antifreeze, to British Standard 3150. Follow handbook recommendations about changing this particularly carefully – it may need changing earlier than other types, not because it'll let the water freeze after that but because it could then let corrosion start. But in general antifreeze will do for a couple of years or so, so long as it's been kept topped up in the same proportion as it was originally added (see page 109). Change it earlier if the handbook says.

When the time comes to replace the antifreeze, make sure you get the type specified in the handbook. If a particular brand's specified, use that: the small amount you'd save on another brand of similar specification wouldn't be worth the potential risk of the car maker pointing at your use of the 'wrong' brand as the cause of any trouble. But in practice differences between brands don't seem important to how well the antifreeze works, so long as the brand is of the *type* specified. Usually the car makers will describe this as 'BS3151' or 'BS3152'. Even a cut-price brand meeting the relevant BS should be satisfactory.

If you're not sure which brand was in before, or if it was a different one, flush the radiator through with plenty of clean water after you've drained out the old antifreeze, and before you put the new one in. This is because the anti-corrosion chemicals in different brands can conflict with one another.

If you spill any anti-freeze on to the car's paintwork, wash it off at once, as it could stain.

If you've a suspicion that because of very hard frost the cooling water, even with its anti-freeze, has started to freeze into a soft mush, you should still have escaped serious trouble. Ideally, let the water thaw on its own. But if you have to run the car, let it idle gently for a minute or two before you drive off. There should be no damage, but increase the concentration so that it doesn't happen again.

EMERGENCY SPARES KIT

You can save a lot of trouble if you always keep a basic emergency kit in your car.

Make sure you've got all you need to cope with a puncture (unless you've got the new 'drive flat' tyres — see page 48). It pays to check the pressure of the spare whenever you check your other tyre pressures — nothing worse than getting out the spare after a puncture, only to find that's flat too. You also need a jack, and a wheel nut brace (probably supplied with your car anyway).

It can be a good idea to keep the basic tool-kit described on page 114 in the boot. Instead of an inspection lamp (unless it's the type which runs off the car's battery), keep a torch with your tools. If you do have to get down to work on some grubby part of your car, you'll be glad too of having hand cleanser and tissues with you.

Bits and pieces which can turn out very helpful are:

Electric flex: a few feet, which you can use to strap up something that's falling off, as well as for its proper purpose

Exhaust bandage: seals noisy breaks in your exhaust — for small breaks and awkward cracks you can also try exhaust sealing compound.

Transparent quick-sealing compound: clear 'plastic rubber' like Silicone Seal can patch cracked lamp lenses, torn rubber, even some leaks in an emergency

Insulating tape: can also be useful for non-electrical faults

'Maintenance spray' such as WD-40: spray cans of very light penetrating oil, useful for seized nuts and to spray over the ignition system if your car won't start because it's damp

Light nylon tow rope: again, may be useful not just for towing

Useful spares to keep handy are a fanbelt, fuses; bulbs for brake light, side light, direction indicator, tail light; if your car has an ordinary toughened windscreen, not laminated, a temporary plastic roll-up windscreen

'Jump leads' are insulated cables with clips, which can be used to connect a dead battery to a healthy one, getting the broken-down car started. They cost a few pounds. If you want this extra precaution against being stranded in winter (or abundant opportunities of being a Good Samaritan), make sure you get a sturdy pair with really strong fastening of clips to cables. Also, keep the clips well smeared with Vaseline. AA and Ripaults Booster Cables came out well in *Motoring Which?* January 1979 brand tests. Using them, make sure the other car's voltage is the same as yours (most are 12 volts). Check carefully that absolutely all electrical equipment is switched off in both cars (though you'll have to leave the clock). Make sure the cars aren't touching. Put both in neutral, with the handbrakes on. Then connect the jump leads one at a time, taking great care that one lead connects the positive terminal of one battery to the positive terminal of the other; the next lead connecting negative to negative. Make sure that the last connection made is to the flat battery. When both batteries are connected, start the engine of the healthy car, and leave it idling. Then try and get the second car running.

Clutch Problems

There should usually be a small amount of free play in the clutch pedal: it shouldn't disengage the gears until you've pressed it down by an inch or so.

If you have to press it down a very long way before you can change gear, or if the gears seem to clash a bit even though you've got it pressed quite far down, the reason depends on how your clutch works. If there's a cable or system of rods between the pedal and clutch itself, this probably merely needs adjusting (your handbook should show how to do this). But if it's hydraulic, using pipes like brake pipes connected to a little reservoir under the bonnet, the fluid may need topping up: check by unscrewing the top. If the fluid's so low that there's none left in the little container, you'll have to get a garage to do it, as by then there's probably air in the pipes, which will have to be bled out.

If the opposite has happened – so that the clutch frees the gears the moment you start pressing the pedal –

it's probably best to have the adjustment done by a garage. To reach this state, the clutch plate lining will have worn down, and it might be best to have it replaced before it starts slipping if adjustment doesn't cure the problem – at least, if you're planning a long trip.

Clutch slip is when the car behaves as if your foot's on the clutch when it's not – so that even when you're in gear the engine speed can increase without the car going faster. It's most likely to show either when you try to pull away up a hill, or when you are accelerating very hard and change gear briskly. It's something that usually starts in a small way and gradually gets worse, so shouldn't leave you broken down if you have it fixed when it first starts. It's worth trying adjustment of the clutch linkage in the way described by the handbook before you go to the expense of a full clutch overhaul.

Breakdown services

Even in a fairly young car, there's quite a high risk of breakdown – the odds are about two to one against, in any one year, and get worse as the car gets older, until after five or six years there's nearly an even chance.

That's much the commonest reason for people joining the AA or the RAC. Breakdowns are not, on average, common enough for you to be likely to recover the cost of your subscription by using the breakdown service. Calling out a commercial garage (very likely, the same as the one that would do the job through the AA or RAC) should – over the years – work out cheaper. But if you're at all worried by the prospect of a breakdown stranding you, the peace of mind you'd get from being able to call in AA or RAC would be worth while. On the basis of previous *Motoring Which?* readers' experience, there's perhaps more chance of your getting back on the road without delay using the AA than using the RAC (or just relying on a local garage). These two long-standing breakdown clubs have recently been joined by the National Breakdown Recovery Club, which deals with breakdowns, and getting you home if your car's beyond repair, in much the same sort of way. Although it's rather cheaper than the others, it doesn't have the other services such as touring information, legal help, route plans, technical advice,

DIAGNOSING TROUBLE

This book's not the place to learn how to pinpoint exact trouble-spots, and fix them yourself. But it can be relatively easy to tell whether some fault is safe for you to go on driving with, or whether you should stop dead there and then to get help. And, using a bit of care and logic, you may be able to put your finger on some common faults. Moreover, even if you're not going to try to deal with it yourself, the more care you take to note the symptoms of some fault, the easier it'll be for a mechanic to deal with it (see overleaf).

GET HELP AS SOON AS POSSIBLE IF:

Ignition light stays on when the engine is switched off.
This probably means that there's a bad short somewhere. Disconnect the terminal of the battery that leads to the car's bodywork at once, to prevent any risk of fire. Get expert help.

Oil warning light comes on.
Stop immediately, check for leaks, filler/dipstick fit, oil level. If no obvious and simple solution, get expert help.

Knocking noise from engine, and low oil pressure.
If the noise is worst when you take your foot off the accelerator, a "big end bearing" has probably failed. Major engine trouble: stop and get help.

Car starts faltering or stuttering and slows down.
Clouds of steam when you stop. Overheating — check the fanbelt (see page 120). Check for leaks or split hoses. Wait till it's cooled down to remove the radiator cap, and when you do muffle it and protect your hand with a cloth. Topping up with water (very hot if possible — otherwise wait till it's cooled down a lot) will probably let you drive on, if a hose hasn't disintegrated. When you reach help (or after fixing

fanbelt or hoses yourself) check that the oil level hasn't dropped. If it has, top up (and listen carefully for strange engine noises over the next few weeks).

Steering suddenly feels very strange.
Probably a flat tyre. Replace it before you drive on — driving on a flat one will wreck it. If not a tyre, and if the road's quite well surfaced, suspect a serious steering or suspension fault and call for mechanical help.

Knocking noise from gearbox.
If it happens only in one gear, stop using that gear and drive on. Otherwise, stop and call for mechanical help right away. Probably broken gear wheel teeth.

With most other faults, if the car actually moves it's safe to drive it at least to the nearest place that you can conveniently get help.

IF YOUR CAR'S ENGINE WON'T START:

Starter motor sounded very sluggish?
YES   Probably flat battery: try jump leads, charge it, maybe try to get started by having the car pushed in third gear — or get help
NO,   sounded as brisk as usual — so try . . .

Weather damp?
YES   Suspect damp ignition: try water-dispersant maintenance spray (see page 132), or remove distributor cap and leads, and dry them in a barely warm oven
NO — so try . . .

Electrical connections all ok?
NO   Tighten them firmly, and try again.
YES — so check if . . .

Distributor has obvious fault (Check for contact-breaker points not opening)?
YES   Fix it, try again.
NO — so check if . . .

Petrol getting through to carburettor?

NO   Suspect empty petrol tank: if not, maybe faulty fuel pump – tap it sharply with soft-headed hammer; otherwise, blocked fuel line, which you'll probably need mechanical help with
YES – so have a sniff . . .

Strong smell of petrol?

YES   You've probably 'flooded the carburettor'; push the choke back in, gently press the accelerator down, and let the starter spin the engine a few times
NO – so one last check . . .

Accelerator and choke cables to carburettor secure?

NO   Fix them
YES

If you still haven't found the trouble, it's most likely poorly set, faulty or dirty ignition, or perhaps a faulty sparking plug. If you feel competent, take out each sparking plug in turn, lay it on its side on top of the engine, with its lead attached, and get someone else to press the car's starter. A snappy blue spark means that plug – and everything in the ignition system leading to it – is ok. Even with one faulty plug, the engine should probably have started but if the spark's weak on just one plug, that plug might be dirty; its gap might be incorrect; the lead to it might be faulty; less likely, the contact for it in the distributor itself could be dirty or out of adjustment. If one plug has no spark, try another plug in that position. Still no spark means that the lead to it is probably not connected properly; but the contact in the distributor cap may be wet or broken. If none of the plugs spark, suspect the lead from the ignition coil to the distributor; the contact breaker; the contact on the distributor's rotor arm; the ignition coil itself, and its connections.

But probably, if the first few simple checks don't show the culprit, it's best to call in expert help.

If the car stops dead:

First, check for fuel (most likely, there'll have been some splutters, as a warning). Next, check all the fuses. Then see that a lead hasn't suddenly slipped off the ignition coil or the distributor. Check the petrol pump, as above. If it's none of these things, and if the electrics – lights, etc – are still working properly, it's probably a trickier ignition fault. You could try tracing it as suggested above: but most likely, if it's not one of the first few obvious things you'll need expert help anyway.

If the engine doesn't tick over evenly:

On older cars with adjustable carburettors, this is probably a sign of faulty adjustment. It may simply be an unhealthy battery. But more likely it's an ignition fault. The ignition timing may be too far advanced; ignition contact points may be dirty; the sparking plugs may be dirty, or their gaps may be set wrong. Less likely nowadays is dirt in the carburettor itself. If there's a light tapping noise from the engine, suspect incorrectly adjusted valve clearances. The fault, though irritating, can wait till a routine service.

If the engine won't run smoothly at speed

Things you might be able to deal with yourself include spark plug dirt, incorrect gaps, or failure; the choke still being in operation (either because you've forgotten it, or because its linkage is out of adjustment). But probably it's dirty or pitted ignition contact breakers, ignition timing too far retarded (or a sticking automatic ignition advance); a faulty ignition coil or condenser; faulty carburation; valve clearances out of adjustment; or a dirty carburettor air cleaner. It also could be dirt in the fuel lines (or the breather valve for the petrol tank); the generator not working properly; or weak valve springs.

Again, unless the engine gets very jerky, a bit of trouble here can be left till it's convenient to put your car in for repair.

handbooks and so forth which you might want from the Big Two. It's address is Freepost, Bradford, West Yorks BD7 1BR.

Garage repairs

For any but the simplest repairs, it could be worth getting an estimate from more than one garage. This is certainly so for a big job. If you know exactly what needs doing, you can probably get an outline costing over the telephone – and if you live in a big town it could be well worth trying at least one garage well outside the town, as its labour rates could be a lot lower.

Especially with electrical faults, it will probably pay you to go to an electrical specialist (usually in telephone directory Yellow Pages under 'car electrical equipment repairers'). Often even if you did take your car to a general garage they'd contract out the electrical work to one of these specialists, anyway. Some garages also specialise in radiators. Tyre dealers usually have wheel balancers, and may have wheel aligning equipment. You should get very good prices from exhaust system specialists, and (if you can find one) from shock absorber specialists.

Otherwise, the rules suggested under routine servicing hold for repairs too: both finding a garage, and trying to get the best possible work out of it.

You may get help from the fact that the MAA/SMTA/OFT Code of Practice (see page 112) says that garages doing repairs should guarantee them for a specified time – and put right anything that turns out to be inadequately done.

When you get an estimate, make sure that it includes the cost of all parts that will be needed, *and* the cost of labour (about one in six that turn out to be wrong have missed out one or the other); and VAT. With expensive parts, it's particularly worth checking what the maker's recommended price is, maybe by phoning a parts distributor or the maker's service department.

Major spare parts will almost certainly cost you more than you thought they could. In general, spares for British cars (in relation to the original cost of the car) tend to be cheaper than those for foreign ones. French and German cars tend to have more costly spares,

Sweden and particularly Italy even more costly in relation to the basic price of the car itself. Some Japanese spares are startlingly expensive but others cost little more than for British cars. Of course, within these general trends there are many particular exceptions. And in general, the more expensive the car the less costly its spares – bearing in mind its price. That's to say that even though spares for a Rolls-Royce cost much more than for other British cars they aren't *so* much more as you'd have expected from the price of a Rolls.

When you're shopping for a spare, always try to get a maker's exchange unit – it should work as well as an ordinary new unit, but is much cheaper. If the garage quotes you for a major item like a new engine or clutch or gearbox, check very carefully that you really need the whole thing. You may again save a lot by just having the one part out of the assembly that truly needs replacement. But with some cars you may have to give up trying to get the faulty parts only, and have to buy a complete assembly instead – the chief culprits are drive shafts (not just the constant velocity joints which fail), propellor shafts (not just universal joints), distributors, starter motors and exhaust systems.

If the part's one that you can check for quality simply by looking at it, try car breakers (see page 92). But you'd need a good deal of mechanical expertise and confidence to get a working, moving part from this source – though it's very much cheaper than from any other.

Once you've tracked down the cheapest way of having your repair done – or decided on a garage because you know you can trust it to do a good job, which is the best choice possible – your troubles *may* be over. But two people out of five have found rough estimates are exceeded; nearly one in five who've had firm estimates find that the garage spends more. One moral is to get a 'firm' rather than 'rough' estimate – much less likely to be wildly wrong. Better still, get a 'quotation', which should be legally binding on the garage.

If the estimate has been exceeded without consultation, you've got a legitimate cause for complaint – see below.

Perhaps more serious, about one in five major repairs have not been done successfully – at least as far as owners have reported to *Motoring Which?*. This too is obviously ground for complaint.

Rows with your garage

If you've serious grounds for complaint against your garage – most likely, an estimate being exceeded without your permission, or the repair work itself being unsatisfactory – the first step is to try and sort it out, in a firm but friendly way, with the garage itself. When you collect the car, you may be able to reach agreement with the sevice receptionist or manager. Next, write to the garage's service manager by name, if it's a big firm; or its managing director or owner, if it's smaller (or if you know him). Make it clear that you know that the OFT Code of Practice says that you should have been contacted if the estimate was going to be exceeded by a significant amount; that you know a 'quotation' is legally binding on the firm, and cannot legitimately be exceeded (if that's what you got); or that under the Code the repair quality should be guaranteed. Also, make clear that although you don't want to be unpleasant you do feel hard done by – and you intend to press firmly for your rights.

If that doesn't work, consult the consumer protection or Trading Standards department of your local authority: some have been particularly active in attending to garage standards in their area. If the garage belongs to its trade association, write to that: for England and Wales –

Investigation and Advisory Service,
Motor Agents Assosciation,
201 Great Portland Street,
London W1N 6AB

for Scotland –

Customer Complaints Service,
Scottish Motor Trade Association,
3 Palmerston Place,
Edinburgh EH12 5AQ.

Both have been very concerned to improve people's satisfaction with garage standards.

For bodywork repair disputes, the trade association is the Vehicle Builders and Repairers Association, Belmont House, 102 Finkle Lane, Gildersome, Leeds LS27 7TW. They run a similar Code of Practice for their members.

Next, consider arbitration (the MAA or SMTA may suggest or arrange this). Both you and the garage would have to agree to accept the findings of the arbitrator which then are legally binding. That's to say, if the arbitrator found against you but you still felt you were right, you couldn't then go to court. There'd be no appeal. You have to put down a small deposit with the independent Institute of Arbitrators, through which the scheme is arranged.

Instead, you can go to the county court. If the amount involved is £200 or less, you can use its small claims procedure (see page 000), at virtually no cost – and whether or not the garage agrees to your doing this. From £200 to £2,000, you have to use the full county court process – see *How to sue in the county court*, published by Consumers' Association. In Scotland, the relevant court would instead be the Sheriff Court.

Doing major repairs yourself

If you feel competent to undertake big repair jobs yourself, you don't need me to tell you which tools you'd find useful. But you may well be surprised at how cheaply you can hire special tools from hire shops. They're listed in telephone directories under Hire Contractors – Tools and Equipment. Some car tools may instead be hired by accessory shops, or even on a special arrangement by a garage.

For example, you may be able to hire a chain hoist for £4 or £5 a week; a compression tester for £1.50 a day; a stud extractor for £1 or £2 a day; a valve seat cutter for £2 or £3 a day; a torque wrench for £2 a day, not much more for a week; a heavy-duty engine crane for £10 a week.

You may also be interested in the MKOK 10-bay nonprofit workshops you can use in Milton Keynes, or a similar commercial outfit called Autoplus in Nottingham.

7. GOING ABROAD

Taking your car abroad is quite straightforward. But a little planning saves a lot – of money, maybe of trouble.

First, your cheapest route may be quite different from the way you'd go without a car – and exactly how to travel will depend on how many of you there'll be in the car. As cross-Channel fares change frequently, get quotes for your party and car for both ferry and hovercraft – and check more than one ferry company, especially on the longer routes. Hovercraft scores over ferry for speed, and waiting to get off (but is more prone to cancellation in bad weather). Though there's often an extra charge for travelling at the weekend in high summer, you may escape this by booking really early – and early booking's essential anyway, if you're planning to travel at a really popular time.

Before you finally book, check on the cost of a holiday package which includes air fare and car hire, as this can work out cheaper than taking your own car – if you include your driving-there costs, with en-route accommodation. But you may feel that the drive down is all part of the holiday. On that basis, it's cheaper to drive yourself; fly-drive is chaper *only* if you don't really count your holiday as starting until you've reached your eventual holiday area.

Holiday Which? gives up-to-date travelling cost information for the main European resort areas, including driving yourself.

Some countries tend to be hit worse than others by petrol shortages. If there's trouble, check ahead with the country's national tourist office here. They will know what the position (and petrol cost) is, and may have special schemes for tourist petrol.

If you're particularly worried about petrol shortages, but really want to take your own car, consider the (rather expensive) long-distance motor-rail arrangements. With these, your car is taken by train which you board somewhere like Ostend, Boulogne or Paris. You can get details (at the same time as some ferry details) from Sealink, 52 Grosvenor Gardens, London SW1.

You should take your normal papers – your own driving licence, the car's registration document, and your passport. You must also have a GB sticker at the back of your car. For a few countries (including Spain) you will need an International Driving Permit, from AA or RAC; check with them – AA, 01-954 7355, RAC 01-686 2314. For Italy, you need a translation of your driving licence (again, AA or RAC).

You should also get an insurance 'green card'. Your normal policy gives you basic 'Road Traffic Act'-type cover (see page 102) in other EEC countries, and they will be happy with your normal insurance certificate. But to make sure that your policy covers you as fully as here in those countries, you still need to fix it up in advance with your insurers. And in other countries, outside the EEC, you still need 'green card' cover – which includes the actual green card you need to produce at frontiers to show your insurance covers you there.

For Spain, arrange a 'bail bond' with your insurers.

Otherwise you can be put in prison there, with your car impounded, immediately after an accident, regardless of whether or not it's your fault. (If you hire there, the bail bond is included in the hire insurance.)

Take a collapsible red reflective warning triangle, such as you may have seen used for broken-down lorries. They're generally used abroad in breakdowns, and are obligatory in many countries.

If your car has separate headlamp bulbs (rather than integral light units), change them, for yellow ones (although you're allowed to have white headlamps, drivers in France will flash you interminably if you do). Otherwise, fit dip-conversion headlamp covers, or stick-on beam converters.

Most important, check your car's condition with extra care. Pay special attention to these parts:

● radiator and all hoses, fanbelt
● tyres (replace if three-quarters worn or more)
● battery, electrical connections and wiring, lights
● change engine oil and filter
● check ignition contact points, sparking plugs, valve clearances
● brake travel and wear
● clutch adjustment
● steering wear.

Besides the list of routine spares which was suggested as an emergency kit (see page 132), you should also take the following:

● phrasebook including common mechanical parts and faults; list of dealers for your car
● ignition contact breaker set
● distributor cap and rotor arm
● water hoses
● condenser
● full set of sparking plugs
● headlamp spare bulb (or complete unit, if yours are sealed beam units – pair of units, if you have separate main and dipping lamps in a four-headlamp system)
● HT lead for sparking plugs
● cylinder head gasket, or gasket set
● radiator sealing compound.

You may be able to arrange for a touring spares kit, including these and maybe other things, with a garage or spare parts distributor for your car. If so, it'll usually be on the basis that you pay for what you used, and return what you didn't; with an additional hire fee.

You can insure against the risk of breakdown abroad, either with AA or RAC (you don't have to be a member), or with Europ Assistance (252 High St, Croydon CR0 1NF). Breakdown insurance usually includes recovery of your car after a serious breakdown or accident, on-the-spot towing and repair assistance, emergency car hire fees, extra hotel or travel costs, perhaps a chauffeur if you're too ill to drive. And it includes arrangements to fly out spares at short notice, though you have to pay for the spares (*Motoring Which?* tried these arrangements – many years ago – and found they worked smoothly and quickly).

On the whole, breakdown insurance seems a good idea.

DRIVING AND THE LAW

Which way to keep on the right side of the law, even for learners – plus how to get good value from your insurance

1. LEARNING TO DRIVE— OR DRIVE BETTER

There's no magic formula for passing your driving test. Professional driving lessons are certainly a good idea. But a typical course of 20 one-hour lessons might cost well over £100. Many people can pass the test with far fewer lessons, though – while some might need 40 or more. The more practice you get, the better – especially in the straightforward process of actually making the car work. A great many driving test failures are caused by people not being able to carry out the manœuvres which the test calls for: reversing into a parking slot, say; doing a three-point turn; reversing into an entry and driving off again. So the basic manœuvres need practising repeatedly, until they come almost automatically.

The point about getting professional lessons, instead of being taught by someone in the family, is chiefly that even the most experienced driver may well have lots of little faults, or at least foibles that go against the grain of the driving test. If they're passed on to you, the examiner will find them sticking out like a sore thumb. By all means practise as much as possible with all the drivers in your family – but don't let them 'teach' you. There are subsidiary reasons for learning from a professional. Very likely, you'll find the pro far more patient – he won't get into a flap when you make the little mistakes that every learner's bound to do. Unlike dad, he shouldn't get so edgy about his pride and joy if you mangle the gears. The pro will have a keen eye for your faults, too: notice things you're doing wrong in a way that an examiner will (and that your family

and friends probably won't). And if you learn from a driving school in the area in which you'll be taking your test, the teacher will take you through the same sort of roads and streets that the examiner will use, so that you won't feel it's all unfamiliar territory when you finally take your test.

Take time to learn the Highway Code, too. It's not something to cram into a frantic swot, but really something to live with while you're learning to drive, to be looking at every day so that you're thoroughly familiar with it. Then, when the examiner tests you on it, answers will be there ready without your having to search for them.

Don't be upset if you don't pass, first time. About half the people who take the test fail it – more women fail than men, incidentally. But virtually everyone gets through eventually. If you do fail, the examiner will give you a form which sets out those things you'll need to do better, but he's not allowed to discuss them with you. It's most unlikely that you'd be failed for making some single basic mistake. And the examiner will probably expect you to be a bit nervous. But what will fail you is a general air of inexperience – if you give the impression that you really don't know the car yet, and aren't at all familiar with driving and traffic.

As soon as you start learning to drive, find out what the waiting list for tests is locally (sometimes it can go up to six months or more). This will let you book a test for when you want, without too long a wait – something the driving school can do for you if you're learning with one.

Some important points:

● when you book a course of driving lessons, make sure you like your instructor – if you can meet for a chat beforehand, so much the better; otherwise, ask for a change after your very first lesson if you don't get on perfectly together

● ideally, learn in the car you'll be driving regularly – and the one you'll be practising in (you may get a discount for this)

● try to start your lessons at the driving school – if the instructor meets you somewhere else, you'll either have to pay extra, or (more likely) have his travelling time lopped off your lessons

● make sure you can see perfectly: in the test you'll have to read a number plate in good daylight 25 yards away, and to drive well you should be able to see considerably better than that

● unless you're certain you'll never want to drive one, learn to drive on a manual-gearchange car; if you take your test on an automatic, you'll only be licensed to drive automatics

● always remember the really common failure-points:
 – precautions before starting the engine; the way you use the controls; correct procedure before moving off
 – correct use of mirrors
 – careful observation at junctions
 – reversing into a narrow opening and around a tight corner
 – slowing down for junctions
 – correct use of signals
 – three-point turning
 – smooth progress with the general flow of traffic
 – correct position ready for turning left or right
 – correct action regarding other traffic (especially at junctions)
 – careful anticipation of what pedestrians and other road users may do
 – giving parked vehicles safe clearance.

● when you go for your test, make sure the car's in good condition, with all its lights and indicators working for instance, and with the L-plates properly in place.

Learning more about driving

Passing the test doesn't automatically make you a good driver. Most obviously, you don't need to do any night driving for the test – and you're not allowed to drive on a motorway until after you've passed the test. But there's much more you can do to improve your driving.

Whether or not you're a learner, if you want to drive better you'll find the Department of Transport handbook, *Driving* (HMSO, £2.25) full of sound sense. For learners, its step-by-step guide to the driving test will be valuable. But more important, it will ground you firmly in the three essential principles of truly good driving – observation, planning and method. These are the foundations of advanced driving courses which may be run by some driving schools and motoring clubs. They are developed very fully in two useful manuals, the Institute of Advanced Motorists' *Advanced Motoring* (Macdonald and Jane's, £2.25), and the Home Office police drivers' manual, *Roadcraft* (HMSO, 95p). There are also comparable versions of both for motorcyclists.

Many drivers find that some aspects of advanced driving techniques tend to develop naturally, with experience. This is particularly true of the concentrated observation which seems to learners almost like a mysterious sixth sense. But it's not that. When the skilled driver has already started braking long before the child jumps out from behind a parked van, it's because he was automatically checking under the van beforehand for tell-tale feet. When he's ready for the cyclist swerving across to the right in front of him, it's because he noticed the cyclist looking briefly over his shoulder first. When he leaves plenty of room for the taxi which without warning stops dead in front of him, it's because he saw a pedestrian waving it down. When he's ready for a sharp unsigned bend just over the brow of a hill, it's because he had been watching for the line taken by telegraph poles or roadside trees.

But even after picking up this careful attention to

143

roadside detail, and to the actions and intentions of other road users, few drivers then add the other two essential ingredients of true driving skill – planning and method. Planning ensures that your car will be in exactly the right part of the road, and moving at exactly the right speed, for each manœuvre or incident. Common faults shown for example by the IAM's advanced test are people being too close to the nearside when they're about to overtake or turn right, and too close to the middle of the road when they're not; being too close to the car in front; using the brakes too sharply or too late – all avoided by thinking carefully, all the time, about what you're going to do next. But above all, really smooth and safe driving demands strict method. The great virtue of the books mentioned above is that they will drum method into you. The basics of driving method, to cope with a traffic manœuvre like turning, or with an incident like some other road user's action or a road hazard like a deviation, are these:

Step 1   – check mirror
      – give signal if necessary
      – SELECT POSITION AND COURSE, so that you will be correctly placed, ready for the manœuvre or hazard

Step 2   – check mirror
      – signal
      – BRAKE to correct speed for manœuvre or hazard

Step 3   – if necessary, change to correct GEAR

Step 4   – check mirror
      – if necessary, further SIGNAL
      – if necessary, warning HORN

Step 5   – last 'lifesaver' mirror check, and
      – MANŒUVRE, or negotiate hazard.

A technique which some police driving instructors use is to get their pupils to 'talk through' their driving. You will probably find this useful – even if you do it while you're alone in the car. On the one hand, describe

the things you see which might have a bearing on your driving: 'Lorry four cars ahead starting to brake . . . double white lines . . . ice cream van parked on left . . . van waiting at junction 60 yds ahead, driver looking at me . . . dog lifting leg on lamppost . . . old lady approaching zebra crossing . . .' On the other hand, describe your own driving method, as you approach hazards, corners and so forth: 'Mirror, well into left lane . . . mirror, left indicator, brake . . . 2nd gear . . . mirror, 'blind' turning so horn . . . last check behind so that no cyclist's coming up on my nearside, and turn into side road . . .'

A few talk-to-yourself lessons like that may give you a lot of clues to ways you can tighten up your driving. But the advanced-driving books are really worth while.

ADVANCED DRIVING TECHNIQUES

Books on advanced driving often use this technique to illustrate what you should assume lurks out of sight, when you're 'road reading'

HIGHWAY CODE TEST

Unless you've learned to drive very recently, you should take the trouble to read through the latest edition of the Highway Code from time to time. You may be surprised by some of the things in it. Try this test:

1. A white number 40 on a plain blue circle means:
 a) 40-ton weight limit for heavy lorries
 b) 40 mph speed limit for heavy lorries only; others can drive faster
 c) 40 mph limit for heavy lorries *and* buses only
 d) you've got to drive at 40 mph or *faster*

2. If pedestrians want to cross a busy road junction:
 a) they're not allowed to — they must find the nearest zebra crossing instead
 b) they're not allowed to after lighting-up time
 c) they'll have priority over traffic there

3. A little red arrow pointing upwards, beside a big black one pointing downwards, means:
 a) you've got to give way to anything coming in the opposite direction
 b) you've got priority over anything coming in the opposite direction
 c) low bridge coming (with its height printed separately)

4. The minimum depth of tread which you must have on your tyres is:
 a) 1 mm
 b) 1½ mm
 c) 2 mm

5. White zig-zag lines leading up to a zebra crossing mean:
 a) you can't park there
 b) you can't overtake a car there
 c) once a pedestrian's crossed, you can't pull away before the car beside you, if it stopped first

6. At night (except in a one-way street) you can't park on the right-hand side of the road:
 a) ever
 b) unless you leave your sidelights on
 c) if the road is subject to a speed limit higher than 30 mph

7. Generally at roundabouts you should give way to:
 a) traffic coming from your right
 b) traffic coming from your left
 c) heavy lorries

8. Overtaking on the left is normally allowed:
 a) in one-way streets
 b) on dual carriageways (excluding motorways)
 c) on dual carriageways *and* motorways

9. Criss-cross yellow lines at a junction mean:
 a) you may wait on the yellow lines if heavy traffic stops you clearing the junction
 b) you may only wait on the yellow lines if you want to turn right and oncoming traffic blocks you
 c) you must never wait on the yellow lines.

Score like this:

1.	d=3	**6.**	a=3	**8.**	a=3
2.	c=3	**7.**	a=3	**9.**	b=3
3.	a=3			(c may be prudent, but	
4.	a=3			scores no marks as it's not	
5.	a=3			recommended in the	
	b=3			Highway Code!)	
	c=3				

If you scored:

33 Congratulations: you either know the Highway Code by heart or wrote it.

27–30 Good: but it would still pay you to look at the Code again.

21–24 Well, you've now got next weekend's reading lined up!

under 20 Don't drive to the bookstall to buy your Highway Code — walk!

ACCIDENTS

If you have an accident – even a very slight one – you may well be in such a state of shock that, although you think you're perfectly all right, you say or do something silly . . . something which in the end makes it all much more expensive for you.

So it's important to know in advance the key things you must do besides switching off your engine.

First, keep a pencil and paper or notebook in the car, always (useful for other things, as well as crucial if you do have an accident). Make an immediate note in this of the numbers of any cars or other vehicles there at the time, whose drivers might have seen what happened. If you do need witnesses later, you can write to DVLC, Swansea SA99 1AR to find where you can get the owner's address (there's a small fee).

Better still, get names and addresses of people who saw the accident, and who stay on the scene (be quick about this too, because they tend to go – approach them before you approach the people waiting to have an argument with you in the other car, say). Many people don't like getting entangled in possible court cases, so don't bandy words like 'witness' about. If they're obviously reluctant, you could say something like 'just so that my insurance company don't think I'm making it all up'.

Then get details from any other driver involved. He's legally obliged to give you his name and address. In case of some funny business over that, you should be sure of getting his car's number, too. And it will make your account of the accident, later, sound much more competent if you also note the make and model of car, and anything obviously defective about it (bald tyres, say, or a really filthy windscreen, or a load in or on it that would have obstructed its driver's view).

If there's any injury involved, the other driver must show you his insurance certificate – or at any rate tell you the name of his insurance company. Whether or not there was injury, it's worth asking him for this.

Make a plan of the scene of the accident: the position of cars involved, including distances from the side of the road, positions of junctions, 'street furniture' like lampposts or traffic bollards that could have had an effect. Photos help with this, too. And note down what happened: direction of vehicles involved, what other people involved did, state of the road surface, whether it was raining or not, how good the light was, time of day, whatever other people – especially those involved – actually said.

POINTS TO REMEMBER

Get witnesses; make notes; don't admit anything.

Above all, don't say anything which could be interpreted as an admission that you were to blame. Of course, if someone else has been hurt it's impossible not to show normal human sympathy. But don't say anything like 'I'm sorry' – whatever you feel. An in-

MAKING A SKETCH OF THE ACCIDENT

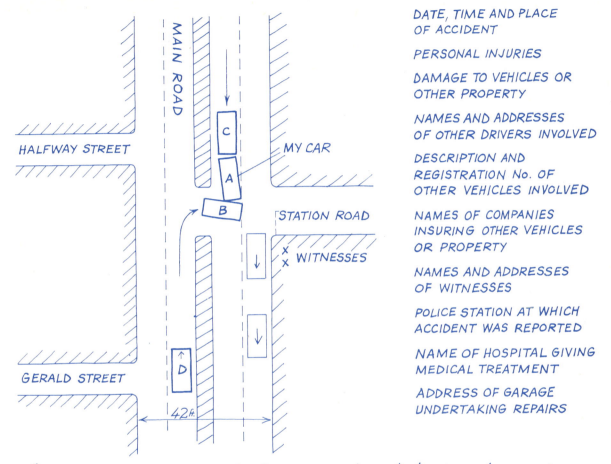

DATE, TIME AND PLACE
OF ACCIDENT

PERSONAL INJURIES

DAMAGE TO VEHICLES OR
OTHER PROPERTY

NAMES AND ADDRESSES
OF OTHER DRIVERS INVOLVED

DESCRIPTION AND
REGISTRATION No. OF
OTHER VEHICLES INVOLVED

NAMES OF COMPANIES
INSURING OTHER VEHICLES
OR PROPERTY

NAMES AND ADDRESSES
OF WITNESSES

POLICE STATION AT WHICH
ACCIDENT WAS REPORTED

NAME OF HOSPITAL GIVING
MEDICAL TREATMENT

ADDRESS OF GARAGE
UNDERTAKING REPAIRS

I was driving along Main Road at 8·30 a.m. towards London, when car B suddenly drove out in front of me. Estimated speed at collision was 30 mph. Car C, driven by Mr Robinson, hit the back of my car. Witnesses were from car C and car D, plus two pedestrians on corner of Station Road.

surance company could theoretically even refuse to cover you for claims against you, if you'd admitted blame.

You don't have to call the police, unless someone's been injured and insurance certificates haven't been shown. However, if it's beyond doubt that the accident was caused entirely by someone else, and especially if it seems clear that he was driving carelessly or otherwise breaking the law, do get the police. You're much more likely to be able to recover the cost of any damage to your car without losing your no-claims discount (see page 103) if the other driver gets convicted of an offence to do with the accident.

Take a note of the police officer's station, his number and preferably his name. If you're quite certain that you're clearly blameless, it's safe to say what happened: be brief, but as helpful as possible. But if there's even a shadow of doubt in your mind about blame, don't say anything. You're not obliged to, and nothing will go against you if you say something like 'I'm sorry but as a result of the accident I feel rather shaken. Although it wasn't my fault and I did nothing wrong, I've read in the *Which?* book on cars that it's best never to say anything after an accident.'

If someone's hurt:
Make sure that an ambulance is called, even if the injury seems very superficial. Unless you've medical knowledge, don't move the injured person. If you don't give your name and address, and show your insurance certificate, you have to report the accident to the police – with your insurance certificate – within 24 hours.

You must also leave your name and address, or report to the police within 24 hours, if you run down or injure a dog, horse or farm animal (not counting poultry – cats don't count, either).

Accident repairs
If you're fit to drive, and the car still works, cautiously get it home. You have to report the accident right away to your insurance company. See page 103 for how to decide whether or not to recover the cost from them, if you've a comprehensive insurance policy. If you

are going to claim on your policy, it's probably best to ring them up, rather than write, so that you can ask them what to do about repairs.

If you're not going to claim, or if the insurance company leaves choice or repairers up to you, you've then got to find one. (And see page 104 for what to do about recovering the cost from anyone else who's to blame.)

Garages which specialise in body repairs are listed in telephone directory Yellow Pages under Car and Coach Body Builders, Car Breakdown and Recovery Services, Car Painters and Sprayers, and sometimes Garage Services. Choosing one is much the same as choosing a servicing garage: ideally, rely on trustworthy recommendation or personal experience; failing that, get several estimates, and look for one that has a clean and efficient air about it – with what looks like flawless work leaving its workshops.

If you couldn't drive the car away from the accident, the police may have arranged for it to be towed to a nearby garage (or perhaps to somewhere where it can be inspected for roadworthiness, if they suspect that its condition contributed to the accident). But if you've got to arrange for a tow, 'Car Breakdown and Recovery Services' is what to look up in the directory.

If you're a very long way from home, have the car towed to safety at a nearby garage, but don't yet commit yourself to having repairs done there. Garages nearer your home may be so eager for the work that the quotes they give you – even including the tow – are lower than the distant firm's. And of course, it would be convenient for you to have the car done closer at hand. Wherever the car's left, try and remove as many things as possible from it.

FIRST AID

If anyone seems badly hurt, try not to move them unless it's essential for safety. Someone breathing but unconscious is best put on their side, with their face and mouth facing down (to keep their breathing clear). Anyone with obvious chest injuries is best gently moved on to their side, too – with the injured side *underneath*, not on top. Try and stop any severe bleeding: push a pad of bandage say, firmly against the wound, clamping down with your hand until it stops (don't peep for at least 15 minutes). This is better and safer than trying a tourniquet. Unless it's an obviously hot day, keep anyone injured warm. If they're conscious, stay with them, and talk to them soothingly: try and make sure that vulturish onlookers or worried panickers are kept away.

If someone thinks they're all right, but seems pale, maybe a bit faint, and either panicky or rather listless in a not-all-there sort of way, they're probably shocked. Other signs are a cold but sweating skin, and big pupils. Get them to sit or – better – lie down, again keeping them warm. It's important to do this: good anyway for the shock, but essential if it turns out (as it might) that they've some head or internal injury.

Don't be tempted to try and straighten bent or broken-looking limbs.

Best of all, enrol in a first-aid course so that you really know what you can do. As well as courses you can go to in your own time, you may find that your firm will send you on one in working time: ask your personnel office.

In November 1977 tests, *Which?* found that the best value was to make up your own first-aid kit, rather than buying one. Here's what it should have:

sterilised wound dressings; 2 medium (BPC 14), 3 large (BPC 15)
3 triangular bandages
5 tissue wipes
10 assorted sticking plasters
1 stretch bandage
dozen safety pins
small scissors
clean cotton handkerchief, kept in polythene bag.

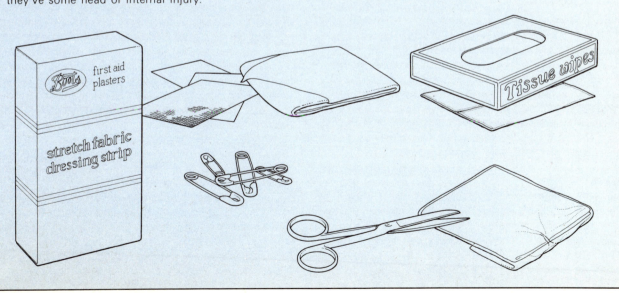

2. THE POLICE

If you do have the misfortune to be in an accident that wasn't your fault, or if your car's stolen, you'll very likely find the police sympathetic and kind, beyond the straightforward practical needs of their job. For example, they may well help you record the details of the accident. If there's bad news to break after an accident, the police traditionally shoulder the burden. And you can get practical help from them before disaster strikes, too: they will advise you on anti-theft protection.

There's a risk, though, that your encounter with the police could be less friendly.

At worst, you may be arrested. The police can arrest you without a warrant if they see you driving dangerously, carelessly, recklessly or even inconsiderately; if you're under the influence of drink or drugs (they've got to be in uniform); or if they suspect that you've caused death by dangerous driving, manslaughter, or driven while disqualified. And if they're in uniform they have the right to stop you at any time, and take your name and address ... your age, too.

If you're arrested, and charged, you can ask for bail as soon as you've been questioned. You may not get bail if your case is serious and can be heard within 24 hours (or 48, at a weekend). You don't have to answer any questions or make a statement, and can ask to see a solicitor first. If you do make a statement, read it through carefully before you sign, to make sure it's exactly what you meant to say.

If you have not been arrested, you don't have to go to the police station even if asked, unless you want to. But it's best to go along if they insist, though you may want to complain about it later. Ask to contact a lawyer or friend if you want, and (unless you're charged) ask to leave when you feel you've been at the station for long enough.

If you're in your car, or even just near it, the police can insist that you take a breathalyser test, if they think you're drunk. It can be an offence to refuse. If you fail, you have to go to the police station and take a blood test or urine test (whichever you'd prefer). You're entitled to an extra sample to take away if you want it analysed separately – though the results are likely to be the same. Refusing the test is an automatic offence, regarded more seriously by courts than just failing it. After the test, you can go (not driving), unless you've been arrested for some other offence.

If you're just stopped by the police, you have to show them (if asked) your insurance certificate, MoT test certificate, and driving licence. If you don't have them, you must produce them within five days. The police aren't supposed to look in the covered part of the licence for any endorsements.

The police can search your car if they think it's been involved in any crime, or carrying drugs.

If they ask to test its condition, you don't have to let them there and then. If it's inconvenient, you can fix an appointed time instead (maybe welcome breathing space – see below for possible penalties if there had been three defective tyres, say).

The courts and traffic offences

If you've broken the law and been caught, you may be lucky and get off with a warning. The policeman on the spot may simply warn you not to do it again. More formal written warnings are sometimes issued, and police are being encouraged to use these rather more instead of prosecution.

If you hear nothing within six months, you've probably escaped the net: you cannot be taken to court after that, except for causing death by dangerous driving (which has to be tried by the Crown Court, not the usual Magistrates' Court). And (unless an accident was involved) you must have had at least the written warning of a prosecution within a fortnight, for reckless, careless or inconsiderate driving, dangerous parking, speeding, or disobeying most traffic or police signals.

If you are taken to court, you may as well plead guilty unless you're certain there's been a mistake. The overwhelming majority of people tried for motoring offences are convicted, and as the cost of legal representation will probably be as high as the cost of your fine you'd really just be doubling your penalty.

The Magistrates' Association, with the approval of the Lord Chancellor and the Lord Chief Justice, suggest penalties for motoring offences. Their suggestions, reviewed every few years, represent a broad consensus view on a just and reasonable average, for first offenders. But they make it clear that individual courts shouldn't use the figures as a 'tariff', and should take into account not just the circumstances of the particular case, but factors like income levels (the richer you are, the more you should be fined), and the severity of the offence.

In the past, many courts have sentenced in line with Association suggestions. But when fines have been different from the suggestions, they have been much more likely to be lower than higher.

Here are the suggested penalties, for some common offences. If endorsement is mentioned it's usually compulsory. The offences are listed on the left, the penalties on the right – starting in the next column, and continuing on to the next page.

Driving offences:

careless driving (say, not checking that the road's clear)
£60, endorsement

inconsiderate driving (say, splashing pedestrians)
£60, endorsement

reckless driving (say, dangerous overtaking; carving people up)
£120, endorsement, and 6 months' disqualification

speeding
£1.50 per mph over the limit, endorsement

failing to comply with traffic lights
£25, endorsement (consider disqualification)

failing to stop at a pedestrian crossing
£25, endorsement (consider disqualification)

disobeying double white lines
£25, endorsement (consider disqualification)

disobeying other traffic or police signs
£20 (endorsement for some offences)

driving with insecure load
£30, endorsement

reversing on motorway sliproad
£40, endorsement

drunk driving   **£100, endorsement, compulsory disqualification** (suggested 12 months 80 mg–150 mg/100 ml; 18 months 151–200 mg; 2 yrs 201 to 250 mg; 3 yrs over 250 mg)

refusing blood or urine test   **£100, endorsement, compulsory disqualification** (18 months)

(penalties are lower, and disqualification is only optional, for people who were in charge of a car but not actually driving it and have been convicted of alcohol offences)

Parking offences:

not supplying 'statement of ownership' after fixed penalty notice   **£20**

causing obstruction   **£10**

parking on pedestrian crossing zig-zags   **£20, endorsement**

parking in dangerous spot   **£25 endorsement**

stopping unnecessarily on motorway hard shoulder   **£25** (and another **£15 to £25** if you take a walk)

night parking on wrong side of road   **£8 to £15**

Vehicle offences:

faulty brakes   **£25, endorsement**

driving without lights   **£20** (**£10** if street lights)

without proper headlights on unlit road   **£15**

faulty steering   **£25, endorsement**

no MoT certificate   **£8** (more if long overdue)

faulty or over-worn tyres   **£25, endorsement** (for each tyre)

no excise licence   **duty lost, multiplied by three**

other vehicle faults   **£25**

Driving licence, insurance, accident offences:

failing to stop at an accident   **£50, endorsement** (consider disqualification)

failing to report an accident   **£25, endorsement**

driving after disqualification   **£120 or prison; endorsement** (and consider longer disqualification)

no driving licence   **£40, endorsement, if you weren't even entitled to it; otherwise £5**

learners on motorways   **£40, endorsement**

learners without L-plates   **£15, endorsement** (consider disqualification)

learners without supervision   **£25, endorsement** (consider disqualification)

no insurance   **£60, endorsement; and disqualification** (unless it was an oversight).

The endorsement goes on your licence and into court records. If within three years you tot up three endorsements, you are automatically disqualified – for at least six months for each endorsement after the original two. The dates that matter for this are the dates of the court case, not of the actual offence. (So if you're on the margin you must obviously try your hardest to have the case delayed.)

Straightforward disqualification (not totted-up endorsement) runs from the moment you're convicted. If two such disqualification sentences overlap, they don't follow on from each other. So if for instance the same court disqualified you for a year for drunken driving, and six months for reckless driving, on the same day, you wouldn't lose your licence for 18 months, you'd just lose it for the year. But 'totting-up' disqualification does follow on, as a rule. So if in that case you'd been endorsed for both offences, and you'd already got two current endorsements, the extra six months for each endorsement would follow on after the 18-month disqualification. You'd then be disqualified for $2\frac{1}{2}$ years in all, unless the magistrates waived the usual rule on grounds of special hardship.

Can we be of any assistance, Sir?

INDEX

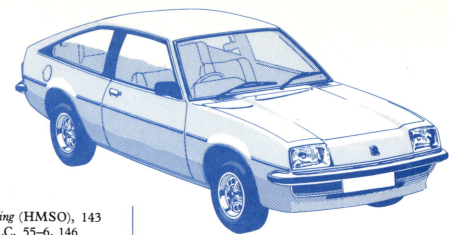

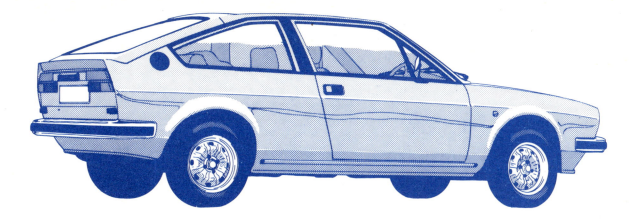

Printed and bound in Great Britain by Butler & Tanner Ltd, Frome and London

NOTES

NOTES

NOTES

NOTES